Pelican Books

Living in Cities:
Psychology and the Urban Environment

Charles Mercer was born in 1943 and educated at
Denstone College, Uttoxeter. He studied civil
engineering at Manchester University for two years
before teaching sex education at a local technical college
while simultaneously studying zoology. He then
became a student of psychology at the University of
Wales. After graduating he remained in Cardiff as a
lecturer at the Institute of Science and Technology of
the University of Wales, where he has been ever since.
He writes that he 'very soon became involved in
promoting psychology to non-psychologists – namely
architects, paramedics and social workers – and realized
the as yet untapped potential of psychology in many
applied fields'. He is currently involved in population
research.

Charles Mercer and his wife spend most of their time
renovating their Victorian house in which they live with
their two daughters.

Charles Mercer

Living in Cities:

Psychology and the
Urban Environment

Penguin Books

Penguin Books Ltd, Harmondsworth,
Middlesex, England
Penguin Books Inc., 7110 Ambassador Road,
Baltimore, Maryland 21207, U.S.A.
Penguin Books Australia Ltd, Ringwood,
Victoria, Australia
Penguin Books Canada Ltd, 41 Steelcase Road West,
Markham, Ontario, Canada
Penguin Books (N.Z.) Ltd, 182–190 Wairau Road,
Auckland 10, New Zealand

First published 1975

Copyright © Charles Mercer, 1975

Made and printed in Great Britain by
Cox & Wyman Ltd, London, Reading and Fakenham
Set in Monotype Baskerville

This book is sold subject to the condition that
it shall not, by way of trade or otherwise, be lent,
re-sold, hired out, or otherwise circulated without
the publisher's prior consent in any form of
binding or cover other than that in which it is
published and without a similar condition
including this condition being imposed on the
subsequent purchaser

To Jill, Jessica and Nemone

Contents

Preface

Two hundred thousand years ago there were probably nomadic groups of people in Britain. Their numbers were few and their impact on the physical environment insignificant. In 1971 54·1 million people occupied the same land and most lived in a physical environment that was man-made. This physical environment was progressively shaped over generations and in its turn shapes and is further shaped by those that follow. This book is about the relationship between man and his modern, largely self-made physical environment. How *does* the physical environment influence our behaviour and experience? how do we shape it? – these are some of the central questions of environmental psychology.

Psychologists have been late starters in making a contribution to understanding this relationship. Architects, planners, geographers and sociologists have already achieved significant understandings each from their own perspective. In this book I have adopted a specifically psychological perspective in the hope that progress towards a further and deeper understanding can continue.

I have yet to meet the author who has written a book without the moral, emotional and intellectual support of others. I am no exception. I thank my wife Jill for her support and inspiration, Julia Vellacott, my editor, for her patience and understanding, the Newsons for their assistance, Professor Lee for his comments, Kathie Osborne, Anne John, Robert Slater, Roy Davies, Chris and Sue Minay, David Canter and Alan Lipman for their critical reading of parts of the manuscript and all those people all over the world who provided so courteously and generously – as befits members of a scientific community – their published and unpublished works and encouragements.

Charles Mercer,
Cardiff, August 1974

I

Important Questions in Environmental Psychology

If you live in a town or city ask yourself how many strangers share it with you and what acreage it covers. Now repeat the questions, but imagine you are living about 2,000 years ago, in the Roman settlement that might have stood in the same place. The difference between the two sets of figures contains the reasons for an environmental psychology – population growth and urbanization. Take my own city, Cardiff – the capital of Wales – as an example. The Romans built a fort here during the eighth decade of the first century A.D., enclosing within its walls 8·8 acres and having a population numbered in hundreds rather than thousands. You could stand on any of the fort walls and take in the whole scene. You could also relate to, or at least know, a sizeable proportion of the total population. A better or worse place to live? Or perhaps there wouldn't be any difference?

When the Romans evacuated their Cardiff fort, its fortunes and its population fluctuated somewhat, but even during early Norman times you could stand on the castle wall (now rebuilt) and still take in the whole scene, which now consisted of not only the castle but also the small walled town. The population numbered under 2,000 – a figure which remained fairly steady from Norman times to the late eighteenth century. Even with 2,000 people one could still know or be on nodding terms with a significant proportion of them.

Now, however, the situation is very different. The 1971 census showed that 279,111 persons were living in Cardiff. One was me, another three the rest of my family, leaving 279,107 to account for. Take off another 300 or so for friends, acquaintances, etc., and it still leaves well over a quarter of a million people – all strangers. The present acreage of Cardiff is very nearly 20,000, so that, unless you see it from the air, it is impossible to *actually* take it in, visually, all at once. And there must be a very tiny minority of people who could accurately point out the boundaries of the city – a task which would present no difficulty in Norman times – with its walled delineation. Does it matter? Do such factors make any real difference to people?

If one looks at the man-made physical changes that have taken place in Cardiff, the majority have occurred in the last 190 years: the building of the canal through the middle of the city to facilitate iron and coal transportation from Merthyr and the North to the Quay, 1794; the development of the Quay into proper docks to cope with coal exports in the early 1800s which allowed Cardiff in 1913 to become 'the premier coal port in the world'*; the supplementing of the canal by the Taff Vale railway, 1841; the iron and steel works adjacent to the docks, 1891; the diversion of the River Taff, 1851; and, because of the massive industrialization and need for labour and the tenfold increase in population in fifty years (from 2 to 20 thousand), the inevitable development of row upon row of back-to-back narrow alley housing.

But what irony! Cardiff now exports no coal, the remaining docks operate at a fraction of their potential and a stranger to Cardiff might attribute what remains of the canal, running as it does through the parkland by the castle, to an unimaginative landscape architect. Moreover the back-to-back houses fall regularly under the bulldozer, and the erection of tall, reinforced concrete office blocks and suchlike is commonplace. Cardiff is forging out a new role based on a greater diversification of industry. Its physical face is, likewise, changing. Do people like it better? Does the physical fabric *really* make any difference? Does it matter if the office where you work is 200 feet off the ground and open plan instead of being at ground level and cellular?

Every town or city has, of course, its own very individual history. Thirty-four large towns in Britain have a very short history, having come into existence practically overnight –

*See Rees, 1969.

the so-called 'New Towns' developed since the Second World War (Evans, 1972). But whether the history is short or long every town and city can only come about through massive environmental upheavals and transformations. At this point in human history these are not only much larger but also greater in their potential impact on human life than at any other time. Many of these changes, however, are being made on the basis of completely untested theories. The New Towns, for example, have embodied the idea that it is good for people to live in neighbourhoods with easily perceived physical boundaries, that it is necessary to have a certain proportion of the land left as open space, that a certain density of population should not be exceeded or else the likelihood of all sorts of social pathology will greatly increase and so on. Some actual evidence might be enlightening.

The ancient Roman towns and cities were, of course, centres of culture. Places where man could explore his intellectual and spiritual life, where civilization could be nurtured. They were seen as positive forces in the creation of a cultivated man. Nowadays, however, the most prominent analogy for a city is either a concrete jungle or a human zoo. City life is likely to evoke associations with all sorts of social problems like crime, loneliness and alienation, together with all sorts of environmental outrage like air and water pollution, while the positive cultural side of city life is ignored. It is because the physical changes that have occurred and are occurring in our cities do so with such *obvious visibility* that they become the scapegoat for any kind of undesired behaviour or social phenomenon. Thus it is said, our cities are inhuman, lacking in warmth, discouraging of human relationships, not because of the socio-political system under which they labour, but because their layouts are wrong, or the architecture is misguided, or the transport systems insufficient or because of some other *physical* deficiency that in some way assaults the basic nature of man.

This is a simple explanation. Being simple it tends to be believed. It also has the advantage of making it unnecessary to collect evidence and so avoiding a lot of hard work. *But it is not sufficient.* Even at this early stage in environmental psychology we can say with certainty that the relationship of man to his self-created physical environment, whether at the level of the single room or at the level of the city, is enormously complex. This book is about these complexities.

Let us consider some of the differences between the city of today and the city of time past, which is often assumed to have provided a more fitting physical matrix for man.

Firstly, the perceptibility of the city. The Roman settlement was easily perceived, because you could see it all at once. The image of the modern city must, by necessity, be a compendium of *separately* perceived areas, because it is too large to be taken in all at once. The experience of the city must therefore be less *immediate.* But so what? It could be argued, surely, that this lack of immediacy makes the modern city a more interesting place to live in and to visit, because it is in the nature of man to seek variety. The modern city supplies just this quality.

Secondly, the modern city-dweller is in closer proximity to a greater proportion of absolute strangers than formerly. On the other hand, via the mass media, he is far more familiar with, and accurate in his perceptions of, places he has never been to. Thus the local environment is potentially more hostile (being filled with strangers), while the far off environment can be very familiar. Is the proximity of large numbers of strangers really a hostile situation? Or is it, perhaps, far worse to be alone at Stonehenge in the middle of a moonless night with a person you know to be mentally unhinged? Being part of a group – however anonymous the individuals in the group may be – *can* impart feelings of security, as well as providing greater scope for human relationships.

Thirdly, the 'build-use-demolish' cycle of the modern city is likely to be shorter than formerly. Technologies, changing land uses and greater population migration potential are all factors which act against the prolonged permanence of buildings and the physical fabric of cities. Need that be bad? Buildings exist to serve human needs and not to stultify them. Surely it is not coincidence that the few remaining 'primitive tribes' of the world have finished up in psycho-social evolutionary dead ends and use building forms that remain unchanged throughout human history?

Fourthly, the modern city has not only more buildings but the functions they serve are more specialized – for example, the factory, office block, psychiatric hospital, old people's home, school and so on. So we have an increase in the distinctions made in society. Role differentiation – a very important part of Roman life – permitted the development of culture. Such differentiations are being increasingly captured in the specialized buildings of the modern city. Because of this, may not the speed at which man continues to civilize himself be accelerated?

And lastly (although this list is not intended to be exhaustive), there is a faster movement of people over greater distances within the city. Far from imparting rootlessness or anomy, it could be considered as a continuing reinforcement of man's adaptability. This is the very quality that so markedly singles man out as a unique species.

The justification for an environmental psychology, then, does not lie in a proven assertion of the overwhelming importance of the physical environment in people's lives. It springs from a desire to provide some scientifically derived and reliable information about what man is doing to himself and, just as important, what he thinks he is doing to himself by his self-created physical environments which today are so different from a time not long past. We urgently need this information at this point in time because of the escalating and unfounded assertions currently made that man is overreaching himself with his massive environmental transformations. Maybe we will find that such assertions have a scientific validity but, maybe, on the other hand, we will lose our fear that we have trapped ourselves in a concrete human zoo and, instead, where psychological and social problems do exist, pinpoint the real causes and effect the real remedies.

2

What is Environmental Psychology?

The cave drawings of early man some 35,000 years ago show that even then man was aware that there was more to life than mere survival. Ever since his self-created shelters became homes, as opposed to places for simply keeping out the elements, he has been concerned about the experience that can be communicated through his hand-built edifices which became increasingly necessary as societies grew more complex. Places of worship had to engender a feeling of a presence greater than man himself; places of government had to look and feel like centres where power could be seen to be concentrated; or New Towns had to engender a feeling that all was well in the urgent modern urban society.

Architecturally the emphasis throughout history has been on the aesthetic experience or mental associations that the built environment evokes rather than on the evocation of behaviour: with the image rather than the result. Buildings or large developments are designed to convey some message – a New Town is a nice place to live: an old persons' institution is not an institution but a home, and so on. Recently, however, the question of image (which anyway, until recently, received little scientific investigation) has been joined by the question of what kind of behaviour *actually* is encouraged or discouraged, facilitated or prohibited by the physical matrix man makes for himself.

Ironically the concern about the relationship of the built environment to behaviour probably owes its existence more to those occasions where some undesirable behaviour has been found in association with a physical environment than vice versa. For example, mental illness has been associated with particular urban areas (Faris and Dunham, 1939), neurosis with high-rise living (Fanning, 1967) and vandalism and marital disharmony with New Towns (Goodey, 1974). If environments can have negative effects like these, then surely, if we could understand the processes involved, we could create environments that had *positive* effects? The underlying assumption is that the physical form of the enclosure can *itself* be an influential factor in promoting behaviour change and human growth in the widest possible sense. The desire to find out whether this is possible marks the beginning of environmental psychology. But of course this utopian ideal of creating a *better* physical environment places environmental psychologists in the position of developing criteria of evaluation of not only environments but also of behaviour. Not very long ago people who were mentally ill were simply removed from society and contained in large colonies – for their own and society's good. Now mental illness is seen very differently – as something which is potentially amenable to therapy. Thus the ethos behind the design of a modern psychiatric hospital is not now one of containment but one in which active therapy can be pursued. A 'good' design nowadays would be very different from a 'good' design 150 years ago. Just as the *Zeitgeist* of society changes so will the evaluative criteria of the environmental psychologist. He should be aware of how deeply rooted in the society these values are, *and* he should be aware of how easy it would be to make recommendations about environmental transformations which look to be scientifically valid and based on research without acknowledging the value-derived assumptions on which they rest.

But what exactly is environmental psychology and how can it be used to create a better physical matrix for society? I want to answer these questions by looking at the ideas and activities of people who are working or who have worked in the field of environmental psychology and I also want to examine the collaboration between such people and the people who have the responsibility for making the actual physical modifications. There are three titles at the present time acting as umbrellas for examining the relationship between man's behaviour and his environment: environmental psychology,* architectural pyschology† and ecological psychology.‡ Of these three, the title 'environmental psychology' is preferable in order to 'profit from the rich connotations that the term "environmental" has acquired through many recent efforts to analyse systematically the character of the total contemporary physical environment' (Craik, 1970). It is an unrestrictive title, unlike 'architectural psychology' which is more concerned with specifically architectural issues as opposed to general environmental ones. The central concern of 'ecological psychology', on the other hand, is much more with a way of *doing* psychology rather than with particular questions. Its aim is to see man in the context of his environment. It would be as well to start with his ecological contribution since it is having a very powerful effect, not only on environmental psychology but also on psychology as a whole, an effect which will do much to expand the narrow horizons of a great deal of modern psychology.

Professor Roger Barker is one of the major exponents of ecological psychology and he maintains that the psychologist, in his search for an understanding of human behaviour, can act in two ways (Barker, 1965). He can act as a transducer – that is as a 'docile receiver' of psychological phenomena. He categorizes or interprets natural behaviour as it occurs. The data that is generated by the transducing psychologists Barker labels T-data. The other role the psychologist can play is that of an 'operator'. Most psychologists, claims Barker, act as operators. As an operator the psychologist creates the situations to which he then asks his subjects to react. He throws questions at them, makes them memorize things or thrusts them into prescribed social situations and records what happens. Were it not for the psychologist, it would be pretty certain that the subjects would not be in that situation

---

* Craik, 1970, 1973; Kaplan, 1972; Proshansky *et al.*, 1970; Wohlwill, 1970.

† Canter, 1970; Taylor *et al.*, 1967; Wells, 1969; Kingston Polytechnic, 1969.

‡ Barker, 1965, 1968.

and therefore not behaving in that way. The data generated by this operation Barker calls O-data. Barker says 'Operator data generating systems are, in essence, experimental methods', but goes on to add, 'we have not used the term, however, because of its common restriction in psychology to operations carried out in laboratories, and hence its exclusion of clinical methods, a restriction and an exclusion that do not apply in any degree to O-methods'. This is an important point. Situations which might not be considered as experimental by outright experimental psychologists are nevertheless O-data generating systems. A psychological tester asking a child what he means by courage, as part of an intelligence test, and evoking a response from the child is – even though it cannot be described as experimental – a situation in which the psychologist is acting as operator. Barker (1965, 1968) rhetorically asks himself why psychologists should bother to act as transducers when they have previously shown themselves only satisfied with 'vigorously defined and controlled data generating arrangements'. T-methods of course could easily be confused with the naturalistic observations, the preliminary studies, the reconnoitres that are the usual prelude to the 'hard' experiment – the 'gathering observations' stage. They could be easily dismissed as the necessary 'fooling around' before the 'real' work of experimentation begins. Although naturalistic observations have been a core method in anthropology, ethology and to a lesser extent sociology, psychologists have been reluctant to take them seriously – perhaps because they fear anything that might throw suspicion on their scientific status. Barker, however, provides a convincing answer to his own question:

T-data refer to psychological phenomena which are explicitly excluded when the psychologist functions as operator. Indeed the primary task of the psychologist as transducer is carefully to preserve phenomena that the psychologist as operator carefully alters, namely, psychologist-free units. We have to say, therefore, that what T methods do, O methods cannot do at all: O methods cannot signal behaviour and its conditions unaltered by the system that generates the data. The primary task of the operator is to alter, in ways that are crucial to his interests, phenomena that the psychologist as transducer leaves intact.

To highlight this difference, Barker quotes the work of one of his students, Clifford L. Fawl. One of Barker's experiments quoted in most introductory texts of psychology (Barker *et al.*, 1941) demonstrated the general proposition that, if a child is frustrated, he regresses – i.e. operates at a younger mental level (e.g. his play becomes less constructive). However, this investigation was conducted in the rigorously controlled confines of a laboratory setting. Clifford L. Fawl elected to study frustration as children face it in everyday situations and found (to quote Barker) that 'frustration was rare in the children's days, and when it did occur it did not have the behavioural consequences observed in the laboratory'. Barker now maintains that the frustration generated in the laboratory 'did not simulate frustration as life prescribes it for children'. This makes inevitable the conclusion that 'psychologists as operators and transducers are not analogous and that the data they produce have fundamentally different uses within the science'.

The 'psychologist as transducer' has at least as large a role as 'psychologist as operator' in environmental psychology since the environmental psychologist's main concern is with the environments in which people enact their lives, not the artificial environments of clinic or laboratory. To illustrate this let us take an example of a three-and-a-half-year child going to play-school. The child, whilst receiving help from its mother in getting dressed (and probably ignoring half the requests like, 'hurry up', 'put this sock on', 'undo your sandal buckle before you put it on', etc.), starts saying 'I don't want to go to school today' – a 'stimulus' which is studiously ignored by the mother. Finally the child does get to school without tears, perhaps due to collusion between teacher and mother, and then proceeds to spend the day playing with other children and *not* playing with other children, responding to the teacher's 'social inputs' not all the time, but some of the time and, when the time for release comes, running off very happily with the mother, with gay shouts and jubilance. Although the child originally didn't want to go to school and responded only spasmodically when there, he has without question passed the 'test' of 'being a child at school'. In other words the overall segment of this child's life – being a child at school – is made up of individual 'behaviour episodes' which in themselves would not be given the same interpretation if taken as discrete units of behaviour with a meaning outside the larger context of occurrence. Barker, for example, finds that the children of Midwest (the *nom de plume* of the town in which a great deal of his work has been conducted) are responsive and conform 'to about one half of all social input'. There is no evidence given for supposing that the children of Midwest are in any way abnormal. But, if *half* of the requests or communications to a subject in a laboratory setting were ignored, that subject would probably be excluded from the experiment. The message seems to be that, if we want to understand 'behaviour as it occurs', we must stop looking at the level of detail that is so characteristic of the experimental (O-data) methods and give up looking for relationships between specific aspects of environment and behaviour. Instead we must think in terms of 'complete behaviour units and of studying them in relation to environmental inputs'.

To understand behaviour in the natural setting Barker proposed 'a theory of behaviour settings'. This theory sees behaviour and the setting in which it occurs as part of the same whole. Behaviour itself cannot even be defined outside of an environmental context (Altman, 1973). The unit for psychological study thus becomes not behaviour as such but behaviour–environment. Barker has over the years developed a language to describe the characteristics of behaviour settings, the ground rules for identifying them and the internal processes and programmes that maintain them. Unfortunately the language he employs is difficult and space prohibits a detailed discussion of his work here, but one finding of importance that has been yielded by his theoretical model deserves attention. A behaviour setting like a school, which

has an identifiable programme (to some extent what happens
in a school is laid down), is 'manned' by a certain number
of people. Within limits a varied number of people will be
able to maintain that particular behaviour setting. Thus we
have a behaviour setting which, although it still works, can
be 'undermanned' or 'overmanned'. Where behaviour settings are undermanned we would expect (predict) certain
kinds of compensatory behaviour on the part of the participants. Barker (1968, p. 166) suggests the following:

a. There will be more forces acting on individuals as the
'same forces are distributed among fewer inhabitants'.
b. 'The range of directions of the forces upon each inhabitant
is greater because fewer inhabitants mediate the same field of
forces.'

He then proceeds to give evidence to support his expectations,
the evidence being drawn from work contrasting findings
'about students in small schools with relatively few associates
within behaviour settings . . . with students in large schools
with relatively many associates'.

Firstly, students in an undermanned school reported being
under greater pressure to participate in the school activities.
They held two-and-a-half times as many responsible positions
in the school. This is perhaps somewhat paradoxical, when
the large school had more varied activities, yet it was the
students of the small school that actually performed more
variously. Also small-school children reported greater satisfaction in the areas related to 'a. development of competence;
b. to being challenged; c. to engaging in important actions;
d. to being involved in group activities; e. to being valued and
f. gaining moral and cultural values' (Barker, 1968, pp. 199–
200).

So ecological psychology does at least three things; it
directs attention to behaviour as it occurs in natural settings
and thus plays down laboratory situations; it re-asserts the
importance of the observing, categorizing, interpreting (transducer) role of the psychologist; and finally it orients our concern towards the ecology of human behaviour rather than

towards trying to understand it *in vacuo*. Since the speed of environmental change and the variety of environments is surely going to increase rather than decrease as time goes on, the environment is going to become an ever greater source of variation in human behaviour, and 'behaviour setting' theory of the ecological approach can provide a theoretical cornerstone.

The other two titles, environmental psychology and architectural psychology, need not be considered separately except to note that everything that goes on within architectural psychology could equally be described as environmental psychology.

1970 marked the appearance of the first comprehensive review of environmental psychology from Berkeley psychologist Kenneth Craik. In an earlier publication (Craik 1966) he defined environmental psychology as 'the psychological study of behaviour as it relates to the everyday physical environment', and as such it addresses basically three questions.

1. What does the everyday physical environment do to people?
2. How do people comprehend the physical environment?
3. What do people do to the everyday physical environment?

These questions are very much within the traditional mode of inquiry of psychology. What is new is the implication that the environment is a source of behaviour variability, that it can be comprehended in lawful ways and that it is an object towards which behaviour is directed. For example, Craik tells us that answers to the first question – what does the everyday environment do to people? – can be provided by straightforward psychological experimentation. Do people work better in open-plan offices than in cellular ones, does the colour of the walls affect typists' performance, do carpets on the wards speed up psychiatric therapy, do windowless classrooms facilitate children's learning? This sort of question can be answered (although it is only too easy to underestimate the practical difficulties involved) by straightforward experimentation. One of the dangers of this kind of work is that enormous numbers of investigations into particular problems will be done without anyone making any attempt to provide a theoretical framework into which they could be fitted. Without such a theoretical framework there will be simply thousands of research findings with a very limited application, and nobody who actually has the job of constructing environments is going to waste time searching through thousands of pieces of empirical research for an answer to their particular problem. Principles of the man–environment interaction must be created out of such work.

Craik's second question – how do people comprehend the physical environment? – is again a traditional psychological question, though it is not usually asked about the physical environment. Craik tells us that, just as people have enduring styles of interacting with other people, so they have enduring orientations to the physical environment. They will probably have clusters of belief systems about the effects of urbanization or high-rise living, and so on. Similarly we might find that people's experiences of the physical environment can be described in terms of relatively few dimensions made up of clusters of very similar experiences. Craik certainly believes in this possibility, and much work has already been done, which will of course be applied practically. Once such dimensions of experience are related to actual, measurable environmental features then it becomes a simple matter to play around knowledgeably with the environment – to make old people's homes homely, or dentists' waiting-rooms friendly, or railway stations even more unwelcoming. Craik takes the idea even further by suggesting that environments can be 'tried out' (using simulation techniques) before being constructed, and he foresees a time when people will be called upon to act as subjects in the same way that everybody now accepts jury duty.

His third question – what do people do to the everyday physical environment? – is on all counts a new type of psychological question. Traditionally psychology is retrospectively analytic. The psychologist is concerned with behaviour that has already occurred in response to some situation.

Rarely does he actively engage in an exercise of possibilities, of how people could, or could be persuaded, to behave, rather it is nearly always a question of how a person *did* behave in a certain given situation (Mercer, 1974). But where we have man bringing about alterations to his own physical matrix we cannot avoid getting embroiled in future possible worlds: the worlds that people don't already have but want. The architect Le Corbusier, for example, had a theory of how man should behave in cities and produced blueprints for the necessary architecture. The New Town development corporations did likewise. As soon as we ask Craik's third question, we are inevitably bound up in the future world that people think they are creating. To study this is a new departure for psychology, and it is also a wide study for it will include all the participants in the process of environmental transformation: management committees, affected residents, 'the wife of a vice-president who took a personal, informal interest in the choice of architectural firm' (Craik, 1966), the urban designer, the architectural draftsman, 'the building code commission', etc. Everybody who plays some role in the transformation will be the object of inquiry. Craik says that 'research done in this domain will demonstrate the truly interdisciplinary nature of environmental psychology, for such studies will be done jointly with sociological, economic and political science investigations'. It is difficult, however, to understand Craik's insistence that such a study must be interdisciplinary, since the designation 'environmental psychology' implies the existence of specifically psychological questions that can be asked about the man–environment interaction as opposed to sociological or political ones. If we want to ask *any* kind of question, then perhaps the words 'environmental psychology' should be replaced by something more general, like man–environment studies, which could draw on techniques of inquiry and method from any discipline. Logically, environmental psychology cannot be interdisciplinary.

In Craik's most recent review of environmental psychology (Craik, 1973) these three questions have settled in various areas of research which he lists as follows: assessment, per-

man–environment studies and particularly trying to lay bare the different strategies that practitioners – designers, architects, engineers, etc. – and behavioural scientists have developed towards such studies. He separates three main dimensions of concern: *places*, *phenomena* and *processes*. 'Places' refer to 'entities' or 'systems', like a city or a hospital; 'phenomena' refer to the concepts developed to explain spatial behaviour like privacy or territoriality, 'process' refers to actual design, construction, use and evaluation of the built environment (see Fig. 1).

If environmental psychology really did grow out of a feeling expressed or perceived by people, that there was some 'problem' which could be solved by scientifically analysing the links between man and environment, then having defined approximately the sorts of things that go on in environmental psychology, the question naturally arises of how the new information, in terms of either data or theory, can be fed back into society's construction programmes. Can environmental psychology actually have an effect on either the way things are or how we want our future physical environments to be?

Altman (1973) directs his attention to this, but before examining his suggestions I would like to take specific suggestions from people who have worked in a collaborative or near collaborative situation with designers. Psychologist Brian Wells was an architectural psychology consultant for the tobacco company W.D. and H.O. Wills. This company was keen on utilizing the best scientific knowledge available for the development of their new factory site, and the psychological consultants conceived their task as broadly twofold: Firstly, 'to obtain a clear idea of what people's reactions were to the proposed move; what specific anxieties existed and what effects the prospects of the move and the new environment might have on staff recruitment, retention and morale'; secondly, 'to find out what employees felt was necessary or desirable in terms of amenities and improved working arrangements' (Wells, 1965).

Wells sees the kind of collaboration that occurred in this

project, between designer, psychologist and client as something of a revolution and suggests that the simple polling of people's opinions, expectations and so on is one of the most useful modes in which the architectural psychologist can operate. As Wells says, 'up to the present time an understandable criticism of psychologists in architecture has been that the architect needs quick and accurate answers to specific questions and that the psychologist has not been able to give them ... I believe that existing firms of psychological consultants are going to be able to fill this need' and in so doing the technology of architectural psychology will be created. However, although the psychologist as pollster might fulfil a valuable role, this won't do much to develop a science of the study of man and his relationship to the environment. Wells is perhaps, in his effort to justify a discipline, rather over keen on providing 'usable' results, at the expense of developing a theoretical framework. Merton foresaw this danger as far back as 1948, in his discussion of the social psychology of housing. Merton mentions the 'hazard of empiricism'. He urges the social psychologist entering the field of housing not to take 'the easy and empty path of quick empiricist findings rather than the more difficult and ultimately more productive path of empirical research orientated toward basic theory'. A similar point was made by Cohen (1951) about social surveys as planning instruments. He says of such social surveys, 'There has been little progress towards developing a sociological framework for these surveys. Quantities of data are being collected on a variety of situations, but without a framework it is difficult to place these findings in a meaningful setting. Much experience is thus wasted, and no systematic body of knowledge is built up.'

The warning is clear, the environmental psychologist must not simply see himself as an information gatherer (important though this activity is), he must also be prepared to systematize and construct theories.

Another approach to environmental psychology which seems to be atheoretical, although not in quite the same way, is that of Rohles (1967). Rohles defines environmental psychology as 'the study of behaviour as it is affected by one or more factors in the physical environment'. One of the first tasks following from such a definition would be to outline exactly what these factors or variables are and Rohles specifies three categories:

1. Physical (e.g. sound, light, area-volume, etc.).
2. Organismic (e.g. age, sex, drive, body type, etc.).
3. Reciprocative (e.g. diet, clothing, social, etc.).

He goes on, 'when we bear in mind that every one of these can vary along a continuum it is small wonder that research in environmental psychology is regarded as a bucket of worms'.

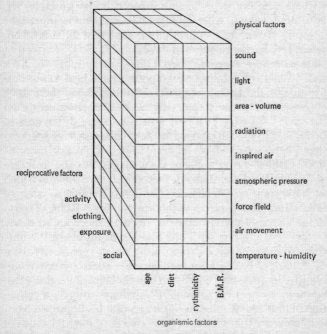

Fig. 2. Environmental psychology, Rohles's eye view. (Variables to be considered for human factors research in altered environments.)

Previously Rohles had provided the concept of 'Standard Man' (Rohles, 1965): 'standard man would define the limits of physiological and psychological functioning under a non-stressful, anxioous and neutral environment. Then when research in stressful environments is conducted, the extent of deviation from the Standard Man could be determined, and would indicate the effect of the altered environment on the particular measure in question.' Apart from obvious difficulties of defining a non-stressful, neutral environment (neutral to whom?) and the attendant difficulties produced by man's adaptive capacities, Rohles's approach seems to favour a taxonomy without a theory – to merely outline changes without relating them to any superordinate principles. In addition to which, when Rohles talks about environment, he is clearly referring to something completely different from what, say, Barker refers to as environment. So we know that 'infants require warmer surroundings than adults' or 'older individuals are "chilly" at temperatures judged to be comfortable by the college student' or 'at adulthood the female of the species prefers a somewhat warmer environment than the male'. So what? Does it give rise to any differences in behaviour? How do men and women cope when sex segregation doesn't seem to have followed from this piece of information? Rohles's programme seems to suggest pure information gathering. Until there is some theoretical structure into which such information can be fitted, the jigsaw remains a system of isolated unrelated pieces without a pattern.* Rohles (1965) himself says, 'In environmental research there are so many factors that interact with one another to influence the outcome of the results it is almost impossible to generalize from the findings.' But without such generalizations (or laws), e.g. relating temperature change to human behaviour, there can be no *science* of environmental psychology – merely a collection of findings. Rohles (1965) hopes that his Standard Man will 'enhance the validity of generalization' but as the idea of a standard man flies in the face of so much established psychology it seems unlikely to achieve its objective.

* See Noble, 1963, for another inventory approach.

So far, then, we have Barker proposing a methodology and conceptual framework and Craik 'doing psychology' (theory building, promoting methods and discovering laws, etc.), but with reference to the physical environment. Wells and Rohles, on the other hand, somewhat overawed perhaps by the desire to be useful to others (in Wells' case to architects, in Rohles's case to engineers), attack specific man–environment problems in the hope of providing if not complete design solutions, at least specific information that can be fed into the design process. Maybe this is the old division between pure and applied science, but, because there exists a high expectation that behavioural science can solve societal problems if only it were applied (a belief quite misplaced), environmental psychologists should beware, in attempting to fulfil this misguided expectation, of falling flat on their faces. As Lipman (1970a) says, 'design may be described as a synoptic process in which particular solutions are sought for specific problems ... the research process is primarily analytical ... the immediate goal is not action but an attempt to identify relationships between phenomena and to explain them in terms of overall theory'.

This raises perhaps the most important problem in the collaborative exercise – that of values. The work of Willmott and Cooney (1963) provides a concrete example. They conducted an investigation into four different types of apartment block in the East End of London, looking specifically at, on the one hand, whether the layout encouraged 'sociability' and on the other, whether there was enough 'privacy'. The results for the four types (a, b, c, d) were:

	Sociable layout Yes (%)	Enough privacy Yes (%)
a	95	79
b	71	81
c	30	95
d	24	100

These data show that the relationship between sociability and privacy is not straightforward. While (a) and (b) are obviously superior environments in terms of overall satisfaction expressed, as Willmott and Cooney ask 'who knows the rate of exchange between privacy and sociability? . . . We do not know how to weigh up the value that people put upon privacy on the one hand, and opportunities for sociability on the other.'

This is not to say that we will never know or that research cannot answer the question, but it *does* raise the question, for the designer, of what values he is to base his design decisions on. Say, for example, that Environment X leads to behaviours, B, C, D, E and that Environment Y leads to C, D, F, G – this is what research has revealed – the designer is still left with a problem of which environment to construct. He still has to exercise his judgement and his professional integrity as to which environment is best, which behaviour he wants to encourage or facilitate. The problem can be further highlighted from Lipman's (1968) research into old people's homes. Lipman found that in the old people's homes he studied the residents regarded particular chairs in their lounges as their own. He hypothesized that such behaviour served two purposes: a. to symbolize the person's social existence or identity, and b. in conjunction with furniture layouts (usually chairs round the wall) to limit social participation to ranges which fall within the emotional resources of institutionalized old people. So if we want to *limit* social participation, we know what to do; if we went to *increase* social participation, we know what *not* to do in terms of arranging the furniture. The first thing to do therefore is to formulate a therapeutic objective which expresses how institutionalized old people are valued. We must decide what old people's homes are for. Are they to be passive receptacles for the dying or near dead, or active agents in prolonging life no matter what? Our furniture arrangements can promote either. If old people are allowed to limit their social participation, they will die sooner; if not their lives can be prolonged. What do we want for them? Research, be it environmental psychology or any other 'ology', will not make this decision for us, it can only clarify the options. Science can serve social values, but cannot create them.

So far we have environmental psychologist as pollster; as empiricist; as maintainer of logical distinction between fact and value.

What about the view from the other side? Sociologist Professor Robert Gutman has spent a good deal of his time trying to 'familiarize himself with the culture of architecture' in order to be able to formulate the expectations that one design profession (architects) has of the behavioural (sociological/psychological) sciences. He has suggested that architects have looked to behavioural scientists for help in three main areas:

a. To help clarify whether a client's objectives are reasonable.
b. To say whether the physical form will fit the activities that are to go on in it.
c. To determine what size spaces for the purposes they are to serve (Gutman 1965–6).

The result seems to have been mutual disappointment, dissatisfaction and disillusionment on both sides. The reasons, Gutman says, are:

a. There are very few behavioural scientists around with any kind of specifically environmental expertise.
b. Architects are not sufficiently aware of the distinctions between fact and value, architects want 'objective' evaluation of value and this (see above) is not a scientific activity.
c. The behavioural scientist is not a futurologist; as he cannot be sure what the variables are in a new physical entity, it becomes an intuitive exercise to predict the behavioural response.

To highlight an aspect of the dissatisfaction Gutman cites a particular example. 'Tell me,' asks a Gutman hypothetical architect, 'whether in my new housing estate where I want to promote neighbourliness, rootedness and a sense of community, should I have linear rows of houses or should I build my houses around courtyards? Which of these two is more likely to give the residents a feeling of responsibility for the community?' And back comes the reply that the variable of site layout is an insignificant one compared to others like the provision and positioning of amenities such as nursery school or community hall; or whether the residents own or rent their dwellings. 'Do you mean to tell me,' the architect re-joins, 'that there is nothing the sociologist can offer in the way of advice about which of these two is better for the inhabitants?' The truthful answer is 'no – your question is unimportant'. This answer from a consultant who is supposed to be helpful and subservient is certainly not going to endear him to many architects, who still have to take the decision.

An extreme form of this argument might run as follows:
Architect to Social Scientist:

I design for people. People have needs. You tell me what people's needs are and I'll design you the appropriate physical environment.

Social Scientist to Architect:

Needs are inferred from the way people behave, i.e. they are arrived at retrospectively. New situations may call forth new patterns of behaviour and, by implication, new needs. Man's nature is dynamic not static. Furthermore, we know that a characteristic of man is that he seeks stimulation and change. Also it is clear that the physical environment is an effective variable only in connection with certain patterns of behaviour. I cannot therefore give you a straightforward reply. You will have to specify more exactly what you are building, for whom, and what social values you are trying to incorporate into your design. When you've done that, the answer I will give will be a mixture of interpretation of 'objective research findings' with a liberal dose of intuition. You just might be better off doing it yourself – after all, you're more practised at the 'intuitive' decision because you're making them all the time.

To further emphasize this it is worth quoting George Rand (1969) who seems to see the request for behavioural help as a shedding of the moral responsibility and professional integrity of the designer:

The planner-architect looks to psychologists for a redefinition of priorities, a finger on the panic button and a rationalization for carrying out his strategies as quickly as possible. He looks to the psychologists to redefine the moral status of life and death so that he may loosen the funds from industry and government to convert each metropolis into a 'Garden of Eden' in accord with his utopic vision of the 'good life'.

Perhaps the most creative attempt to come to terms with this problem of the interaction of the designer and the behavioural scientist is that made by Jameson (1971). He suggests that a useful role of the social scientist, with respect to architecture and planning, is not the traditional one – of retrospectively seeking relationships between known variables – but an active or instrumental one. The instrumental approach will not generate questions like 'what are people's needs?' but 'what can people be persuaded to need?' Jameson claims that 'People do not know what they want; and, when they do know, they have difficulty putting their wants into words – and when they can put their wants into words they cannot imagine a change . . .' What Jameson seems to be saying is that the architect or designer must make what *he* wants other people to want absolutely explicit, without embarrassment. *Then*, using the techniques of – in Jameson's case – marketing, he should test their feasibility. The kinds of methods that Jameson has in mind are: a. the diagnostic interview – or depth interview as it is often called – in which the motives and the 'real' meanings behind what the interviewee says are probed: in which the interviewer adopts a non-directive mode of questioning, becoming something of a cross between a mirror and a sponge; the interviewee is relaxed, '*rapport*' is established and much information is revealed, when interpreted, about how far he can be persuaded to want what the designer wants; b. attitude scales – basic tools of social psychology, which can provide objective information about a subject's held attitudes; c. preference testing – asking the subject to choose between alternative designs (sketches, photographs, etc).

With these data Jameson is then in a position to provide an assessment of what the subject can be persuaded to want. Of course the diagnostic interview procedure is a mode of data gathering that is most open to the injection of the interviewer's value systems. The ways in which an interviewer can – quite unbeknown to himself – guide the interviewee to say what he thinks the interviewer wants to hear (e.g., see Greenspoon, 1955, Rosenthal, 1966) are now a part of 'accepted' social psychology – and one which would lead us, or perhaps *should* lead us, to adopt an attitude of considerable scepticism about people's claims of being able to get at the 'real truth' through diagnostic interviews.

The results one gets using any method can only be as good as the methods that generate them. So, while Jameson's attempt at a new definition of collaboration between scientist and practitioner has a very welcome, aggressively useful flavour, the really radical departure is not a methodological one but an attitudinal one. Practitioner and scientist, he might well have said, have an enormous common ground if the superordinate values that motivate their work – to create a better physical environment – are made explicit, if both are willing to lay open to examination the ideals which underlie their separate activities.

However, Jameson's approach does raise an important problem, and that is about the nature of 'understanding', which in modern psychology is very much a controversial topic. For example, some say that understanding is simply a question of being able to control and predict phenomena and perhaps the most active exponent of that view is the American psychologist B. F. Skinner (see Skinner, 1971). Others, however, would claim that such an approach is superficial in the extreme and understanding should in some way get at root causes. An example from Jameson (Jameson, 1973) will illustrate this. A client wants an architect to design offices for his office workers; the fact-finding social scientist produces the information from office workers that they would like large offices. The client cannot meet this need for obvious financial reasons. How is this to be resolved? The instrumental social scientist now gets to work and finds out that what the office worker *really* wants is not a large office but status, and the size of the office is a good indicator to the outside world of status.

The solution now lies in finding status substitutes – a big comfortable chair, a desk with drawers on both sides, stylish lavatorial facilities and so on – that will satisfy the status need. The problem is solved without the office worker himself really realizing what's been going on, but yet he ends up in a good position. But, although hopefully the problem has been resolved, has it been understood?

Clearly it could be argued that *real* understanding would mean trying to answer the question of why the office worker wants status in the first place, which is a question about how human beings work. It is this kind of question that has received the most attention in psychology so far, and it has done so at the expense of the manipulative understanding that Jameson advocates. Both of course have their place, and once it is realized that both are worthwhile, that 'understanding' need not describe only *one* process, they can feed each other. Equally, however, Jameson's manipulative understanding is likely to be the most useful to designers, at least at this point in time.

Another bold attempt at bringing behavioural science into the design process is made by architect Alan Lipman (1971). Recently 'integrated design' has become a popular idea in design circles. Integrated design demands a commitment by building owners and design and building teams to 'contribute towards a common and comprehensive view of long- and short-term aims. All must share the decision at the inception of the project to consider the integration of design factors for which they are normally individually and separately responsible. Decision making thereafter becomes a concurrent process in all the disciplines involved, and not sequential (and therefore logically isolated) as in the normal case of building design' (Davison *et al.*, 1970). Lipman argues that, as well as plans for the physical climate, explicit formulations of the behavioural and social aims (made with the collaborative assistance of behavioural scientists) should be brought into the integrated design process so that when evaluation studies are made they can be made against these expectations. Thus the behavioural scientist makes a 'value input' at the begin-

ning and, in the monitoring of the behaviour when the building is occupied, plays his more traditional role of measuring
behaviour. A third role that Lipman *suggests* for the behavioural scientist (although I think a dangerous one, in that it
introduces enormous role-ambiguities if he is a *member* of the
team) is that of monitoring the integrated-design team's
behaviour, in order to understand the difficulties created by
this unusual collaborative effort. As Lipman says, this kind of
design-team collaboration has been advocated since at least
1923, but there has been little evidence of its adoption. Perhaps, if the problems that arise when it is used were understood, it could, with the appropriate modifications, become a
more often used technique.

I hope I have shown with these examples something of the
complexity of the relationship of environmental psychology
to the ongoing process of environmental transformation. If
environmental psychologists do continue their attempts at
getting in on the environmental transformation scene they
will also have a high chance of widening the area of concern
and competence of psychology itself. Returning to Altman's
paper mentioned earlier, he very specifically outlines what
the particular communication difficulties are between the
environmental practitioner and behavioural scientist, and by
way of summary I will outline them.

Firstly, the practitioner is 'criterion orientated', there is
some goal to be achieved – for example, how do we house 350
people on this acre of land and provide them with privacy?
The behavioural scientist is what Altman describes as 'process orientated' – what factors contribute to high rates of
vandalism on this or that housing project? The practitioner
is creating a future, the behavioural scientist is trying to
understand a present. Jameson's approach is an example of a
behavioural scientist who is adventurous enough to try out a
'criterion orientation' of the practitioner.

Secondly, the practitioner attempts synthesis in his work.
Putting a great deal of information together and finishing up
with a whole, whether a housing project or a concert hall, he
has to play with and balance many factors. The behavioural

scientist does just the opposite. He attempts to tease out individual factors and discover their importance in contributing to whatever behavioural phenomenon he is studying. He is analytic, not synthetic. Much, if not all, of the training of the behavioural scientist specifically discourages synthesis.

Thirdly, the practitioner is a 'doer' while the behavioural scientist researcher is usually under no obligation to do anything but understand.

These three differences are large differences but, as Altman says, if both sides make an attempt to understand them, rather than eliminate them, they can produce the dynamic substrate which is so necessary for creative thought. And why not, in our educational institutions, train our psychologists and architects and designers to feel at home in any mode, to be criterion orientated *and* process orientated, synthetic *and* analytic, to do *and* to understand? This surely is the most logical way forward.

How does one do it? Altman suggests several ways. Firstly, departments in universities could be set up in which no single discipline dominates but many contribute around an environmental theme – a department of environmental studies for example. Or existing departments, e.g. psychology and planning or psychology and architecture, could run joint courses for students in both departments. Thirdly, a department could incorporate on its staff members of other disciplines to complement the teaching and research (as has happened in this country where psychologists can be found working in schools of architecture). Or a department can set up a speciality, as for example at the University of Surrey where it is possible to take postgraduate qualification in environmental psychology, within the department of psychology. The first option was in fact recommended by Steinhart and Cherniack (1969) in their report to the President's environmental quality control council, *The universities and environmental quality*. In this report they recommend 'that the Federal government support formation of Schools of the Human Environment at colleges and universities ... Their ... purpose ... should be problem-focused education and research directed toward people – their need and desire for a satisfying life in pleasant surroundings. Such schools or programmes can begin the task of providing trained professionals to work on environmental problems, help to define what is possible and help to get it, and provide opportunities for the justifiable desire of many young people to devote their attention to environmental problems.'

Whilst such a recommendation is entirely laudable, it would seem to be a waste not to capitalize on those existing departments in universities which are already involved in or becoming involved in environmental issues. A concern for environmental quality is apparent in a great many disciplines and once operative disciplines and behavioural scientists learn each other's value systems and orientations, great progress towards a 'better' physical environment is not only possible but inevitable.

3

The How of Environmental Psychology

Modern psychology has two obsessions – with statistics and with the laboratory. First let us consider statistics.

The replacement of the present population of the U.K. requires that each married couple has 2·1 children. This figure allows for death by accident, disease and unequal sex ratios. However, the couple who has 2·1 children has yet to be found, because the human being is indivisible – either being whole or not being at all. The statistical abstraction of 2·1 (i.e. an average) enables us to summarize the desired reproductive behaviour of many couples to achieve zero population growth, but is not descriptive of any *one* couple. Some couples will be childless, some will have only one child, some two, three or many more children. Nor does the average figure tell us anything about how the children will be distributed amongst couples. If we want to know something about this – how the couples have to be spread out or dispersed on either side of the average figure – other measures are used, one of which is the 'standard deviation'. The two figures yielded when the standard deviation is added to the average and subtracted from the average give a range in which is contained approximately two thirds of the population. Take an example: if 5 per cent of couples remain childless, 15 per cent have only one child, 50 per cent have two children, 25 per cent have three and 5 per cent have four, this gives an average number of children per couple of the required 2·1. The standard deviation when calculated is 1, so that immediately we can say that two thirds of the population will have a family of between 1·1 and 3·1 children. But again, families with fractions of children do not exist. In other words the statistical abstraction does not fully describe the reality, because the general is being emphasized at the expense of the particular. For psychology the obsession with statistics means that psychologists will tend to collect limited data from lots of people and search for statistical commonalities between people, rather than collect masses of data from a few individuals with the intention of looking at human uniqueness. Thus modern psychology is concerned with generalities that can be squeezed out of large groups of individuals but which cannot then be applied to any one single individual. The biography, autobiography and the case history are not very visible sources of data for the experimental psychologist. Rather, they present a world of independent and dependent variables, of five-way analyses of variance, of control groups and experimental groups, of 'significant' results and rejected null hypotheses, of large samples and rotated factors. The study of individuals as individuals can be safely left to the novelist or playwright who is not self-conscious about appearing to be non-scientific. Frills have been added of course – like telling subjects lies about the experimental situation and pretending to study one behaviour while really studying another, or faking crises, or planting stooges amongst the subjects. Because of the increasing sophistication of the student populations that form the majority of the subjects of modern psychology, many laboratory experiments take on the qualities of a game – the subject trying to work out the *real* purpose of the experiment. If the subject should actually be told the truth about the experiment and its possible outcome, there is a fair chance he will deliberately not fulfil the expectations. One subject (where the 'ethics' of the experimental situation was the independent variable of the experiment), who was informed of the real purpose and possible outcome, when questioned afterwards about his 'discrepant' results replied, 'My only concern was to make it non-boring for the experimenter!' (Resnick and Schwartz 1973).

I am not suggesting that the frenetic statistical activity of modern psychology should be abandoned. It has, after all, considerably increased our understanding of how the mind works and why people behave in the ways they do. What I am suggesting is that such a strategy is one sided. The other side to this search for the generality in human nature lies in the study of the uniqueness of the individual, oneself included. In such an endeavour psychology has made little progress.

In order to show exactly what can and cannot be achieved by the use of statistical methods, I want to consider an example of social psychological research which implicated the physical or built environment in the aetiology or causation of behaviour disorders. The work, now considered to be a classic study of the incidence of mental illness in urban areas, was carried out by sociologists Faris and Dunham in the 1930s in Chicago. The strategy of scientific method they were following is shown in Fig. 3. This is often upheld as the only method of investigation if psychology is to show itself to be scientific. Within such a model there are points of controversy, like whether the scientist can make theoretically untainted observations, whether the hypothesis comes first and so on. The major thesis of the model, however – that hypotheses are tested by experimental means – is rarely challenged. How does the Faris and Dunham investigation fit this model?

The 'observations' from which Faris and Dunham began their investigation were in fact rooted in other people's work and could be detailed as follows:

1. A recognition of a relationship between urbanism and social disorganization.
2. A recognition that some sections of the urban scene were characteristically more socially disorganized than others.
3. A supposition that a city could be divided into 'natural areas' (this idea being rooted in the work of Park and Burgess, 1925). Areas like the business area, the rooming-house area, single-family-dwellings area are examples of 'natural' areas.
4. These 'natural areas' could be identified 'by the use of certain mathematical indices for different types of social phenomena' (e.g. percentage of foreign born, percentage of homes owned, the sex ratio, density of population, etc.).

From these observations they developed an hypothesis which

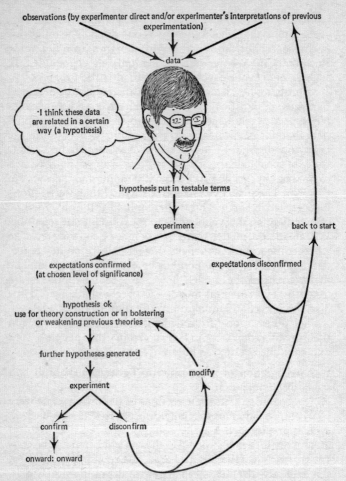

Fig. 3. Model of scientific inquiry.

they put in question form (p. 22): 'In view of the definite relationship which appears to exist between other social problems (e.g. delinquency) and the areas of social disorganization in the modern city, the question may be raised as to whether mental disorder will tend to follow this typical pattern,' and further 'will the different types of mental disorders also follow this same configuration?'

Then – according to our model of 'Scientific Method' – would follow the experiment. In this case it was a matter of collecting data concerning the incidence of various psychoses in the previously delineated natural areas. In fact Faris and Dunham delineated eleven such areas which could be distinguished by the type of housing in each area.

The areas were:

1. Single-home and two-flat area of $50 and more a month – 'one of the most stable of the eleven residential divisions'.
2. 'Single-home and two-flat area with rentals of under $50 a month is also an area of high stability'.
3. Two-flat and single-home area with rentals of $50 a month.
4. 'Two-flat and single-home area with rentals of under $50 a month, while not as stable as the first three areas, still is medium to high in the series'.
5. 'Apartment-house area (native-born white) is located in fairly desirable sections of the city and inhabited by a population which shows little sign of disorganization'.
6. Hotel and apartment-hotel area is occupied by a fairly high economic class, so that, although the mobility is somewhat higher than in the residential areas, the population does not show signs of disorganization.
7. Apartment-house and two-flat area.

Figure 4 shows that the schizophrenic expectancies (what you would expect by chance) for the first areas are all higher than what was actually observed. Area 7 marks the change-over. It is significant that Faris and Dunham say of area 7 that it 'is on the fringe of the slum areas and is in most respects intermediate between the residential and slum areas'.

8. 'Apartment-house (foreign-born) is also on the fringe of the slum areas and shows some signs of the characteristic deterioration'.

9. Apartment-house area (Negro) contains some of the most deteriorated communities of the city.

10. Tenement and rooming-house area is one of the most seriously deteriorated . . . and is part of the real slums.

11. Rooming-house area is in several respects the most unstable and deteriorated in the city.

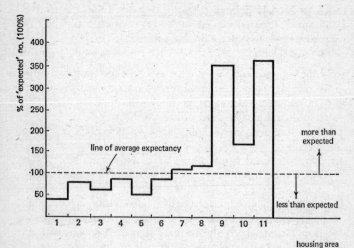

Fig. 4. Showing the percentage of 'observed' schizophrenics in the housing areas 1–11. 100% line represents the average expected in each area.

They then – using statistical correlation techniques – showed how the rates for the different areas varied significantly – at least with regard to a particular disorder, namely schizophrenia. To keep the illustration reasonably brief, only a tiny part of their original data will be analysed now, using a test that they could have used (x^2 or chi squared, which was invented in the early part of this century) but chose not to, because for their purposes this test is not sufficiently refined, though for our purposes it is adequate.

The principle behind the test is to compare the distribution of data that you get from doing an experiment or survey with what you could have expected to get if 'chance factors' alone had been operating. We ask whether our collected data is sufficiently out of accordance with what we could have expected on chance grounds to make it very unlikely to be attributable to chance alone. So we take the number of reported cases of schizophrenia for the eleven natural areas, find the total and – given the population size of each area – compute the 'by chance' number of cases we could expect if the natural areas were not associated with the manifestations of schizophrenia. Table 1 can be constructed.

The value of χ^2 is given by the formula:

$$\chi^2 = \Sigma \frac{(O - E)^2}{E}$$

where O = the observed frequency, E = the calculated expected frequency and the degree of freedom is $k-1$ which is the number of cells or categories that have to be filled in before the final one is fixed. When we consult the statistical tables with our value of χ^2, they will tell us the likelihood of getting such a figure by chance. If the figure we obtain is shown by the tables (which are worked out probabilistically) to have only a one in twenty probability of occurring by chance, we can be pretty sure (nineteen times out of twenty) that chance is not responsible. Expressing that as a percentage we can be 95 per cent certain that a non-chance factor (in this case the environmental factor) has got something to do with it. The figure of 95 per cent is not God-given – merely arbitrary and conventional – and is also referred to as 'probably significant'. To be significant would entail a 99 per cent certainty and to be very significant a 99·9 per cent certainty.

Looking up the value of χ^2 that we have obtained from reworking the Faris and Dunham data, we find that it is highly significant ($p < 0.001$, where p = probability) – we can be sure there is something other than chance operating to pro-

Table 1.

Showing the number of 'observed' (actual) and 'expected' (by chance) cases of schizophrenics from foreign-born populations in the eleven housing areas of Chicago (adapted from Table 9, p. 51 of Faris and Dunham, 1939).

Area	Description	Actual Cases (O)	Foreign-born population	Expected Cases (rounded) (E)
1.	single-home and two-flat over $50	76	526,656	194
2.	single-home and two-flat under $50	110	402,857	146
3.	two-flat and single-home over $50	78	353,353	128
4.	two-flat and single-home under $50	334	1,052,129	384
5.	apartment-house	139	789,097	288
6.	hotel and apartment-hotel	66	212,758	77
7.	apartment and two-flat	323	795,301	292
8.	apartment-house (foreign-born)	191	462,020	168
9.	apartment-house (Negro)	70	54,717	20
10.	tenement and rooming-house	252	407,745	150
11.	rooming-house	237	183,521	66

$$\chi^2 = \Sigma \frac{(O - E)^2}{E}$$
$$\chi^2 = 829 \cdot 16 \quad (df = 10)$$

duce the divergency of schizophrenic rates obtained from those which we would expect (see Fig. 4). This finding, however – which is not altogether unexpected – takes on a new significance when compared to the manic-depressive rates. Manic-depressive psychoses and schizophrenia are the two major psychotic illnesses, and according to Faris and Dunham 'the rates for manic-depressive psychoses by housing areas show a lack of consistency as well as a lack of pattern'. This finding led Faris and Dunham to speculate that the diagnostic categories of schizophrenia and manic-depression must have some validity, because they are differently associated with the different natural areas. It also led them to speculate further about the aetiology of schizophrenia – 'the hypothesis is that extended isolation of the person produces the abnormal traits of behaviour and mentality' (p. 173), and later (p. 177) 'the hypothesis that forms of isolation are significant factors to account for the high rates of schizophrenia in certain parts of the city is strengthened by the studies which have shown that the conditions producing isolation are much more frequent in the disorganized communities'.

Faris and Dunham close their book with the remark that the 'isolation hypothesis' of schizophrenia is worth following up with further research.

So we have come full circle in our paradigm of scientific method. Starting with observations from previous work, a hypothesis was formulated, tested and confirmed. An unexpected finding was obtained and this led to further inferences and a further hypothesis for testing. The circle is complete. Science is at once seen as a *continuous* process, a social process (their hypothesis was seeded from the communicated observations of others) and experimental – data has to be gathered and statistically manipulated. Above all, it is inductive – particular findings contribute to a general theory.

But there are problems. One problem is that of causality. Faris and Dunham imply that social isolation is a causative factor in the aetiology of schizophrenia. The fact is that the data shows only a correlation or an association between two factors. For example, an alternative explanation could be that incipient schizophrenics drift towards the high-rate areas – the areas of social isolation – encouraged to do so by the very nature of their mental illness. Faris and Dunham countered this (p. 163) – 'Many of the cases of schizophrenia consist of persons who were born in and have always lived in deteriorated areas. These did not drift into the high-rate areas.' Many cases? How many cases? How many is sufficient to substantiate the argument? Immediately we are led into making further hypotheses and collecting more data – refining the original hypothesis. 'It is a question whether this drift process, which undoubtedly contributes something to the apparent concentration of rates, is anything more than an insignificant factor in causing the concentration.' Doubtful to whom? Particularly pertinent is the very next sentence: 'No decisive material on this point was obtained in this study.'

Do we see here a little bit of intuition intruding into the investigation? Faris and Dunham in their work *opened up* rather than answered the question of a lawful relationship between urbanity and schizophrenia. They provided some very good grist for the mills of others, a potentially useful way of looking at things rather than a sewn up answer. In lots of cases our model of the scientific process provides not answers but further questions. Perhaps one of the most frequently used endings of scientific papers is the one that runs 'clearly, more research needs to be done on this question'.

The picture becomes even more blurred when we wonder about the seventy-six diagnosed schizophrenics in area 1. Chance would lead us to expect 194, or 118 more than there actually were – but there *were* seventy-six. Seventy-six individuals who became schizophrenic when they were not living in areas of social disorganization or isolation. Our finding that social isolation (or its associate, deterioration of housing) is a 'very significant' factor tends to cloud over the fact that all we have actually found is a slightly different *distribution* from that which we might have expected. And to get this we must talk about large groups of people rather than about individuals. We must specifically *not* be concerned with the individual case if this is the kind of investigation we have decided to conduct: we have no way in this investigation of entering into the private world of the individual schizophrenic. We can, for example, make no predictions about one single person's future behaviour in this kind of situation – only being able to quote odds about groups of people. Now this isn't bad – and I am in no way asserting that the Faris and Dunham work is not a very necessary part of the scientific process. It is bad, however, when large groups, statistical tests, and the rest of the paraphernalia become and are heralded as the *sine qua non* of psychological investigation, and it can lead to trouble particularly when psychologists have to communicate their expertise to people belonging to other disciplines who do not have as great a reverence for the *statistical* generality. Environmental psychologists will have an increasing dialogue with architects, designers and planners. Glancing at books on architecture especially, one is struck by the *particular* case (i.e. building) being given the attention, the unique case being valued more highly than the ordinary or frequent case. This argument, of course, is not a new one. A recent exponent of the view that psychology needs to expand its methodological horizons beyond the naive scientific-method paradigm above, that is so dominant in present day psychology, is James Deese (1972). Taking the rapidly expanding field of psycholinguistics as an example Deese says (p. 22), 'A few years ago some linguists demonstrated to psychologists that one could answer penetrating psychological questions about the nature of human language without experimentation or even the explicit collection of data in the statistical tradition of psychology'. And he went on to say: 'The initial reaction of many experimental psychologists was to say that what these linguists were doing was not science . . . It was not science because there was nothing to which one could apply statistics.'

And later he continues (p. 23): 'Some facts about human behaviour and thinking are so obvious that they scarcely need a laboratory experiment to demonstrate them, and they may be far more important than the facts that come out of the laboratory.'*

* He does not, however, give any examples!

On this side of the Atlantic too, there are sceptics. Liam Hudson (1966) tells us that 'There is a case for enshrining the statistical *exception*. In exploratory science, the odd man out is frequently the one who foretells the next transformation in the experimenter's search for order. He deserves therefore to be handled with special care . . . If psychologists care about exceptions – if they *notice* them even – progress remains a possibility.' Hudson (1970) adds: 'What I would like to see is a slight softening of our resolve to be hard scientists above all things – of our tendency to caricature the Victorian conception of the physical scientist, a model incidentally that physcial scientists themselves have long abandoned.'

It is thus my impression of modern psychology that far too much emphasis is placed on statistical sophistication and elegant experimental design at the expense of the *quality* of problem such tools are serving. The tail is wagging the dog. Where are the psychologists who should be throwing themselves into the pressing urgent problems of the modern world? Problems like population control, overcrowding, environmental quality – the social problems so visible in the dense urban environment. They are – with some very notable exceptions – mainly tucked away, hidden from the public gaze in their laboratories inventing better and better statistical techniques to apply to more and more trivial patterns of behaviour.

Those psychologists who have been courageous enough to become involved in environmental psychology not only have a chance of promoting the welfare of man but also could help jerk establishment psychology out of its ever deepening rut of statistical trivialization. For one of the first steps that environmental psychology has already made is towards moving the analysis of human behaviour from the laboratory to its normal milieu of the real outside environment. This is a very positive step forward, since psychology will be faced with a far greater variety of human behaviour than would be prodded from people (mainly volunteer student subjects) in psychologist-created tasks within the confines of laboratory walls.

At the beginning of the chapter I claimed that modern

psychology had two obsessions: one the statistical predilection discussed above and the other the love relationship with the laboratory. The two are very much connected. Something that emerges very plainly in the history of psychology is an increasing realization of the complexity of the nature of man and his behaviour. It is largely because of this realization that the retreat to the highly controlled situation of the laboratory occurred, because where you have tight control you also have the attractive possibility of applying rigorous statistical techniques. Attractive, because once your investigations or experiments can be presented in a way the ordinary man has not the educational sophistication to understand then you have got one of the hallmarks of a science – a private language. There has been, still is, a great sensitivity amongst psychologists about their scientific status. In the early days of psychology it was manifest by psychologists attempting to demonstrate the worthlessness of 'common sense'. Nowadays it is manifest in the too often unnecessary statistical mumbo-jumbo.

Both the obsessions have of course produced enormous benefits. It is just that the time has come to relax about statistics and to weaken the dependence on the laboratory. The ideas generated in the laboratory – important ideas concerning the nature of man – need now to be taken to the outside world of real people in real living environments, and put to the test. I want to suggest that there are two ways of looking at man – developed from laboratory studies – which are ripe for testing in a man–environment context. These ways of looking at man, or 'models' of man, are: 1. Man as an adaptive animal; 2. man as a stimulus seeker.

But first a word about 'models of man'. Anybody who is professionally involved with people's behaviour must develop general theories – implicit or explicit – to explain the behaviour that is observed, or behaviour that is required. For example, law has 'reasonable man' whereby all actions are presumed to be based on rational considerations (which is not true); economics has 'economic man' whereby buying and selling activities are simply profit-orientated (which is singularly different from the way man actually is). Such models do not give a completely accurate picture of man and thus can serve as stimuli to new and improved models. They can be put to the test, refined or jettisoned, but above all they can stimulate observation and inquiry. For example, Peter Jay (1968), an illumination engineering consultant, has briefly outlined the models of man that architects have used in the past, and have found wanting. An early model was that of 'aesthetic man' who was 'responsive primarily to the spatial and visual aspects of buildings and unconcerned with any other features. After trying "functional man", who was concerned with a school only as a machine for teaching in, and a house only as a machine for living in, they now show signs of replacing him by an even stranger monster "environmental man" who is always ready to work hard and long provided only that the lighting, heating and ventilation and acoustics are just right.' Pointing out that such a notion is silly, Jay claims 'there is no escape from a model of some kind', and suggests 'expectant man', 'who compares what he has with what he has a reasonable right to expect, and is satisfied if the comparison is favourable and otherwise complains'. Furthermore Jay asserts that 'It appears that most people are largely indifferent to those aspects of buildings upon which designers lavish so much care, and their general assessment, where not related to purely sociological and managerial considerations outside the control of the architect, are determined by such things as the size and the luxury of the lavatories.'

Such views make sense. How can we know anything about the likely reactions of people to buildings unless we know what they have been used to and what their expectations are? In other words we need to know something about individuals' prior experience of physical environments: what the person or the group has been used to and what expectancies have been established through this experience. We could look at this question through at least two temporal perspectives; evolutionary and developmental. Surprisingly, considering the very strong biological roots that psychology has, looking at man's perceptions and thoughts as products of evolution has not been a popular activity among psychologists; they are more concerned with the relationships between mental life, behaviour and either the surrounding environment or, at the most, environments within the individual's own life span. Environmental psychologist Stephen Kaplan, however, is convinced that the *way* we have of acquiring knowledge and processing information has evolved with marked biases through man having lived through 'millennia of hardship and danger'. Kaplan explains 'There are several things that he [man] would have to be able to do, and do quickly, in order to have survived under the unfavourable conditions that we have reason to believe hounded his footsteps, a. he must know where he is, b. he must know what might happen next, c. he must know whether these things are good or bad. And d. he must know what to do.' Kaplan then suggests that this ability to know is a visually based process and not, as the current assumption has it, based on words or on verbal abilities. 'It is certainly', says Kaplan, 'a viable hypothesis that man acts intelligently with respect to possible futures when he has available strong, vivid imagery about these futures. Words, a late arrival on the evolutionary scene, may not in themselves be sufficient' (Kaplan, 1972).

Why should these abilities be visually based? Kaplan cites evidence from research done by geographers (e.g. Kates, 1962) that *knowing* that a natural disaster (tidal waves, floods, earthquakes) is about to occur does not have sufficient reality to make people move out of the areas. Similarly, although there is widespread concern over overpopulation, there is evidence to show that it does not much affect reproductive behaviour at family level (Barnett, 1970). Concern over pollution only really gets going amongst people when they themselves are affected (de Groot, 1967). If people can *see* something going on around them, *then* it will be real. If they 'know' it as only an abstract problem, there will be no urgency to do anything about it. But Kaplan points out 'our concern is to avoid futures that we cannot afford to experience first'. If we have to experience the deleterious effects of overcrowding, pollution and general environmental decline before we do anything about such problems, it will probably be too late. If the evolutionary experiment of man is going to continue, we will have to find some substitute for direct visual experience of such situations. Kaplan outlines a whole research programme which follows on from taking this evolutionary perspective of man. The following questions, he says, are in urgent need of exploration: 'What are the conditions under which people plan? Under what circumstances are they more likely to take the future into account? What kind of knowledge is most likely to be influential in planning? What is the role of vividness? What is the relative influence of knowledge characterized by imagery? What kinds of experience lead to knowledge likely to be acted upon? What substitutes for direct experience are most effective?' and so on. Thus this evolutionary, adaptive 'model' of man that Kaplan sets out provides the basis for further inquiry.

Turning to the smaller temporal perspective, to the determinants of present behaviour within the person's past experience, there is a very large body of psychological research to draw on from within the adaptation framework. Although psychology has not drawn on evolutionary concepts much, it has strong roots in the biological sciences and has used certain biological concepts as bases for theories of behaviour. One such concept is that of homeostasis. Homeostasis is the collective name given to the set of processes that ensure the constancy of internal bodily environment. Body temperature, blood sugar level, oxygen content, water content, etc. are all kept within very fine limits independent of the outside environmental conditions provided they do not become impossibly severe. This is achieved by the complex neurological and endocrinological control systems within the body. The concept of homeostasis is really a very dynamic concept although in its operation it nullifies the capacity of environmental influences to change bodily states. If it were not for the fact that organisms voluntarily put themselves in 'adverse' environmental situations, it would be easy enough to see homeostasis as a governing rather than 'following' process. Psychologists, in utilizing the concept homeostasis, tended to use the nullificatory aspects of the process, and see these as an end product, rather than see the end product as the new freedom from external environmental constraints for the organism which allows for the development of a greater and wider behaviour repertoire for that organism. It is not surprising that some psychologists did this, because such a way of thinking was around even before homeostatic-based motivational theories began to be popular.

For example Freud (1915) had this to say of nervous-system functioning: 'The nervous system is an apparatus having the function of abolishing stimuli which reach it, or of reducing excitation to the lowest possible level, an apparatus which would even, if this were feasible, maintain itself in an altogether unstimulated condition.' Applied behaviourally to the man–environment interaction, it implies that the environment is something to be reacted to and mollified rather than acted upon. Such a view is not seriously upheld today and not least of the reasons, I would suspect, is that most people know that for themselves it is simply not true. To get nearer to reality we need a concept of adaptation that is dynamic rather than static and one that could be seen to be at the root of new types of behaviour rather than just bringing old ones into play. Such a concept of adaptation is provided by Helson in his *Adaptation-Level Theory* (Helson, 1964). In this extract he explains how 'adaptation level' differs from homeostasis:

How then does adaptation level differ from homeostasis and from concepts that envisage behavior as always changing in the direction of greater stability? The point of view enunciated here asserts that equilibrium states represent the reference points or zero from which behavior is measured, predicted, and understood, without implying that the *goal* of behavior is a state of equilibrium. The adaptation level represents the zero or origin to which gradients of stimulation are referable. The steeper the gradient is, the greater the impact of the stimulus on the organism and the greater the response to it. Repeated or long-continued stimulation is reduced in effectiveness and sometimes completely neutralized because the organism brings its level as close as possible to the level (a weighted mean) of stimulation. With very intense (and sometimes very weak) stimuli complete adaption does not occur. The adjustment level does not rise high enough or sink low enough to negate stimuli completely, except near the lower absolute threshold. There is survival value in remaining aware of such extremes in the environment as the deafening roar of an explosion or the quiet hiss of a rattlesnake. Since level tends to approximate a weighted mean of all stimuli, it never corresponds to zero or complete absence of stimulation. This is true even in cases where there is no stimulation, e.g. in complete darkness, because of fine and gross bodily activities and residual factors with receptors. Adaptation thus occurs with respect to a given segment or region of stimulation, reducing its effectiveness but at the same time accentuating stimuli above and below the critical region. Thus, far from being only a neutralizing process, as in the classical concept, adaptation is also a sensitizing process that enhances some stimuli at the same time that it negates others. Sensory adaptation thus differs from homeostasis, as do other forms of adjustment, in being labile and in having reference to continua rather than to fixed values. Adaptation level furnishes reference points, as does homeostasis, for understanding complex interactions of many simultaneously operating factors in the organism.

This is an enormous conceptual advance over the more conventionally rooted homeostatic theories of behaviour. Helson goes on to formulate the classes of stimuli on which our adaptation levels depend. These are:

a. Focal stimuli (stimuli at the centre of our attention).
b. Background stimuli (stimuli present at the time of the focal stimuli but not being directly attended to).
c. Residual stimuli (the stored memories of past situations and reactions, attitude, personality, etc.).

The fundamental and important implication of this approach is that the prior experience of the individual is taken into account when calculating his adaptation level. Our judgements, perception, learning, even our behaviour in groups, is conceived of as a function of the stimulus range with which we are presented, the context of the presentation and our prior experience involving related situations and stimuli (residual stimuli).

The geographer, Joseph Sonnenfeld (1967, 1969, 1969a), has already tried to develop these ideas in his work on what he calls the environmental personality. In a 1967 publication, specifically following a Helsonian type framework, he outlines three methods for getting at the 'residual stimuli' – the environmental sensitivities, attitudes and preferences of people – in this case in the Arctic. In a later paper (1969) Sonnenfeld breaks down this concept of environmental personality into four categories – environmental sensitivity, mobility, control and risk. That is, Sonnenfeld specifically first defines an environmental personality – i.e. the way in which a person interacts with his *physical* environment (which, as he suggests, may not contain the same modes of action as his interaction with his social environment and therefore should be conceptually distinguished) and secondly tries to break this down into the four categories above. These categories are related to other variables, for example 'those with least schooling preferred places less exotic and risky and were more consistent in wanting to live in the kinds of places they would also like to visit: the more educated by contrast were much less consistent in their preference for visiting and longer-term residences and much more attracted to risk and the exotic in environment' suggesting by implication that we largely '*learn*' (unconsciously?) our environmental personalities. This means in turn that our adaptation level has a large learned component. The next question of course is how large? Can it be unlearned? How easily? What is its weighting compared to focal and background stimuli? etc. Our adaptation levels to varied and wide-ranging physical enclosures await detailed analysis within this framework. It would certainly seem worth trying.

For the history of the other model of man (man as a stimulus seeker) we need only go back as far as the early 1950s and McGill University, Montreal. There was an increasing concern around that time about the so-called confessions that were being elicited from American Armed Services personnel in Korea during the communist trials. Experiments were set up at McGill University under Woodburn Heron, W. H. Bexton, T. H. Scott and B. K. Doane. Subjects were voluntarily confined, asked to lie on a bed in a small cubicle, to wear translucent goggles (which reduced visual patterning) and to wear gloves and cardboard muffs, to reduce tactile sensation. They were confined in a lighted, semi-sound-proofed cubicle with the only noise being that of the air conditioning. The twenty-nine experimental subjects – male college students – were paid $20 a day and were asked to stay as long as they could, usually two to three days, during which period they 'were prevented as far as possible from finding out the time'. The results of this procedure seemed to be general impairment of many perceptual and cognitive abilities, and in twenty-five of the twenty-nine subjects some form of hallucinatory activity ('perceptions without object') and (this was particularly relevant to 'brainwashing') the subjects became more suggestible and susceptible to persuasive argument. The McGill studies demonstrated the importance of environmental stimuli for the maintenance of brain function because the effects of sensory deprivation 'seem to involve a general disorganization of brain function similar to that produced by anoxia, by large brain tumours, or by the administration of certain drugs' (Woodburn Heron, 1961). Inevitably there followed other 'sensory deprivation' experiments. People were put in respirators (Mendelson *et al.*, 1961), immersed nude in warm water (Lilly, 1956), placed in an absolutely light-proof, sound-proof room (Vernon, 1966) and so on.* As work progressed it became imperative to define more exactly the term sensory deprivation and to attempt to specify exactly the variables in such situations. For example, sensory deprivation covered situations of absolute reduction of sensory input (as in the Vernon series) to a reduction in patterning of sensory input (as in the McGill series) to a situation of imposed structuring or monotony of the sensory input without a reduction of stimuli. It also became apparent that the

*P. Suedfeld (1969) gives a comprehensive coverage of the centres and people involved in s.d. research (in Zubeck, 1969).

definition of an hallucination would have to be clarified, as very divergent reports came in of different rates of hallucinatory activity. In the McGill experiments, for example, hallucinations were counted as such if the mental imagery was 'perception without object' although the subject might have no illusions about it not actually being there (although three people thought theirs were 'real'). In the Vernon Series, on the other hand, for imagery to be counted as hallucinatory, it had to '"fool" the observer with its realism'. Further experiments (e.g. Orne and Scheibe, 1964, Murphy *et al.*, 1962, Pollard, Uhr and Jackson, 1963, Myers *et al.*, 1962) introduced the idea that much of the so-called sensory deprivation effects (the cognitive impairment and hallucinations, for example) could be attributable in part to the expectations on the subjects' part that such effects would occur, and on the experimental situation itself. It also became apparent that the personality of the individual could have a fairly swamping effect on the results obtained.

However, the McGill experiments couldn't have happened at a better time, as in 1949 Moruzzi and Magoun published a paper in which they showed that the efficiency of the cerebral cortex (the part of the brain that has most to do with the 'higher' functions) was dependent in part on its receiving non-specific or general arousing neural impulses from a portion of the hind brain: the reticular formation. This network of cells – the reticular formation – receives collaterals from all the major sensory inputs (except smell) which could stimulate it, and in its turn it could arouse the cerebral cortex which could then act efficiently (see Fig. 5). This was a major breakthrough in our understanding of brain function, as the reticular formation could act as a mediator or filter for incoming information from sense organs – a 'missing link' between incoming sensory impulses and outgoing motor impulses. It could serve as the neuronal mechanism for attention (regulating our degree of alertness, acting as a filter) and for governing sleep and wakefulness. Incoming sensory information, then, could now be seen to have two destinations: one to the sensory areas of the cerebral cortex that were concerned

the appropriate nerve fibres or burning out the activating part of the reticular formation), the sense input will not be dealt with adequately. Applying this to the sensory-deprivation situation, the hypothesis might go that sensory deprivation accomplishes two things: specific sense-modality deprivation (e.g. visual input to the occipital cortex) and general reduction of overall cortical arousal, because the reticular formation is receiving no inputs, or very limited inputs, from sense modalities. Incidentally, the neural equipment we have excels at picking up changes rather than continuations of sensory input, so a non-patterning of stimuli would be expected to be doing the same kind of thing as a reduction of stimuli. If the cerebral cortex did not receive arousing or alerting impulses, its efficiency would be impaired – thus accounting for the impairments in the performance of skilled or highly complex tasks on termination of sensory deprivation. But, on the other hand, if the brain is a mechanism that needs variety in sensory input for adequate function, then what there is in the sensory-deprivation situation (and it would be impossible to cut it all out) would be amplified in an attempt to retain neural efficiency. To assume that living biological systems can act in this way in order to protect themselves is not, I feel, an unreasonable assumption. The assumption seems to accord with results. In one of the most extensive investigations of sensory and social isolation ever carried out (involving 352 subjects) Myers *et al.* (1966) found that after four days of such deprivation there was an impairment in intellectual functioning but also some *improvement* in tasks involving simple sensory discriminations – presumably because what sensations there were in that situation were elevated in importance. On the same lines they reported a 'possible greater irritability or over reactivity to mildly noxious stimuli'. The reported hallucinations (even allowing for the artefactual ones) could be interpreted as internally created stimuli in order to retain cognitive integrity. Hence 'man the stimulus seeker'.

This general theoretical statement has, since its formulation, also been extended into the field of individual differences between people. If man is a stimulus seeker (or has to be because of the way his nervous system works) it would follow (a fundamental Darwinian principle) that some people would be more stimulus seeking than others. Neurally their reticular formations would require a greater variety of sense input to produce the same level of cortical arousal. Such a theory has been formulated, and one of the chief exponents is Professor Hans Eysenck (e.g. see Eysenck, 1967). He postulates, with a quite considerable body of evidence in support, that the extravert is cerebrally underaroused, and therefore has a greater need for sensory variety. Thus the extravert gets bored easily, finds tasks requiring sustained attention difficult and needs sensory variety to maintain alertness. Gale (1969) has shown how the electroencephalographic characteristics of introverts and extraverts differ from one another – the extravert displaying a typically lesser aroused pattern than the introvert – which is in line with expectations.

Thus the theoretical line sparked off by the McGill experiments has provided not only a general way of looking at man's behaviour but one which can also be extended to account for differences *between* people's behaviour. It is also, however – like all pan-theories – wide open to abuse, particularly when combined with yet another idea, the essence of which was expressed in a now classic paper by D. O. Hebb (the original recipient of the grant for the McGill experiments). The idea was put forward in a paper with the title 'Drives and the conceptual nervous system' (Hebb, 1955). Hebb postulates (and this idea has a long psychological history) that there is 'an optimal level of arousal for effective behaviour'. If we consider the second task of sensory input (of stimulating the reticular formation to activate the cortex), we could conceptualize two extreme situations: one in which the input is so impoverished that the reticular formation cannot maintain arousal of the cortex which in turn will cause cognitive impairment; and the other where sensory bombardment is so high that the reticular formation overdoes its bit in *over* arousing the cortex so that it goes outside its efficient functioning limits (see Fig. 6). Thus there is a *range* over which a cortex

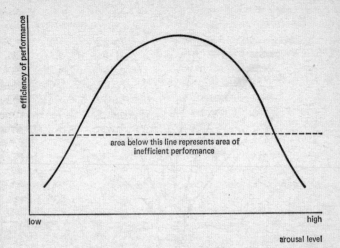

Fig. 6. Graph of efficiency of performance against arousal level, showing that performance can be inefficient at both high- and low-arousal levels.

in a state of reasonable arousal will lead to competent or effective behaviour.

It would not seem unreasonable, if this is the case, to assume that there is some brain mechanism that will promote the containment of arousal within limits. And there is one – namely the corticofugal system. Not only is the reticular formation dependent on sensory input for its functioning, it is also responsive to information sent down from the cortex via the corticofugal system – this can be looked upon as the brain controlling itself. (I've often wondered whether another name for the corticofugal system would be that now psychologically unpopular term – will power.) This means that man will act in ways to increase his sensory input (seek out exciting things to do) if his arousal level is too low, or retire from excessive sensory bombardment if the arousal level is too high. All this in order to maintain an optimal level of arousal. Hebb also threw in the

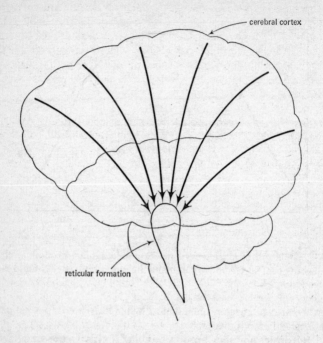

Fig. 7. 'The brain controlling itself.' Corticofugal inputs contributing to the control of arousal level.

idea that doing *both* things might serve as a reinforcer or reward in a learning situation. Thus it can be rewarding to be aroused by a task or it can be rewarding to reduce arousal.

So how far have we got now? Man is a stimulus seeker – he has to be to maintain adequate brain function. Man is a stimulus avoider – he has to be if he is to avoid the consequence of sensory overload. There is an optimal range of stimulus variety over which man works best. And finally people are different, in that the 'optimal ranges' will vary from person to person (e.g. the extravert as against the introvert). One feels one must step back a moment and say 'Gosh, so much

explained with such parsimony!' Almost as good as psychoanalysis. And like psychoanalysis it is in danger of becoming
a part of the conventional wisdom. Once this happens events
will be explained in its terms rather than it being incumbent
on *it* to explain the events. At this moment it either is happening or has just happened. Contrast its use in the environmental field:

> City life, as we experience it, constitutes a continuous set of en-
> counters with overload ... Overload characteristically deforms
> daily life on several levels, impinging on role performance, the
> evolution of social norms, cognitive functioning ... (Milgram,
> 1970)

with an open repeated message of A. E. Parr (1970):

> Our cities have many ailments ... Among which the failings of
> urban architecture must be conceded a prominent place ... while
> psychology was beginning to discover the value of diversity in the
> stimulus field, architecture embarked upon a passionate campaign
> to wipe our urban environment clean of all minor details that could
> have only a psychological justification.

Parr in other papers (e.g. Parr, 1964) suggests a link between environmental monotony (created as a result of the
functional philosophy in modern architecture) and juvenile
delinquency. 'As we make the surroundings more and more
uniform, well regulated and predictable, we force the adventurous to resort more and more to irregular, unpremeditated
or rebellious behaviour as a source of the unpredictable experiences the perceptual environment no longer provides.'

Two very different accounts of 'Man in the City', but both
with roots on the same theoretical base: the city occupying
both polarities on the stimulation continuum. Milgram
claims that the city is over-stimulating, while Parr seems to
look upon some cities as dull, boring and monotonous and
generally mimmicking the conditions of 'sensory deprivation'
and not providing the stimulus variety so important to mental well-being. But surely both accounts can't be right – at

least not at the same time? The endless rows of back-to-back
terraced housing or block upon super block of identical high-
rise flats certainly *might* be monotonous, boring and generally
sensorially depriving, but the high street or shopping precinct
with incessant noise, traffic, burble, variety and people is
surely more towards the stressful, over-stimulation end of the
continuum. We cannot have it both ways. To resolve the conflict, further discriminations are necessary – firstly to get away
from the idea of the city as a unitary entity, and secondly to
sort out the differences and similarities between the conditions in the multitude of different types of sensory-deprivation experiment and the urban scene. And perhaps thirdly
we should put the individual back into all this. Perhaps we
need a concept like 'repetition activity' – doing the same
things even in a highly varied environment might be under-
stimulating. Perhaps we need concepts of deprivation that
attack the effects of specific kinds of sense deprivation:
visual, aural and, most important, MOTOR. Urban dwellers are not physically confined as were the sensory-deprivation subjects except by barriers which are more psychological
than physical, and we know next to nothing about what con-
stitutes a psychological barrier. Surely this is a crucial distinction? And where does *social* stimulation or deprivation fit
into all this? Most of the sensory-deprivation subjects were
confined *alone*. Clearly there is an enormous amount of trans-
lating and extending to be done if this potentially very promising theoretical line is going to give a good pay off in the
man–physical environment scene. Keyfitz (1966), for example, suggests that, although the city is a situation of
'potentially infinitely varied stimulation' the mechanism for
protection developed by man to cope is one of increasing
role differentiation, so that he becomes not a member of an
amorphous city-mass but a useful and important member of a
much smaller body of people which could be interpreted as a
successful adaptation to sensory overload. Looking at man as
a stimulus seeker then, does, as a good model should, enable
us to ask some hopefully answerable questions about the
man–environment relationship.

In conclusion, I have tried to show two things in this chapter. Firstly, that, in looking at the physical environment and man, the psychologist must bring with him his own methodological problems which are, at this point in the history of psychology, in a state of considerable turbulence. Secondly, I have looked at two potentially useful theories of behaviour that have been developed from 'traditional' psychology which until recently has systematically refused to treat the physical environment as a serious determinant of behaviour. These two theories can, if sufficient effort is put into them, form the basis of a tentative theoretical superstructure around which environmental psychology – for the time being anyway – can grow. This of course is a statement of faith. To me it would be an incredible shame not to attempt to use 'traditional psychology' in this way. Binder (1972), however, does not have that faith. He maintains that environmental psychology has more to learn from non-psychological environmental specialists than from 'specialists in basic experimental, quantitative psychology', and that a content of environmental psychology will be richer if it is not dictated by the 'historical development of psychology'. Fortunately, however, unlike physical space, intellectual space is infinite.

4
Architectural Determinism

Norway. Winter. 1900s. Wooden houses, oil stoves, oil lamps, outside, non-flush lavatories. Did these design features as compared to the electric lights, central heating and flush lavatories of the modern Norwegian house make any difference to the way people behaved? Environmental psychologist A. E. Parr, who spent his early childhood in Norway, maintains they did, but in subtle ways. Central heating, says Parr (1970a), allowed for greater use of the spaces in the house because everybody did not have to sit round the stoves in order to be warm. Similarly the electric light allowed the family to disperse within the dwelling. This dispersal of family members under the same roof may possibly have brought about changes in family roles. Formerly, when all siblings and parents in the long winter evenings were confined to one room, the centres of illumination and heat, discipline to ensure quiet for home work or constructive play would be maintained at the instigation of the older children with the parents acting as 'benevolent referees'. When bedrooms became studies such sibling controls became unnecessary, the parents having much more to perform disciplinary functions. In addition the relatively odourless flush lavatory, now indoors and therefore out of the cold, was a far more rewarding place to go for the child who had been recently toilet trained. If the psychoanalytic interpretations of the importance of toilet training are to be believed, this would encourage the development of a more generous, outgoing personality. Parr speculates whether 'the flush toilets in warm interiors may actually be bringing us a tiny step closer to international harmony . . .' Here, then, we see suggestions about the influence that design features can have on behaviour.

When we look at the larger scale, for example the relationships between houses rather than design features inside individual houses, there is some hard evidence. Mate selection – a decision which has extremely long-term consequences in most cases – has been found to be associated with residential propinquity and, oddly enough, in 1931 more Philadelphian marriages were between persons living within five blocks of each other than in 1885, 1905 or 1915 (Abrams, 1943). The same seems to be true of New Haven (Kennedy, 1943) where it was found that 'Propinquity of residence appears to be an increasingly important determinant in the selection of marriage partners . . .'

In 1950, however, what seemed to be an overwhelming case for residential propinquity to be given prominence as a determinant of behaviour was made by Festinger, Schachter and Back in their book *Social Pressures in Informal Groups*. This work, which will be considered below, provided the empirical basis for what Broady (1966) was to call 'Architectural Determinism'. Architectural determinism according to Broady 'asserts that architectural design has a direct and determinate effect on the way people behave . . . It suggests that those human beings for whom architects and planners create their designs are simply moulded by the environment which is provided for them.' It is perhaps more than a coincidence that the philosophy of architectural determinism came at a time when architects were feeling increasingly anxious about their role as manipulators of the physical environment. As other specialists gradually eroded their importance, architects began to see themselves more and more as *social* engineers who could affect the social lives of people through their physical designs. Broady, however, is highly critical of the concept of architectural determinism, seeming to see it as a philosophy that uncritical architects can absorb and trot out as a justification of the importance of their work if that importance is ever threatened. Broady claims that the acceptance of the philosophy by architects saves them 'the trouble and worry of observing accurately and thinking clearly'. A well-known champion of architectural determinism, Professor T. Lee, is reassuring about its implications. 'To assert that our behaviour is shaped by environment is not to concede that we are helplessly moulded, it is merely to assert the need to generate and maintain, on our own volition, a man–environment interaction that will steer the development of ourselves and our children in directions of our choosing' (Lee, 1971). Or, given the *fact* that our physical environment shapes us, don't worry, as long as we understand the process we can intervene to make it accord with our wishes. All this is very cosy except for the fact that architects rarely go back to their creations to see how they are actually performing. The architect's involvement usually ends once the building is erected and is being used. Rarely is any assessment made of how well the building 'works'. It is so rare that when it does happen it is something of an event, as when the Building Performance Research Unit monitored the performance of a school building and in the prefatory editorial remarks preceding the report (*Architects' Journal*, January 1970) it was suggested that the idea of continuing the design process in this way was 'perhaps startling'. Even this paid little attention to the social and behavioural intentions behind the building, for the very good reason that such intentions were not made explicit, which is usually the case. Any behavioural evaluation is thus impossible.

What status should we accord the philosophy of architectural determinism? Does a relatively simple variable like residential propinquity shape people's behaviour? Are Broady's criticisms well founded or is he substituting a sociological determinism (i.e. the overriding importance of *social* structure) for architectural determinism, as Stacey (1970) claims?

In an editorial in the influential *Journal of the American Institute of Planners*, March 1972, the editor talks of the increasingly meaningful dialogue that the planning profession*

* I am aware here of the sudden switch from architecture to planning. There is of course a great overlap – for example, planning has its roots in architecture, and in this country many planners have first been architects. Perhaps instead of 'architectural determinism' it would be more

and psychology are developing. The above mentioned work of Festinger *et al.* is accorded a significant place in this development, as it is in many discussions of the relationship of environment and behaviour. Let us now turn to that work. First to page 160:

> The architect who builds a house or who designs a site plan, who decides where the roads will and will not go, and who decides which directions the house will face and how close together they will be, also is, to a large extent, deciding the pattern of social life among the people who will live in those houses.

And further on page 177:

> The finding that accidental contact which is facilitated by physical closeness is an important determinant of what friendships develop and what social groups form is seemingly relevant to a large number of problem areas. Wherever the physical interrelationships among people are subject to change, either by planning or by accident, we may expect changes in social patterns of interaction to occur. Work groups in industry, the geography of the suburb of a city, the allocation of people in a new housing project or new community, the distribution of facilities in a military establishment, all will have their effect on the formation of informal grouping among the people concerned.

It must have been very pleasant for those 'uncritical' architects that Broady castigates so heavily (who were, paradoxically, aware of social science) to have written for them such a quotable passage by a psychologist of such high reputation as Festinger. However the warning against taking this as a generalization occurs three pages later, on page 163:*

> We emphasize . . . that where the community is heterogeneous one would expect the ecological factors to have considerably less weight than they do in communities where there is a high degree of homogeneity and common interests among the residents.

Easy to miss, short enough to ignore.

----

appropriate to use the phrase 'architecture/planning determinism' or even 'design determinism'.

*First mentioned on page 32.

Festinger's study was an analysis of the friendship patterns
and dynamics of a group structure on an isolated mature
students' (war-veterans) housing project of M.I.T. mainly
for engineering and natural-science students. The students,
all married, occupied two types of dwellings – two-floor,
reconverted navy barracks (seventeen of them) and semi-
detached, pre-fabricated bungalows arranged in nine U-
shaped courts. Fig. 8 gives the site plan.

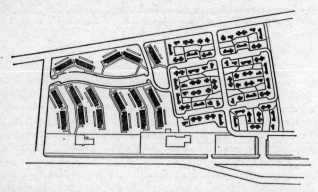

Fig. 8. Site plan of Westgate and Westgate West (after Festinger
et al., 1959).

The bungalows constituted Westgate – the first part of the
project to be occupied (spring 1946) and the converted barracks, Westgate West.* It was completely isolated from
other residential areas and formed a physically very well-
defined community. The dwellings themselves physically
gave no pretensions of permanency, being not very well fur-
nished and having plasterboard-lined walls. Judging from the
photograph of the project, the spaces around the houses were
not cultivated and on the whole the project must have given
an overwhelming appearance of housing a transient population (see Fig. 9). The students and their wives who lived on
the project were very similar to each other in many respects.
They were of a narrow age range of between twenty and

* Occupied in February 1947.

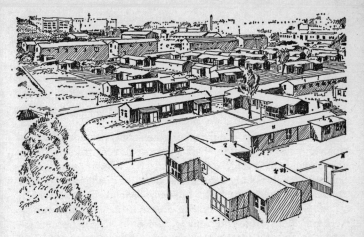

Fig. 9. View of Westgate, schematic drawing (after Festinger *et al.*, 1959).

thirty-five, upper middle class in their residential background (most had been used to large detached family houses), were living at a much lower financial level than they had been accustomed to or would later aspire to. Being students of either engineering or natural history they also had much in common with each other. They could be described as a homogeneous population, although exactly what homogeneity means in the housing context will be examined later.

The data that the investigators collected were obtained by interviewing the wives of the students. From the answers to various questions about participation in the tenant organization and other personal details and preferences the following argument was constructed:

1. The physical layout determines the number of people residents meet 'by chance' (passive contacts).
2. Passive contacts form the basis for the development of friendships.
3. Friendships are the raw material out of which groups are formed.
4. The friendships in groups on the estate provide channels of

communication (Festinger *et al.* followed the course of information distributed on the estate).

5. The content of communications received determines the group's attitude and opinions.

The first and last step is architectural determinism . . . The physical layout . . . determines the group's attitudes and opinions.

The evidence for the first three steps was provided by the answers to the question – asked of the wives only – 'which three people in Westgate or Westgate West do you see most of socially?' Wives only were asked because in the view of the investigators they 'bore the burden of social life [and were] . . . easier to contact', while to do anything else, like interviewing both husband and wife, would 'have hopelessly complicated the interviewer's task'. (In his work on neighbourhood Lee also collected data from housewives: see chapter 7). The friendships ('sociometric choices') so elicited were then plotted graphically against approximate physical distance between dwellings. In the flats the approximate distance between doors was nineteen feet; in the courts the approximate distance of separation was forty-five feet, and in both the flats and bungalows a very clear relationship emerged. The closer together the housewives lived to one another, the more likely they were to be selected as friends (sociometrically chosen). The investigators argued that physical closeness was responsible for the 'passive contact' between housewives; that is, the closer dwellings are to each other the more likely the occupants are to meet each other by accident, and such contact serves as a basis for establishing friendships. So explicit was this 'distance–friendship' relationship that the investigators were able to make (and confirm) certain derivations from it concerning the choices elicited in the flats. Fig. 10 shows, systematically, the access layout out of a Westgate West building and indicates how separated the entrances are from one another. Assuming only that people used the shortest route from door to exit path, Festinger *et al.* made four predictions, an example of which is: 'The people living in the

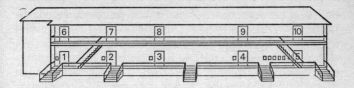

Fig. 10. Schematic diagram of a Westgate West building (after Festinger *et al.*, 1959).

end apartments 1 and 5 on the lower floor should receive from and give to the upper-floor residents more sociometric choices than the people living in any other apartment on the lower floor.' Needless to say, this and the other three similar predictions were upheld.

Step four of the argument – that friendships form the basis of group formation – would lead us to expect that, in Westgate for example, each court would operate as a group, by which is meant that the individuals comprising the group tend to act in a concerted manner, share attitudes, norms of behaviour and have some kind of operative status hierarchy; these are the features that distinguish a group as such from a collection of people. Fortuitously the people of Westgate (the courts) formed a tenants' organization after about nine months of occupancy and this gave the investigators an opportunity to study the operation of such group processes. Westgate West (the flats) was not occupied until after the organization had been founded and thus joined it after it had a chance to establish itself. By rating people's attitudes to the organization, whether they were favourable–active, unfavourable–active, and unfavourable–inactive, Festinger *et al.* were able to determine the types of attitude of people towards the organization both within the Westgate courts and between courts. If group standards were operative, then one would expect similar attitudes towards the tenants' organization within courts but not between courts and, if no *group* standards were operating, no such relationship would be observed. In Westgate this is exactly what was found: that most of the people within a court had a similar attitude to the organization but between courts definite differences emerged. In Westgate West, however, the reactions within and between buildings were similar, suggesting that the group pressures within buildings were not yet in operation. To lend this support, Festinger suggested that other differences between the two should be apparent – and found them. For example, it was shown that in Westgate a 'major determinant of an individual's activity was whether or not others in his group were active', while in Westgate West 'the individuals were reacting more or less independently [of others]' and their activity was related to how much longer they expected to stay in the project. It was also shown that in Westgate there was a relationship between court cohesiveness (a refined measure based on the percentage of 'in-court' choices compared to total number of choices made) and the number of people deviating from the overall group attitude. The greater the cohesiveness the less the deviation. No such relationship was discovered in Westgate West. Group pressures, then, existed in the courts. The status of the deviate was also examined. The term deviate simply describes the person who does not share the group's attitude. It was found that one of the factors contributing to deviancy was the physical isolation of some dwellings. Some of the houses on the courts did not face inwards towards the court but, being as it were on the ends of the U, faced outwards towards the road. It was in these dwellings that there was an undue concentration of 'deviates' – presumably because it was more difficult for the group to exert influence (passive contacts and thus friendships were lower). That is not to say, though, that deviates were not found within the courts also, because they were, but with these the reasons behind deviation were different. Thus it appears that friendships provide channels of communication through which group influences are exerted. This assertion was tested by the experimenters 'planting' information in two courts that were most unlike each other and observing its spread. Two people from one court were told that a national magazine wanted to run a feature article on the tenants' organization, while in the other court two people were told that the organization was to be featured on a national radio network. Nearly everybody was then interviewed to see whether and how the information had spread. It was confirmed that friendship channels had provided communication channels.

From this study of Westgate West it is very clear that the physical matrix in which these people lived exerted heavy directives on group formation, and the dynamics of its processes. However, I believe that this now classic and oft quoted work can be looked at from two standpoints. Firstly, including the first step in the argument, that physical layout and friendship formation follow one from the other (and then the rest of the steps), as an assertion of architectural determinism: and secondly, *excluding* the first step, starting not from the physical layout but from the existence of friendships, it becomes a social psychological theory of group dynamics which could be seen *outside* the context of a particular physical matrix. In other words there are possibly two separate assertions – one that friendship is determined by physical proximity, and the other that groups (outside of any particular surrounding) can exert influence over members through friendships once they are established. It would be my contention that the more *important* standpoint from which to view the book is the second – as a piece of socio-psychological theory – rather than the first – an assertion of architectural determinism. And this is surely confirmed by the actual *title* of the book, *Social Pressures in Informal Groups*, which makes no mention of any physical determinant. However, the book is more often quoted in environment–behaviour discussion from the first standpoint: that its *central* assertion is of the importance of the physical layout – the theory either remaining unmentioned or receiving scant attention. There are in fact a number of passages in the book which refer to the possibility that the ecology of the estate would be of minor importance if the population were a different one, i.e. not as obviously homogeneous (e.g. pp. 32, 59, 153, 160, 163). As made clear on page 176, the prime concern was with 'basic theoretical interests', but with some of the findings having practical application. The only finding of any architectural note was that the physical layout of a housing estate is important in friendship formation of homogeneous, physically constrained, transitional populations. This is not a finding of great generality, but one for which support was certainly provided.

Other investigations have been equally convincing. For example, an investigation very similar in many respects to the Festinger study was carried out by Caplow and Forman (1950) without, until both teams had completed their study, either having knowledge of the results and methods of the other. Caplow and Forman also chose a student housing project (University Village) consisting of fifty married couples with children (it will be remembered that not all Westgaters had children.) All the couples were between the ages twenty-one to thirty-nine, all the husbands were veterans, all were white and all, of course, transient. Caplow and Forman make a strong case for University Village to be considered as a non-stratified society – a community where acknowledged status differences were non-existent or at least so fine as to escape quantification. The question of stratification in Westgate was also, by implication, virtually non-existent. In University Village, say Caplow and Forman, with all status obstacles (occupation, income, family composition, housing type) to 'free' interaction removed 'interaction rises to an extremely high level and organizes itself with almost molecular simplicity in terms of the spatial pattern of the community'.

Using the Festinger and the Caplow studies as a basis, Byrne and Buehler (1955) wondered whether physical factors would determine friendship patterns indoors. They chose to study a college classroom. Taking thirty-three freshman psychology students over a twelve-week period, they found that 'new acquaintanceships were found to be significantly in terms of neighbours as opposed to non-neighbours', and went on to assert, 'It is apparent that with the assignment of classroom seats, an instructor is arbitrarily determining future acquaintances, to a significant extent'. This study has particular significance for me as in my first-year zoology class at university my immediate neighbour later became my wife!! Again, however, in this study a population that is transient, relatively status-free, homogeneous and captive is being considered.

This point about captivity is nicely illustrated by the study of R. R. Blake's *et al.* (1956) of the differences that show up in the social interactions of the occupants of a military barracks when closed-cubicle living arrangements are contrasted with open-cubicle living arrangements. They selected three barracks of open type and three of the closed type. Each barrack contained sixty men and in both open and closed barracks the bunks were segregated into units of six each. The difference between the two was simply that the closed barracks had walls round each unit (with no door in the doorway) while the open ones had no such dividing walls. It was shown that social interactions were affected in predictable ways. For example, the walls served to push up social interactions during 'free time' between members of the same cell or cubicle but to decrease social interactions with men outside the cubicle boundary. The walls, the investigators suggest 'though constituting no legal or geographical boundary limiting interaction, do serve as *psychological* barriers'. The closed-cubicle arrangement also serves to increase the cohesiveness of a cubicle group making 'penetration' by 'outsiders' more difficult.

What these above studies undoubtedly show is the veracity of 'architectural determinism' but *only* when social factors are brought so closely into line with each other that they cease to exert a pull on individuals' behaviour. If all people are equally similar across a wide range of social variables and equally likeable, what other factors are there to influence friendship formation? If one looks back on one's own life and the friends that one has made, it surely must be fairly obvious that most of them were 'circumstantial' friends in no way in possession of particularly special qualities without which friendship would be impossible. They were simply a small range of people picked out from a potential vast array of probably similar people in terms of class, age, interest and status. Friendship formation could perhaps be pictured as a process of cumulative sorting. In the wild one might *seek out* (rather than be passively presented with) persons of similar age. Having made that selection the next search within that age-band might be status similarity, within that interest similarity or perhaps occupational similarity (see Lazarsfeld and Merton, 1954). But while this would be within a framework of propinquity it would not be controlled, merely constrained, by such a factor. When, however, the age, status, interest, occupational criteria are fulfilled in persons who are also close by (as in Westgate and University Village) then it *appears* that proximity is a dominant influence. The dominance, however, is illusory, it is important merely because all the other criteria have *already* been fulfilled. Selection then follows the law of least effort. Another example is given by Park Forest studied by Whyte (1956) where observations very similar to Festinger's were made.

Thus, if the above is true, it would follow in a less-selected or self-selected group of people in which there was a heterogeneity of population that proximity factors would be far less influential. And indeed this would appear to be the case. Carey and Mapes's (1971) recent study of social activity on new housing estates shows that similarity of people in terms of age and stage in life cycle means more visiting and more friendships. The physical factors play a minor and unimportant role. So much for architectural determinism!

When I first became aware of the way which, I felt, Festinger's work was being misused I also became aware of the *lack* of use of another of his works (Festinger 1951) which also had something to do with housing, and had, for architects at least, the far more alluring title of *Architecture and Group Membership*. This was the study of the 'Regent Hill' housing project for shipyard workers. Regent Hill was a government-sponsored project of 100 houses (the same size as Westgate) built specifically for shipyard workers. On this project Festinger found 'an inadequate social life . . . social isolation' and further 'a surprisingly great amount of hostility expressed towards neighbours'.

The reasons Festinger put forward for this were not in terms of physical layout (of which no mention was made) but because 'the great majority of residents keenly felt that they had been forced to live in the project by circumstances beyond their control'. And for others 'war exigencies . . . had forced them to live there'. For the rest? '. . . it was the acute housing shortage and impossibility of finding other places to live that had made them come to Regent Hill'.

This led, continues Festinger, to a resentment at the group memberships that were forced on them. And what is more they did not find any satisfying group membership outside the project, imagining that, as they looked down on it themselves, so would other people. Clearly one must know something about the people before claiming authoritative control over their social behaviour through environmental manipulation.

A similar lesson can be extracted from the equally impressive (from a social psychological point of view) work of Deutsch and Collins (1952). They wanted to investigate 'the effects upon prejudice of . . . publicly supported, non-segregated, interracial housing projects'. Obtaining the cooperation of housing authorities in Newark and New York, they set to work. Newark operated a segregationist policy where Negro and white families were segregated, whilst in New York the occupancy pattern was integrated. 'Integrated' was the term they used when white and black families lived in the same building, 'bi-racial' when white and black lived on the same project but in different buildings. Passive contacts between white and Negro will inevitably be higher in an integrated project.

From interviewing housewives, Deutsch and Collins found that in the integrated buildings as opposed to the bi-racial buildings:

1. There were more instances of friendly neighbourly contacts between black and white.
2. There was a social atmosphere more favourable to interracial associations.
3. There was a more closely knit network of associations.
4. More favourable attitudes by whites to Negroes were expressed.

5. Prejudice against other minority groups (e.g. local Chinese) were less marked, and housewives were more favourably inclined towards living in an interracial project.

It should be made clear that before integration most of the housewives did not like the idea of living in the same building as Negro families.

Deutsch and Collins ascribe the lower prejudice expressed by the white housewives in the integrated project to three main factors:

Firstly, that the physical and functional proximity interracially was greater in the integrated project making interaction possible and likely. But, as well as this, the social norms implicit in official policy were favourable to integration and the social norms of the project and those of the broader community were at variance. This served to bring the members of the project closer together, to, as it were, close ranks against a hostile community. It was these *social* factors acting in an appropriate *physical* matrix that increased interracial togetherness. It is not only short-sighted but erroneous to consider one without the other, or to elevate the importance of one at the expense of the other. Thus Broady's (1966) statement, 'architectural design, like music to a film, is complementary to human activity, it does not shape it' and Lee's (1971) equally extreme assertion 'that our behaviour is shaped by environment' can both be seen as dependent on context rather than generally applicable statements.

As with all behavioural-science generalizations we must pause and ask: about whom are we talking? in what social structure are we intervening? and so on. Architectural determinism as a philosophy will be perfectly adequate in certain fairly constrained situations; in others it may well be irrelevant. Its danger is its simple-minded quality. Its central assertion, that physical design is shaper of social processes, taken out of context, without the qualifications that I have shown to be necessary, might lead the unwary to a naïve policy of environmental transformation in the hope that change in behaviour will inevitably follow. Thus the thinking would go: if we find a lot of social pathology in slum areas, then clear away the slums, provide a 'better' environment and social pathology will decline. Dean (1949) has argued strongly against this 'myth', showing firstly that the social pathology – slum relationship is only correlative not causative, that it doesn't explain 'why many families living in sub-standard conditions do *not* experience divorce, or delinquency, or alcoholism ... why in a given family in sub-standard housing one boy may be delinquent, or mentally deficient, or unhealthy while his brother has remained free of these maladies'. This is not of course to say that substandard housing should in any way be tolerated, but it is to assert that removal of such conditions is a very *small* step to amelioration of the social pathologies. Wilner (1962), for example, carried out an investigation of 1,000 families (5,000 persons) between the years 1954 and 1960. Two samples from this population were surveyed eleven times during the study. A test group, who were originally slum dwellers, were subsequently moved to a new public housing project. A matched control group remained in slum dwellings for the duration. (Interesting to note again that the interview data were secured from the *female* heads of households.) This study provided many examples of how interwoven are the environmental, physical and social factors. Concerning the school performance of children, it was shown that school promotion tended to depend on regular school attendance. Greater freedom from illness amongst those children who were moved out of slum conditions to improved physical conditions made this possible. Wilner also raises the question of a new improved physical environment altering a person's self-concept. Wilner hypothesized that the improvement in housing quality 'might give rise to upgrading of self-perceived class affiliation' and because of this 'families might also acquire heightened aspirations'. The first part of the hypothesis was confirmed; the second 'with a few exceptions' was not.

The perception of self and how such perceptions are formed are questions with which psychologists should concern themselves. Searles (1960) maintains, for example, that our culture consciously ignores the psychological importance of the 'non-human' environment while at the same time being unconsciously 'over-dependent on it'. It is perfectly possible that the physical environment provides a rich source of data not only on how we are expected to behave (see Barker, 1965, 1968 in chapter 2) but also for development, maintenance and flexibility of a person's self-concept. Theories of child development often lay stress on the process of a child learning to differentiate itself from its environment, of learning the boundaries of its own body. If early environmental experience is restricted, then it might follow that the development of a self-concept is retarded, variety of experience being a determinant of the development of the perceptual processes (Held and Hein, 1963). But these ideas remain to be explored, and are a long way from architectural determinism. The point is being made that individual psychological processes intervene between the environment and the social behaviour within that environment. It is by studying these psychological processes that the relationship may be illuminated.

Much has been made in the foregoing discussion of homogeneity and heterogeneity of populations. It is easy to accept these terms unthinkingly and be led to believe that what they describe is easily discernible. However, as I will attempt to show, it is not that simple. The question of exactly what characteristics of a population have to concord before it can be called homogeneous was indirectly raised by Gans (1961), an American sociologist and city planner. In this paper, Gans was arguing the pros and cons of whether planners should promote heterogeneous or homogeneous populations in newly housed communities. It is probably true to say that the tendency is for planners to plumb for heterogeneity rather than homogeneity. Gans, however – and he is not alone in this – sees the establishment of heterogeneous communities as *not* the best way of ironing out some of the more gross social inequalities in the pluralistic American Society but as simply an opportunity for destructive social conflict: 'Total heterogeneity is likely to be so uncomfortable that only those who want no social contact with neighbours would wish to live under such conditions'; or else special conditions have to be fulfilled, as in the Deutsch and Collins study discussed above. Gans also maintains that 'Complete or near-complete homogeneity, as in a company town where everyone has the same kind of job, is clearly objectionable.' Gans recognizes the generality of these statements, and asserts that this is a result of how little is known about the consequences of heterogeneity and homogeneity.

I, however, would assert something different – namely, it reflects how little we know about the *meaning* of the terms rather than their consequences. Homogeneous means consisting of parts all of the same kind; heterogeneous composed of diverse elements. In the Festinger study it meant similarity in age, class, aspirations, stage of life cycles, interest, future occupation (profession), present student status, marital status and transiency. In the Caplow and Forman study it referred to family composition, absence of servants or relatives, student status of husband, age range, place of birth, skin colour, etc. The question is, how similar is similar? Given that all human beings are unique, *how* little do they have to differ from one another and still comprise a homogeneous population? Do certain demographic or sociological variables carry more or less weight than others? For instance, is it more or less significant if your neighbour has a very different job from your own, or is it more important that the neighbouring household's child-rearing strategy is similar to your own? Some variables are clearly more important than others. Child rearing patterns more important than age? Job more important than ethnic origin? and so on.

Perhaps the overwhelmingly important variable is that of class, if only for the reason that it includes so many characteristics either by definition or implication. But social class is of course notoriously difficult to define. The Newsons (1965, 1968), whose work on child rearing will be considered in the next chapter, chose one single criterion to determine the social class of their subjects – that of father's occupation. This has certain advantages as it clearly correlates highly with other characteristics, like income, residential area, education and the like. The Newsons indeed found strong correlations between class as a single criterion and the child-rearing strategies under investigation. Kinsey (1948, 1953) in his pioneering studies of sexual behaviour chose educational level as his criterion, as it not only correlates with ultimate occupational class obtained by an individual but 'has proved to be the simplest and best-defined means for recognizing social levels'. Jane and Roy Darke (1969), however, take a different view. To quote them: 'Traditionally, class distinctions are based primarily on occupational differences and this remains generally true to the present. However, recent empirical work has begun to show that simple one-variable models are rarely useful. Class and status depend on a number of variables and these hierarchies tend to operate in parallel, making for a complex interlocking model instead of the unitary model which seemed sufficient in the past.' They tell us, for example, of the necessity for conceptually distinguishing between class and status, class referring to an individual's capacity to gain income (through skill or possession of property) and status 'not only to the chances [to] receive esteem but also the life chances . . . that result from status prerogatives', i.e. a difference between occupation/income against style of life. These distinctions and the general search for conceptual clarity about such terms are of course necessary, but up to now planners have tended to use the single criterion of occupation as a social-class indicant as synonymous with population homogeneity and vice versa. And the discussion of whether communities should be planned for homogeneity or heterogeneity has been in these terms.

The New Towns Committee (H.M.S.O., 1946) were 'frank' about the 'problem' of 'class distinction' and also ideologically committed to producing balanced communities – 'as long as social classes exist, all must be represented in it' (paragraph 22). But, as Heraud (1968) put it – 'It appears that a recognizable degree of social segregation is an invariable concomitant of any housing development, whether or not this is guided by attempts to reduce such segregation.'

It is within the very nature of social processes that people in a group are seen by each other as different from one another. As Bruner *et al.* (1956) say, in their study of thinking, 'Human beings have an exquisite capacity for making distinctions'. As we saw in chapter 3, man is a stimulus-seeking animal, who in the absence of stimulus variety will amplify that which is available. Thus a so-called homogeneous community will very soon be seen by the people in it as a heterogeneous one, because the people will inevitably make distinctions. It is a fairly well-known fact that very small differences between people can be amplified to enormous proportions particularly if the situation is one that is long-standing and involves some degree of constraint. The extreme versions of such a situation are prisoner-of-war camps and the like. Our nervous system is built in such a way as to be responsive to change rather than monotonous similarity. It seems that when enduring groups are formed – and a group can be anything from a 'family' to a 'community' – for that group to be so designated, certain criteria will be seen to be fulfilled. One of these criteria is that it will have a 'pecking order' or a status hierarchy (Sprott, 1958, Argyle, 1967, Kretch, Crutchfield and Ballachey, 1962 and many, many others). People will be differentiated according to the power or influence they vest in the group. Leaders, whether formal or informal, will emerge, and there will be created a network of likes and dislikes. People will not be seen just 'as people' but as people having certain qualities, capabilities, and as distinctly differentiated from other people in the roles they play. Thus groups in one way or another become stratified. Form (1951) presents a well-argued case exactly on these lines. Where we have an apparently socially homogeneous population there are, says Form, enough variables over (see above) to form the basis of a stratification process – aspirations, recreational pursuits, etc. In other words the homogeneous society, when viewed from the inside, is a myth. If it exists, it exists in that short period before people have had a chance to make distinctions which they will, eventually, inevitably make. Had we gone back to Westgate after a period of ten years and found the same students there, gone would be the straightforward proximity–friendship relationships.

Another point should be made. In chapter 3 the work of Helson was discussed. Helson has developed the concept of adaptation level which is a continuously changing origin on which stimuli impinge and are referable. A person's adaptation level is itself related to three different classes of stimuli: focal, background and residual. If we see 'other people' in a housing community as the focal stimuli, then how we adapt to them (our adaptation level) is also dependent on what we've been used to and the sort of person we are (the residual stimuli) and also on our perception of the other local housing communities (the background stimuli). What we've been used to is an important variable. For example, Jahoda and West (1951) tell us, concerning the question of bi-racial housing 'that those prospective tenants without actual bi-racial housing experience are more likely to prefer segregated housing and to expect conflicts between the races in non-segregated housing'. Thus to be able to make an intelligent comment about homogeneity of a community entails entering into the world of the person who is (by his/her very nature) making distinctions in that community. The planners' penchant for conceptualizing the balance of a community using social class as a crude measure of population homogeneity imposes a measure on that community which that community itself may not even recognize as valid or accurately descriptive. It might be that such a measure can and does serve some purpose – after all most measures in psychology are imposed without a person's knowledge or acquiescence – but could it be that a measure of homogeneity, developed from the conceptions that the people *themselves* hold, would allow a far greater understanding of what goes on.

Roger Brown (1965), an eminent American social psychologist, even goes so far as to assert that social classes have no functional reality at all – at least in the United States. One of the reasons for this argument is that, if classes did represent some social reality, there would be sharp discontinuities between them in terms of people's consciousness of class, the structure of interactions between persons in such classes, and style of life. From his review of a considerable body of evidence, Brown concludes that such discontinuities do not exist and that the functionally real social categories are *roles* not classes.

Whether or not Brown is right it would certainly seem that homogeneity can have two meanings: looking down from the outside, using social class as an index, or from the inside using the persons' own perceptions of the other members of the group – their similarities and dissimilarities to each other. One could call the first, external homogeneity, and the second, internal homogeneity. Jane and Roy Darke (1969, 1969a) suggest something similar, claiming that an incorporation of personalized meanings of class can be an aid in understanding 'class' differences.

With this in mind let us go back to the U-shaped courts of Westgate and the 'deviates' therein. Whilst there was a definite concentration of deviates in the outward-facing houses, there *were* deviates in houses facing onto the court. There must surely have been something about the personalities or styles of living of these people that brought about their relative rejection. Everybody is not equally likeable even though there is 'external' homogeneity. How much more interesting the Festinger data would have been if sociometric data had been gathered on dislikes as well as likes! Some information might have accrued on how nasty a person has to be to outweigh the effectiveness of the propinquity variable!

One recent and very important work which appears to be, at first sight, in the simplistic, architectural deterministic tradition is that of Oscar Newman (1972), although he himself is adamant in disclaiming such an affiliation.

Newman, an American architect, is concerned with urban crime: not the tax evasions of the middle class, nor the well-planned, expertly executed and highly rewarded bank robberies, but the muggings, the petty thieving with assault, the senseless violence in deserted lobbies of high-rise flats, the vandalism and the opportunist break-ins on anonymous government-sponsored housing projects; with those crimes, in fact, which seem most indicative, many believe, of the decaying moral fabric of our society; crimes which seem to provide the most visible and depressing manifestation that man has over-reached his capacity to adapt to urban living.

It is difficult, says Newman, to be socially cooperative with your city neighbours, because the city has such a wealth of diversity of people and value systems that a common ground may not be immediately obvious. Shut away on the thirteenth storey of a high-rise flat, it seems easier to be lonely than to risk life and limb getting involved in the prevention of the vandalism and misdemeanours that are taking place around you. This is Newman's starting point. He asks what modifications can be made to the physical environment to make the residents *want* to get involved in its protection and upkeep, want to eradicate violence and petty crime from within the living enclaves of high rise blocks or government–sponsored housing. The reason for withdrawing from community life, says Newman, is because residents cannot identify with, or exert any control over, any of the space outside their own front door. As such space is 'public' and nobody 'owns' it, nobody will 'defend' it against interference. The task confronting the architect is to make such spaces defensible, to extend to the residents ownership of, and responsibility for, the spaces outside the front door that were formally regarded as public. Once this is done, residents will be able to challenge outsiders, knowing that their neighbours would do the same in similar circumstances, and, in times of great threat, all would be able to call on one another for support. How are the 'public' spaces made defensible?

Firstly, such territories must be defined and delineated. The landscaping policy for most high-rise developments is one in which such territorial definition and delineation has been deliberately designed out, the surrounding space being made to look as unowned and 'public' as possible. This must be counteracted. The area around the building must be seen to belong physically to the building and come under its influence. If the high-rise blocks are in a cluster then the surrounding land should appear to belong to the cluster and become, in effect, an external extension of the internal living spaces. This can be achieved by the erection of physical barriers like hedges, fences and so on, to enclose areas and 'attach' them to buildings. A further claim to ownership can then be made by including within these enclosed areas amenities which the residents will use – playgrounds and sitting areas, for example. A non-resident now, in such an area, will be made to feel like, and be treated as, an 'outsider'.

In addition to the *establishment* of territories and zones of influence, constant *surveillance* by the residents is also required. It must be made easy for the residents to see what is going on within the enclosed areas, so that they can immediately spot 'strangers' or be alerted to suspicious behaviour and take prompt action if necessary. By constant surveillance Newman does not mean the residents maintaining around-the-clock watches but just the ordinary incidental activity of taking a look out of the window occasionally. If a stranger does enter these areas, the residents will immediately be in a position (with territorial right on their side) to challenge him, direct him to his destination or, if his status is suspect, make it known that he is unwelcome. Clearly territorial delineation and surveillance will only work as mechanisms of defence if they operate together. You cannot defend what you can't see is being attacked and you are unlikely to defend what you do not feel is yours. Another feature of many low-rent housing projects in the States (and the same is true in the U.K.) that exacerbates the crime statistics is that they tend to be designed so that they stand out from the surrounding context by virtue of their starkness and lack of architectural embellishment. It is almost as if they are being set up as a target for attack. The interiors, too, tend typically to be 'institutional' in character, with tiled walls, uncarpeted floors and 'vandalproof' fitments. The message is defiance, a physical challenge to those who do not wish to be contained to show that they are superior to their symbolic prison walls. Newman argues that such environments make the residents devalue themselves, lose their self-esteem and self-respect and so create a vicious circle of damage and repair and greater damage.

Newman bases his thesis on data gathered in New York,

where the variety of housing provides for a 'natural experiment'. Unlike many other cities New York has both high-density and low-density housing in the central and outlying areas which permits the study of the effects of physical design independent of urban location. Low-density housing is usually only typical of non-central city areas and dominated by middle- to-high-income families and vice versa. The New York housing pattern allows for the 'controlling out' of the factor of urban location, looking exclusively instead at the effect of physical design.

Do Newman's ideas work? The answer appears to be an overwhelming yes. Modifying living environments to make them defensible does cut down the crime rate. Newman, however, denies the existence of a straightforward causal relationship (architectural determinism) between environmental modification and lowered crime rates. Implicitly, he evokes a particular 'model of man' (see chapter 3) to make the connection understandable. Firstly, he says (and it is mainly said between the lines) that man is a territorial animal, that he needs territory like he needs water, in order to be able to live a satisfactory life. Secondly, he claims that man is not basically criminal – preferring social cohesiveness to anarchy, social harmony to tension. Providing surveillance over defensible spaces allows man to be the animal that he *really* is rather than forcing him into an unnatural environment where he cannot survey and defend simultaneously. This two-pronged model of man is certainly an adequate basis on which to build a programme of crime reduction, but it does raise other questions. One question concerns the genesis of crime. Newman claims that much of the sort of crime that he is concerned with is 'crime of opportunity' rather than premeditated. Remove the opportunity and the crime disappears, or rather is displaced to other environments that are less defended. In fact Newman admits that crime displacement *does* occur (where modification programmes have been carried out) but not to the extent that would be expected. To achieve the maximum possible crime reduction, therefore, *all* living areas (the problems of industrial areas, etc. are

somewhat different) will have to be *equally* defensible. But it
would be very naive to think that, if this were achieved, the
crime problem would disappear altogether. The premeditated crimes would still occur and perhaps the hardened,
violent criminal psychopath would be excited by the increased
danger that such defensible environments afforded. This is a
point that Newman seems to overlook. Throughout his book
the criminal remains completely anonymous – a faceless and
nameless anarchist, without parents, spouse, home or identity. At one point in his book he discusses a particular park
which 'attracts all the bums and addicts in the neighbourhood' and, at another, comments of an environment that has
been made defensible that 'The addicts have . . . been driven
elsewhere'.

But who are these people – the addicts and the bums? Certainly they were once someone's children, but why did they
become addicts? What are the reasons behind their bum-
hood? Where do they go now? Newman has simply taken up
the slack. He has cut down or displaced those crimes where
the opportunities provided by the physical characteristics of
the environment played a significant part. He has offered a
more humane, and in the long run cheaper, alternative to
crime prevention than is provided by increasing police
strength. He has placed greater control within the hands of
the community and coincidentally, but just as importantly,
allowed the underlying cohesiveness of the community to be
articulated. But he has not told us anything about crime or
the criminal. He has made it more difficult for the criminal
to operate, so that the less committed may yield to the increased difficulty, but the rest he has forced elsewhere.

This must not be construed as a criticism of Newman's
ideas concerning defensible space – indeed I think they give
good reason for hope of a better future for many millions of
people – but it is meant simply as a caution against thinking
that 'defensible space' means the end of urban crime. Behind
each crime statistic is an individual. Some individuals are no
doubt 'determined' in their criminal activities by the degree of opportunity available. Others, however, and perhaps

these present a more serious threat to social cohesion, will seek out or create such opportunities for themselves. It is these individuals to whom defensible space will be just another occupational risk, another obstacle over which to triumph. And it is also these individuals who must be intensively studied if urban crime is to be eradicated. As long as they are faceless they will remain. What Newman has done in tightening up the physical environment is to allow us to shift our attention away from the environmental arena to the criminal himself. At the moment it remains to be seen just how much of a problem there will be and what exactly will be its nature, but Newman's policy of metaphorically giving people their own back yards could release the architects and planners from their share of the burden of guilt for, particularly, vandalism and other 'crimes of opportunity'.

Is Newman's thesis 'architectural determinism'? His main reason for disclaiming such a description is based on his belief that for 'true' determinism the physical environment–crime link would have to work both ways. If it is possible to generate crime-free living enclaves through physical design, the converse should also be true. A 'malignant authority' should be able to create crime-laden living environments through the reverse procedures. Newman doesn't seem to think that is what has already happened (perhaps because the malignancy is unintentional) but instead quotes the extreme case of the now demolished Pruitt-Igoe housing project in St Louis, U.S.A. This project turned out to be so bad in terms of crime, vandalism and so on that finally people voted with their feet and simply moved out or refused to be housed there. If the environment really is bad, says Newman, people will not tolerate it, at least they will not tolerate it for long. I do not accept this argument of Newman's because it does not sufficiently take into account the adaptability of man nor the extent to which his current levels of what is acceptable are drawn from the available personal experience (as discussed in chapter 3). Thus, while a bad environment will not be tolerated by those who have known better, there will be a greater chance that it will pass as 'normal' for those who have no other experience. Second- and third-generation high-rise dwellers will be bound to perceive their buildings differently from first-generation dwellers. After all, it was not the people themselves who articulated the concept of defensible space – it was Newman. *He* tapped a feeling and gave that feeling form. I don't think there can be any doubt that Newman is talking architectural determinism. His protestations are altogether unconvincing. However, it *is* a more sophisticated version than was developed out of the Festinger study – not simply because it seems to give reassurance against a galloping social collapse but because it incorporates an identifiable theory of man as a territorial animal needing to live in a socially cohesive society. Such a model can help us to further explore the man–environment relationship. Also, by focusing so clearly on the physical, environmental determinants of crime, and their control, it will allow others, if they choose to take the advantage, to sharpen *their* focus on some of the *other* determinants of this undoubtedly multifaceted problem. For these reasons Newman's work represents a very positive advance towards a greater understanding of urban life.

So what started out as a seemingly straightforward relationship between propinquity and behaviour, and the philosophy of architectural determinism to which it gave rise, has gained in scope and complexity. The questions we can now ask about the man–environment relationship can be much more sophisticated. The following chapters each make an attempt in this direction.

5
Space and Human Development

Bring your children up in the middle of a rural environment. Now start all over again, but this time bring them up in the middle of a city. How different would they be? Do different types of physical environment have different effects on the developing child's view of the world, which might form the basis for later adult modes of thought or action?

One approach to such a question would be to follow through a large group of children from their earliest years from very different physical backgrounds (i.e. do a longitudinal study) in an effort to tease out, from the myriad of factors involved in the child-rearing process, the specific part played by the physical environment. One could speculate, for example, that rural children experience a very different overall socialization process than do children reared in the heart of a busy industrial city. Some very obvious differences might include the number of other children around, the amount of physical space to roam without 'trespass' and without danger to life (e.g. from cars), the involvement of children in father's occupation and so on. It has also been suggested (Parr, 1967), that the modern urban environment compared to the urban environment at the turn of the century has very different implications for the child-rearing process. Today because of motor traffic the urban environment is a far more dangerous one for the child and consequently he is far more restricted in his explorations. Also 'the opportunity for frequent and independent visits to cultural treasures and centres of informal education are virtually eliminated by the urban spread'. There is perhaps the tendency to experience the world second hand through television rather than having a first-hand involvement. Thus the child becomes conscious of an enormous world 'out-there', but experiences it from within smaller and smaller actual physical confines. Are the television children of today in any way different from the children of yesterday whose experience of the world – though more limited – was more *actual*? These questions are not about particular small-scale variables but about atmospheres, climates and possibilities created by major societal systems, e.g. the rural social system as against the urban one or the horse-drawn world of yesteryear compared to the electronically dominated world of today. Is it, or will it ever be, possible to determine the specific effects of specific factors or will we have to wait for historians to explain to us retrospectively how our psycho-social evolution is unfolding?

Although future historians will undoubtedly be able to say something about the effects, at this point in time, of an ever more rapidly increasing world urbanization, I believe, from work that is being done now, that certain trends are becoming apparent. These trends rest on certain assumptions which fortunately can be made explicit.

Firstly, that the habitable space on earth is finite, and that the population of earth is increasing exponentially. From this follows that on *average* each individual will have available a smaller space to inhabit.

Secondly, that the early years of life, and particularly the first five, are crucially important for the development of an adequate adult personality.

And thirdly, an important arena of learning for the preschool child is play, particularly play with other children. Such play gives the child the ground rules for social interaction with contemporaries or 'peers'. Clearly, how children should interact with peers can be the subject of parental guidance, but it is only by actual interaction that the child develops his own styles of personal interaction.

The trends I want to discuss are based on the work of psychologists Drs John and Elizabeth Newson of Nottingham University (1963, 1968) whose work I will now consider.

The Newsons' aim is to collect information about how children are being brought up in this country at the present time, in an effort to provide a solid empirical basis for understanding the child-rearing process. No such basis (although much speculation) has existed previously. Their view is that the most informed expert on a child is the child's mother. The mother sees more of the child in more situations than anyone else, expert or not, and it is the mother therefore who is in the best position to understand her child. The Newsons wanted to know what parents *do* as opposed to what it is thought they do, or what they are told to do. Their studies have three specific aims:

1. To obtain a complete picture of the child at successive stages of development from childhood to late adolescence in his actual surroundings.
2. To obtain a clear picture of the mother's behaviour and attitudes and feelings in relation to her child.
3. To look for cross-sectional (related to age) and longitudinal patterns (cause and sequence) in the data (1970, p. 13).

From the voluminous data which the Newsons present we are interested in only a small part, namely the part that the physical or environmental factors seem to play in the interaction of the mother and her child, and the child and other children.

The information was collected by intensively interviewing 709 mothers of one year olds in Nottingham (the 1963 study) and then 700 mothers of four year olds, 275 of whom were followed through from the original 709 (the 1968 study).

The fact that the Newsons used the interview as their research tool is noteworthy as is also their attitude towards this kind of research. They claim, for example, that in the past psychologists, in attempting to understand the child-rearing process, have spent too much of their energies looking at specifics (e.g. bottle feeding v. breast feeding) rather than the more important considerations such as the kind of relationship the mother has with the child. The general atmosphere of the home and the total climate of the child's upbringing are the important influences and if this fails to show up in the researches of psychologists then, say the Newsons, it is the methodology that is at fault. As mentioned in chapter 3 psychologists have been (and still are) insecure about their status as scientists in the past and one way for psychologists to allay this insecurity as scientists is to invent measuring devices which no one else can understand: measurement being, of course, at the very kernel of the scientific process. However, the Newsons are *not* insecure about their status. The best way of finding out how a mother treats her children is, they say, to talk to the mother, to allow her, without fear of censure, to say exactly what she does, feels and thinks about bringing up her children. The interview is taped and the classifications and categorizations are done from the recording *after* the interview is complete, so there is nothing to interrupt the mother's flow. Their work represents a genuine curiosity to find out rather than an attempt to prove or disprove hypotheses, which has been the characteristic mode of psychology's past. Although technically it would be classified in a Barkerian scheme (see chapter 2) as an 'operator method', it is close in spirit to a transducer methodology. It attempts to get at the 'psychologist-free' units of behaviour. As the Newsons say, their research was not guided by 'preconceived hypotheses', instead they look for 'meaningful patterns in the material as it emerges' (1970, p. 21).

One very strong pattern to emerge was the relationship between social class and parent–infant behaviour, both in the one-year-old study and the four-year-old study where the Newsons note that 'class affiliations remain pervasively powerful even in the minutiae of the four year old's daily life'. This is vital from our point of view, as these social-class differences between four year olds are very much related to the different physical world in which children of different social classes live.

The Newsons' definition of social class is taken from the 1960 Registrar General's *Classification of Occupations*, slightly modified to give them five social classes:

middle class $\left\{\begin{array}{l} \text{I – and II – professional/managerial} \\ \text{III w.c.} \quad \text{– white collar} \end{array}\right.$

working class $\left\{\begin{array}{l} \text{III man.} \quad \text{– skilled manual} \\ \text{IV} \qquad \text{– semi skilled} \\ \text{V} \qquad \text{– unskilled} \end{array}\right.$

This was exactly the type of classification (i.e. social class using only one criterion, in this case occupations) that came in for criticism from Roy and Jane Darke (1969, 1969a) in the last chapter, but it is one, however, that despite its crudity illuminates the Newsons' findings. Having adopted this working definition of social class, they then divide the housing types 'rather arbitrarily' into three categories – central, council estate and suburban. The central area is predominantly a working-class area of tightly packed small terraced housing (see Figs. 11 and 12) or larger houses converted into flats. The council estates are fairly well self-contained with most amenities within their boundaries. Finally, the suburban group is a 'frankly miscellaneous grouping including all housing which belongs neither to the tight grids of streets in the centre of the city nor to the . . . estates. As well as the smaller council-house groups, it takes in all varieties of private ownership, from small 100 per cent-mortgage, semi-detached villas to large detached houses in spacious gardens, worth £10,000 and more by 1964 values' (p. 31). It should be pointed out that class 1 and 2 on the council estates are in the main providing specialist skills to the estate (clergyman, doctor, policeman etc) and 'their homes are likely to be specially planned for their profession, and rather grander than the normal run of council estates' (p. 32).

Inevitably the classes are not distributed evenly among this variety of housing as table 2 shows, but the working class dominate the central housing, the middle class the suburban housing, with the council estates somewhere in between.

Table 2.
(From Newsons' Table 1)

Types of residential background of four year olds by occupational class.

	I and II	III w.c.	III man.	IV	V	all
central area	6	16	43	41	45	34
major council estates	14	34	34	35	38	32
suburban	80	50	23	24	17	34

All figures are percentages

The Newsons attempt to delineate the physical differences of these environments, and discuss: the plan of the houses; physical layout – gardens, communal back yards, outside privies, etc.; areas for children's play; location of activities in the houses (e.g. eating in the kitchen); furnishings (whether home has carpets, books, etc.); cleanliness of the home; absence or presence of plumbing, etc.

One factor which seems to be of overriding importance is the amount of space available to a child, and it is quite clear that the working-class four year old has less space both inside and outside the house in which to play as compared to a middle-class child. Concerning the amount of space and its importance in the child-rearing process, the Newsons note, 'The change to a slightly larger house can mark a new stage for a mother in her dealings with her children' (p. 39). A decent play-area for the children, protection of the children from traffic and a corner in the house (in some cases a room) 'which the child may regard as his own' (p. 40) are all spin-offs from having more space. *That is, extra space makes possible a different attitude to child rearing.*

But the average working-class child, as well as having less space than his middle-class counterpart, is crowded on another count. He is more likely to have more siblings. As the

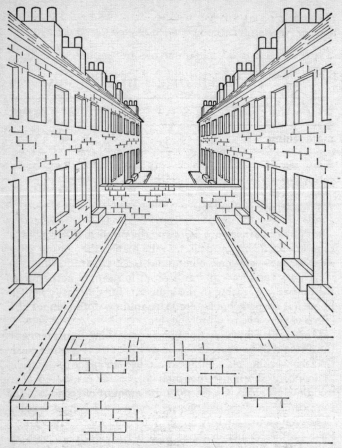

Fig. 11. '... tightly packed small terraced housing ...'

Newsons say, and as table 3 shows, 'families with only one or two children are more likely to be found in the middle classes. Families with four or more children are more likely to be working class, while those with five and over occur six times as often in class V as in the middle-class group. The majority of middle class families have two children or less.'

The Newsons go on to warn, 'This factor of family size needs to be borne in mind . . . when class comparisons are made'.

Table 3.
(From Newsons' Table 3)

	I and II	III w.c.	III man.	IV	V	all (random)
only children	17	19	10	9	1	11
2 children	49	44	31	33	22	35
3 children	19	25	26	25	20	24
4 children	9	7	11	13	19	12
5 or more	6	5	22	20	38	18

From this it can be seen that a working-class child lives in a more densely populated environment, and is therefore more likely to get under his mother's feet, 'more likely to have siblings of an age to play with him, more likely to have much older ones as well, of an age to mother him or boss him around . . . (is) less likely to have play space of his own inside the house, and such space as there is will tend to be over-crowded' (p. 42).

Thus middle-class and working-class children live in very different physical worlds and these physical differences play an enormous part in the socialization of the child. The Newsons' argument (from the data of their chapter 5 – Social Learning and the Control of Aggression) can be summarized step by step as follows:

1. The working-class child lives in a more crowded environment – more siblings and less space.
2. The play of the working-class child must perforce take place in the street or other communal areas and *not* on the home territory.

Fig. 12. Middle-class housing.

3. The working-class child is therefore more likely to come into contact with all sorts and a greater number of children.
4. The working-class child's choice of friends is not guided by the parents, as all children play on communal areas.
5. For the same reason the play of the working-class child is not generally supervised by adults.
6. The working-class parent is reluctant to interfere in children's play, because this may lead to conflict with other parents who are also neighbours.
7. Conflict with neighbours is less easily tolerated in the

working-class environment because of the greater propinquity of families and the fact that working-class parents could not help but come into contact with the offended neighbours and meanwhile the children would have made it up anyway.

None of the above applies to the middle-class child.

As a result (p. 138):

> [The working-class] child is born into an environment which is likely to be described as a 'bit rough'. *There is nowhere to play except the yard or the streets, where supervision is negligible*; so that once outside his own home the child encounters a social free-for-all from which he can only expect rough justice. He learns from infancy that when 'playing out' he must fend for himself, surviving either by his wits or his fists.
>
> At the other extreme, we have a professional-class child whose whole sphere of social interaction is closely supervised by an adult ... In a m.c. [middle-class] area *the children do not play out in the street as a matter of course ... and many will never venture outside their own garden gate unless accompanied by a responsible adult.* [my italics]

Thus, the Newsons claim, working-class children learn that 'might is right, the weakest to the wall', while middle-class children, under constant instruction from adults, since they are under constant supervision from them, learn moral principles, fair shares for all and receive 'copious verbal explanation of the principles [they] must follow'. Also 'Mummy ... reserves the right to exercise some selection in the choice of her children's playmates, thus she will discourage *and discourage successfully*, a child who has the reputation for being over-aggressive, untruthful or light-fingered' (p. 134).

While we can now say there is some sort of relationship between the physical environment and what is learned through play, we can also say that that relationship is not a simple one. Class attitudes intervene between the two. There are 'fundamental and deep-seated differences in attitudes towards the general theme of controlling child behaviour' between working- and middle-class mothers. To support this view the Newsons compare working-class mothers' attitudes towards children's quarrels with the type of housing they occupy.

Table 4.
(From Newsons' Table 14, p. 137)

Differences in working-class mothers' attitudes towards childrens' quarrels, as a function of residential district.

	working-class mothers in central districts n=194 %	working-class mothers in new estates n=164 %	All working-class mothers n=463 %
a. mother accepts role as arbitrator	23	14	20
b. Half and half	40	47	45
c. mother lets children settle own differences	37	39	35

differences not significant statistically

The council-estate mothers as compared to central-area mothers have more space for their children's play and in particular have a garden with a gate which shuts so the 'toddlers can play in the open area but away from the traffic' (p. 37).

As table 4 shows, despite the big differences in physical environment, there are no corresponding changes in attitude towards children's quarrels, *but* as the Newsons themselves say (p. 133) 'we would explain these results in terms of a cultural lag hypothesis; that is to say, it takes time, perhaps measured generations, for a new physical environment to modify firmly established beliefs and values. A shift towards middle-class material standards is not automatically accompanied by a shift towards middle-class attitudes.'

In so saying, the Newsons are implying a cause–effect relationship (more accurately, a cause–delayed effect relationship) between physical environment and children's concepts of justice on which, later in life, their moral behaviour will depend. This is a reasonable and eminently testable hypothesis, and for the purpose of this thesis the Newsons' work thus far has heightened our awareness of and sensitivity to the correlation between physical environment and certain aspects of behaviour. What I want to emphasize from this study are the different types of moral bases of behaviour *which are made possible* by different configurations of the physical environment.

One more point remains to be discussed from the Newsons study. Looking again at table 4, at the frequencies of the mother accepting role as arbitrator, we see that only 14 per cent of working-class, new-estate mothers as against 25 per cent of working-class, central-district mothers accept this role. Now although this is an insignificant difference statistically, the trend which it expresses is the reverse of what one would expect. As the Newsons say, when the working-class, central-district mother moves to a new estate she can then actually more easily indulge her working-class pattern which is generally one of non-involvement. That is, when 'released' from the cramped physical environment, the working-class mother is now in a position *never* to arbitrate, because neighbour contact can be avoided (or more easily avoided) than it could when they were all living on top of one another. The new physical environment is making possible an exaggeration of a former attitude. Why the mother does subsequently adopt, or shift towards, middle-class values and attitudes – as a cultural lag hypothesis predicts – only further research will clarify.

In summary we see that there is a class-related style of control of four-year-old children's play. Also, such control mechanisms as there are, are themselves related to the physical environment in which they are enacted. It would be impossible for a middle-class mother to behave in her middle-class way in the sort of physical environment most working-class mothers live in. This would not (does not) operate vice versa.

The whole process of child development and socialization is one in which the child moves from being a totally dependent person to a person whose behaviour, feelings and thoughts become autonomous, but within a social context, rather than being generated by the social context itself. To be a mature adult is to operate as an autonomous agent, and *not* to operate in this way – to be dependent on others – is to risk being labelled 'neurotic' with all the attendant consequences of not being treated by others as an equal. But like every other human characteristic autonomy will vary in degree, in the speed at which it develops and so on. But the speed at which independence or autonomy in social interaction with peers is strived for, encouraged or inflicted is in part related to the facilities provided by the physical environment. It is difficult to protract the period of dependency in the working-class environment because as the child's orbits naturally expand they have to take in physical areas which are outside maternal jurisdiction. As the middle-class child's orbits similarly expand they do not have to go outside physical areas which are maternally controlled. These areas are the enclosed gardens of mother and her circle of friends, who can be entrusted to exercise motherhood roles by proxy. Thus 'inside' and 'outside' the home for the working-class child is a much more definite distinction, without intervening gradations, than it is for the middle-class child.

I am of course, for the sake of argument, deliberately conceptualizing this as more black and white than it actually is, in order to raise the question of whether – through physical design, or physical contingencies – such patterns of behaviour can be promoted or discouraged. Could we deliberately set out to create an environment which would foster in the growing awareness of the child a sharpness of distinction between codes or moral behaviour towards and within the family as contrasted to codes which would be used *outside* the home? Lee Rainwater (1966) provides some interesting data that relates to this question, titling his paper 'Fear and the house as haven in the lower class'. Rainwater was the director of a five-year investigation of the social and community problems of the Pruitt-Igoe public housing project in St Louis, U.S.A.

Based on interviews carried out there and other places, Rainwater suggests that different social classes have different attitudes and feelings towards their houses and that they serve very different needs. The 'lower class' – equivalent to the Newsons' Class V – see their homes as fundamentally to provide shelter and freedom from the very real environmental threats just outside, both human and non-human: from violence and assault to rape and 'trash'. The more privileged classes – taking such things absolutely for granted – use their houses, not as havens but as a basis for the elaboration of a richer social life, and as a means to establishing symbolically the material values of American society. Interestingly Rainwater points out that the environmental threats which are *just* outside the front door for the lower class, for the more privileged lie at the boundaries of the neighbourhood itself: their perceived 'territory' thus extending beyond the confines which they actually inhabit. For the lower class, inside is private, outside is public and therefore dangerous. Yancey (1971) writing of Pruitt-Igoe puts the lack of neighbourly relations down to the lack of any *semi*-public space, which is necessary for such informal connections to be established.

Rainwater goes on to describe the typical results on child rearing of environmental threats being *just* outside: 'Two of the most common', he tells us, 'are a pervasive repressiveness in child discipline, and training, and, when that seems to fail or is no longer possible, a fatalistic abdication of efforts to protect the children.' Once the children realize that protection from parents is not forthcoming they 'lose faith in them, and come to regard them as persons of relatively little consequence'. As in the Newsons' working-class pattern the children are removed from the moral strictures of their parents (mother) and learn a much more practical morality. An enforced severance occurs separating child from mother's moral influence.

Separation of mother from child, or parents from children, is of course nothing new. Since the industrial revolution children have been compulsorily removed from the family unit to be educated; removed to hospital for treatment when sick; put in nurseries to allow the mother to work in factories away from the family home; and the recent discovery that pre-school 'play groups' are a good preparation for school adds another separation to the lengthening list. The present urban family structure and activities are very different from the pre-industrial revolution family unit – a unit that was the site for both production and consumption (Dominian, 1968). Separations such as these can be seen as part of the ongoing psycho-social evolution of greater and greater social complexity, of greater and greater role differentiation within society, making it necessary for the child to receive its instructions in the ways of the world from the hands of more and more people. In these separations, however, the children are not being given up but given over to people with special training. Rainwater's Pruitt-Igoe and the Meadows in Nottingham are examples of where there is both separatism *and* a relinquishment of adult control. Pruitt-Igoe consisted of thirty-three, eleven-storey, slab-shaped buildings running in six parallel rows, each building containing seventy dwellings. With no space inside for a middle-class type controlled play situation, separation here will be much more distinct. When going out to play involves not only the usage of lifts, etc. but also tremendous physical and functional distance between child and parent, all the casualness and voluntariness of 'going out to play' is lost. As the Newsons (1971) say:

In a house with a yard or garden, however small, the toddler is enabled to make a slow development *at his own pace* towards independence. At one stage he will not tolerate being in a different room from his mother and will move with her as she moves around; then he makes his own sorties, first into other rooms, then outside on to the step, then to the gate to watch the world go by – but the point is that this development is voluntary, that the child increases the duration and distance of his absence at will, and that the separations alternate with casual interactions between mother and child. When 'outside' means seven floors down and is totally separated from 'inside', 'going out' becomes impossible except under formal conditions of 'being taken' and the child loses both the voluntariness and the casualness of this aspect of development. We suspect the second loss is quite as important as the first; that children need periods of casual parental contact just as much as they need periods of full attention.

Small children in high-rise buildings have of course been a topic of concern for a fair period of time now – the consensus seeming to be that high rise do not provide a proper environment for the rearing of young. Jephcott (1970, p. 80) in looking at high-rise flats in Glasgow notes the 'Glasgow tenants' almost universal comment that high flats were "nae use for bairns". Whether the speakers were young parents or ancient grand-dads, they seemed to feel instinctively that multi-storey life was somehow alien to the children.' And she continues, 'So did most of Glasgow doctors, psychologists and social workers . . . and the housing officials, architects and sociologists met with here and abroad.'

And the N.S.P.C.C. study (Stewart, 1970):

> The bulk of research indicates that the great majority of families with children in high-rise or low-rise flats are not satisfied with the accommodation, with living off the ground or with living in a flat and many could not be said to be happy. No matter how roseate the spectacles of the researcher this impression is inescapable.

And to particularize, Burbridge (1969) notes:

> from the large amount of material on the effects of high-density living on younger children the conclusions emerge that those in high flats tend to be more restricted in their activity patterns and

that, to counteract this, they should all live close to adequate and safe play spaces. *But the gap in the evidence is the real effect of this activity restriction on the child's development.* [my italics]

The provision of adequate play space for children in high-rise flats has been seen as very much a priority, but no amount of play space – supervised or not – will, if it is on the ground between blocks, prevent the greater emphasis of the division between 'being out at play' and 'being indoors at home'. If high rise are going to be successful it is that problem which must be solved. Saying this does not of course mean that adequate play space away from home and at ground level should not be provided, but it is to assert that it does *not* solve the major problem which is the emphasizing on the 'in-here: out-there' division and the severance of casual contact between mother and child.

The following are examples of suggestions that have been made to improve the quality of life for children in high-rise dwellings, all of which overlook these major problems.

1. The National Council for Women of Great Britain published a paper (1969) with the title 'Guidelines for happier living in high blocks', in which they outline some of the problems of high-rise living and some suggestions for resolving them. They write that 'By asking Man to live in high blocks of flats, we have taken him away from his natural biological environment and therefore made him feel subconsciously insecure.' In particular there are problems with young children. Apart from suggesting that they should not be housed in high rise at all, they suggest 'more playgrounds . . . to involve the mothers as well as children . . . play spaces with traffic-free approach' and so on. All highly laudable – but what about those interminable hours of the child's 'free time' when it is not in a formal play session, when it's just playing around, increasing its distance from its mother *voluntarily* and having *casual* maternal contact? Play groups, safe play spaces, are not going to provide the necessary conditions for that.

2. The National Playing Fields Association in their publication (1953), 'Playgrounds for blocks of flats', noted not only the paucity but also the poor facilities of playgrounds. In the recommendations for playgrounds for children between two and five they suggest that such a site should be 'within sight of the mothers', but 'it should not be so near ground-floor flats as to cause a nuisance from noise', and that within it there should be a space partitioned off 'and a self-closing gate provided (with a self-latching catch on the outside), so that toddlers can be left on their own for short periods while their mothers get on with their work'. Admirable in intent but again completely neglecting the nature of the child's play. Also 'within sight of the mother' may not mean that the mother is or even could be in sight of the child. And anyway in sight is very far removed from within easy reach. Again a solution which looks good but in fact emphasizes the 'in-here: out-there' distinction so much at the basis of a 'might is right' moral code.

3. That the 'within sight' recommendation might be followed to its literal, logical extreme is the implication in a scheme outlined in *Housing Review* (1966, p. 54), to quote: 'An unusual feature of the Chalcots estate in Adelaide Road, Hampstead, may be the installation of closed-circuit television to enable mothers to watch their children in the playgrounds below four (twenty-three storey) tower blocks ... The London Borough of Camden are considering whether in this way they can overcome one of the disadvantages of housing families with children in multi-storey dwellings.' On their own television set they will get, on two channels, two views of the playground. Mothers will be able to watch in the comfort of their own home their children bullying or being bullied, and generally having a fun time with their peers without in any practical way being able to intervene. And if mothers did, imagine Mrs Brown smacking Mrs White's little boy on stage in front of cameras and watched by literally hundreds of pairs of eyes!!! (What about having an instant-replay facility?)

4. In the publication *The Needs of New Communities*, H.M.S.O. (1967), the authors note that 'opportunities for play are essential for the normal growth and development of a child', but that 'Even with improved standards of space in the home there is seldom a room available in which children can play without interruption. The gardens of new and expanding town houses are frequently small, and the more pride is taken in them, the less likely are they to be a place where children can play freely'. Thus parents, or rather their children, will have to use other facilities – school, park or recreation ground. Again, separation. The committee do suggest, however, that experiments should be made, like 'private gardens opening on to a communal space in which children can play in complete safety'. (One could of course wonder why not just have a bigger garden?)

What I am trying to show with these examples is that, although most people recognize the value of play for the proper development of children, they do not recognize the gradualness of the child's increasing independence from the mother, nor that the provision of play space away from the home base is intervening in this gradual development, breaking it into discrete elements. Consider the following quote from a report of the National Swedish Institute for Building Research:

In studies of the play habits of children it has been stated that children under school age stay near their homes most of the time they are out of doors, near the entrance, irrespective of whether the planners intended it or not and irrespective of whether the forecourt is a playground or a parking space. The children's choice of places in which to play and their fields of action seem to take very little account of the layout of the plan. This must therefore to a very large extent take into consideration the patterns which appear to apply to the general outdoor habits of children under school age. A play space which is thus essential is 'Free space in the immediate vicinity of the dwelling for younger children's daily play'.

In high rise as at present designed such a requirement is

not fulfilled and, as Rainwater pointed out, the response could be either excessive repression or relinquishment of control. The implication of repression can be drawn from a study by Maisels (1961) in which it was shown that mothers would not let their children out to play unsupervised until they were a lot older than they would have to have been had they lived in houses. Only 5 per cent of children below four were allowed even downstairs alone. Compared to the house-dwelling Newson children this is indeed a small percentage.

Mrs Brown put some cloth on this statistical skeleton in replying to Des Wilcox on a B.B.C. *Man Alive* programme (1968) on the high-rise flats in Silvertown in London's East end:

The children are tied to the flat all day and, if you go out in the hall, you've got the lifts coming up and you cannot let them out there, and if they accidentally go into the lift they cannot reach the buttons and therefore you have to be on constant guard all the time because they mustn't go out in the hall to get shut in the lifts at all.

and she goes on: 'the children get out on to the verandah – or the windows – there is always the chance that they could fall.' Mrs Brown continues: 'I think when you've got children you do need a garden – I mean all children like to dig dirt, they like to play with water, but here you cannot do that because they haven't got the facilities.' As Rainwater found at Pruitt-Igoe, 'There is a constantly expressed desire for a little bit of outside space that is one's own or at least semi-private'. Or to take Liverpool, Leeds and London (M.H.L.G. 1970) where, in the high-rise projects surveyed, 71 per cent of house-wives with children under sixteen would have preferred a house, mentioning in the majority of cases the desire for a garden or saying it was because it would be better for the children.

But is it really all so bad? Perhaps one of the difficulties about high rise is the constant expectation that as living enclosures they should be able to mimic exactly the facilities of small houses with gardens. Could it be that, to make them work, these expectancies should be revised?

High-rise living is a totally new concept and a very recent one in the evolutionary history of man, and it is likely to become more not less common; so it would therefore be a pity to condemn it without first trying to understand the nature and quality of life of those therein contained. Would cave-dwelling Neanderthal man have held up his hands in horror at our present idealization of the neat semi-detached or detached house as the 'right' environment? Desmond Morris (1969), in a salutory reminder of just how far we have come in so short a time, tells us that a piece of land 400 square miles would 'a mere few thousand years ago' be the territory of a handful of sixty human beings – today the 'handful' of human beings is likely to number 6 million. We cannot go on expecting to live out social codes suited to vastly different socio-physical environments of a former time. We must adapt. Pearl Jephcott (1971), for example, points out: 'Those who fit easily into life in a high flat are people who are self-sufficient and socially rather "above average". The wider their experience of men and affairs the more they can cope with sharing services and undertaking mutual obligations with a large number of other people. The more advanced their level of education the more likely they are to recognize the risks associated with this type of home. And the higher their income the more they can afford to spend on compensations.'

Elsewhere (p. 105) she speculates: 'Would it be a fair assumption that "living high" caters best for the household and individual who, in very broad terms prefers order to growth?' And further, that women seem to tolerate high rise better than men, that high rise is particularly hard on the socially below average, as the props which might exist in terms of neighbours and friends in on-the-ground housing are less likely to be in evidence in high rise. As we might be led to expect, some people will adapt to this housing form better than others; it will bring out those qualities *in some people* which would otherwise lie dormant. Take the case of Mrs Jean Young, reported by Molly Harrington (1964). Jean Young was in her twenties and had considerable social skill, insight into people's personalities and above all a 'clear and articulate conception of neighbourhood life'. She managed to promote on her floor of a multi-storey block of flats a close-knit, mutually aiding, little community. She did so, claims Harrington, as a reaction formation to her childhood hostility to her mother and deep affection for her father, whereby 'the original wish to come between the parents has been denied, the drive behind it being diverted to maintain the opposite position. What results is a need to keep people together, to build on the positive qualities of loyalty, protection, love and kindness.' It matters little for this thesis *why* Jean Young is the way she is; what matters is that she was able, with her clear conception of what she wanted, to enlist neighbours to pro-duce it. This implies collusion on their part and a certain malleability and, as Harrington remarks (p. 281), 'people without a guiding image of what they want or with hazy expectations of life in a new environment are probably only too glad to collude with someone who offers them a "design for living", whatever the motivation of that person might be.' The echoes of Jameson (1971) in chapter 2 seem remarkably pertinent – what can people be persuaded to want?

It is extremely noteworthy that the neighbourly system so skilfully generated by Mrs Young had implications for child care. Joint responsibility seemed to be one of the values that this group adhere to – a 'code which allows any adult to reprimand any child, and makes the adults responsible cor-porately for all the children'. And this is something which the children themselves recognize. A five year old returned from school one day, walked in on Mrs Young's and asked the three women there, 'Who's watching me?' – sure evidence of the child's accurate perception of the situation. Also difficult and unpopular children are not excluded, other children are not insulated from them and so on. Although similar in many respects to the working-class, Newsonian pattern discussed earlier, the big difference is in the *shared* responsibility of caring for the children.

What makes Harrington's study particularly interesting is the comparisons between Mrs Young's group and a similar collection of people similarly housed in a near-by block. The general picture here was one of 'unease in social relations': strife about the state of the building, and about the children, and general hostilities. After considering differences between the populations in the two blocks, Harrington suggests that the one big difference is the presence of Mrs Young. Mrs Young is the driving force behind the neighbourliness and its original initiation, even though she was not the first to arrive but one of the most recent. So again, as in the last chapter, we see the importance of considering the dynamics of this group situation in terms of the psychology of its individual members; for the populations in the two blocks were, at a sociological level, homogeneous. The qualities necessary for successful adaptation to new housing forms would not appear to be completely contained in such sociological variables.

I began this chapter by promising to extract trends from the work outlined above. It is now time to make these trends explicit.

The work of the Newsons show us that the moral code the pre-school child learns is inextricably bound up with the physical space in which he is brought up. It seems that people living in very close proximity, with no semi-public or semi-private space over which they feel they have authority, relinquish directing control over their children's play. The children in their turn are taught by their peers rather than their parents during that generally acknowledged formative activity of play. However, the children can still maintain casual contact with parents on their road to independence.

This casual contact with parents is important: the child can develop at his own pace. But in the high-rise housing form even that is lost. The high-rise housing form adds a new dimension to the might-is-right/close-proximity code by disallowing (or heavily discouraging) even that casual contact. Thus, so runs my claim, the differentiation in the child's mind between 'playing out' and 'being inside' is made very distinct. Mothers recognize that they have to be around for their children in order to provide a base of operations and security from which the children can go out and explore the world. Thus their adaptation to this enforced distinction is to either keep them in more than they would otherwise do or relinquish control totally. Both of these would produce bad psychological effects (this is surmise). Enforced physical proximity can mean, therefore, increased psychological apartness between generations, with, as a result, more and more social pathology (delinquency and the like). A gloomy picture indeed.

However, there is one assumption upon which the whole argument above rests, and indeed the Newsons made it quite explicit in the beginning of their account of the four year old. Namely that the *family* is the main vehicle through which a child is socialized. 'The family is the basic group to which humans give allegiance,' say the Newsons, and continue, 'the nuclear family excludes outsiders for a relatively long period, so that, for English children, the process of socialization will tend to be mediated through social interaction of a most intense and intimate kind within the family right up to school age'.

But what if we tried to modify the traditional nuclear family? What if we set up a social structure where children were socialized by a *group* of adults instead of as is now the general case only two? What if we, in effect, extend the familial boundaries, so that the family is not two parents plus children but ten adults with *all* their children? Would it work? Of course it would be essential for everyone to live in close proximity to one another, a requirement fulfilled by high rise. Gone would be the might-is-right code of outdoor play, because any adult would be sanctioned to intervene. Gone would be the distinctiveness of out and in, as there would always be a parent surrogate with whom the child could have casual contact. Gone would be the withdrawal from intimacy that physical proximity encourages. All this may sound very extreme, especially for a country where 'the Englishman's home is his castle', but weren't all the elements there in Mrs Young's circle? The joint responsibility for children, mutual caring, the ever-open front doors?

Perhaps we should get away from trying to live out a rural life with the extended territorial rights that it implies and adjust to the urban scene of closely packed living. Adjust by adjusting the *way* we live; instead of retreating from intimacy, embrace it. *If* – and it is a very large if – high-rise urbanization is inevitable (on an extended time scale), the psychological question becomes not the traditional restrospective one of, what are its bad effects? but the instrumental one of, what is it that prevents people from adapting? When those were answered we would be in a position of creating a genuine 'Urban Man', a position where we would be in control of our own destiny.

6
Space and the Small Scale

Residential propinquity may or may not be at the root of friendship formation; close proximity may generate psychological distance or greater intimacy; what sort of spaces children are reared in may affect their adult moral conduct. These are some of the general statements which have emerged from previous chapters. In this chapter I want to focus attention on some of the concepts that have been, and are being, developed which help explain why man has such a complex relationship with space; why it is that not all spaces are equal; and why certain types of behaviour are likely to occur in certain types of space and not others.

One of the fairly recent 'discoveries' about man is that he is a 'territorial' animal. It may seem odd to anyone who has felt the irrational anger at the trespasser in the front garden, or the irritation when someone comes and sits too close on the holiday beach, or when a guest unknowingly sits in 'your' chair, that it is only recently that behavioural scientists have discovered man's territoriality. After all, in other animals the marking out of territory, the defending of it and the migratory returns to exactly the same place have long been an accepted part of the study of animal behaviour, and much of modern psychology owes its existence to studies done with sub-human animals. How is it that man's territoriality was left out? Even as late as 1958 Carpenter, in his review of the concept of territoriality, closed with the remark, 'the territoriality of man is [a] theme which remains to be systematically studied'.

The reason is that psychology took a wrong turning during the first half of this century – a wrong turning that can be laid squarely on the shoulders of the behaviourist movement started by J. B. Watson in 1913. Watson was all for making psychology objective and quantitative. To this end he suggested there was little point in trying to deal with the processes of consciousness but rather one should go for the measurement and quantification of behaviour. Nor did he like using human subjects in experiments because he thought the whole business artificial and unnatural. (This aspect of the experimental situation is itself now a matter of study by psychologists.) Much of his work was therefore with animals. By using animals it was thought that the basic or fundamental behaviour mechanisms could be studied, as it were, in the raw. The justification for this was provided by Darwin (1859, 1871), who showed that physically and mentally man was just another animal. All man's behaviour, said Darwin, even the most human of his behaviours like his morality and altruism, had precursors in lower forms. Thus the psychologists began to study animals as though they were a simpler version of human beings (e.g. Thorndike, 1882). Such an attitude is exemplified by Kohler (1925) in his preface to his work on *The Mentality of Apes*. He tells us that, although apes are a long way behind man in their ability to behave intelligently, 'it is precisely for this reason that we may, under the simplest conditions, gain knowledge of the nature of intelligent acts', and that in ape performance, 'we may see once more, in their plastic state, processes with which we have become so familiar that we can no longer immediately recognize their original form: but which, because of their very simplicity, we should treat as the logical starting point of theoretical speculation'. Animals came to be treated by psychologists not in their own right, but as simple human beings who could be prodded to perform simplified but basically *human* tasks like learning the path through a maze! If the fundamental laws governing a process like learning are the same, as was the claim, then it clearly becomes irrelevant what animal you study. Sure enough this became the case, and with few exceptions (Bitterman, 1965) the rat became the animal (Lockard, 1971; Wilcock, 1972). The study of animal behaviour in its own right was left to the ethologists (e.g. Tinbergen, 1951; Lorenz, 1966).

This is ironic. Animal psychology, with its roots in Darwinism, completely neglected one of the fundamentals of Darwinian theory: that evolution took place by a process of natural selection which worked on the genetic variability within a species. The overriding influence the animal psychologists studied was the effect of environmental variables on behaviour rather than genetics. Indeed genetic explanations of human behaviour have been unpopular in psychology ever since Watsonian Behaviourism became an influential force. Watson unashamedly over-emphasized the importance of environment (Watson, 1925), and his influence has impeded the progress of behaviour genetics for many years. In 1972 there appeared in the most widely read American journal of psychology, *American Psychologist*, an open letter signed by fifty behavioural and biological scientists, including four Nobel Laureates and many psychologists of very high international standing, in which they found it necessary to draw attention to the 'great influence played by heredity in important human behaviours' and to note that 'Recently, to emphasize such influence has required considerable courage, for it has brought psychologists and other scientists under extreme personal and professional abuse at Harvard, Berkeley, Stanford, Connecticut, Illinois and elsewhere' (Page, 1972). As it is fairly obvious that many territorial behaviours of sub-human animals must be genetically controlled, this fact also presumably militated against studying territoriality in humans, because to do so would be to risk asserting a genetic basis for human behaviour. In view of this, and the fact that animals were treated as simple human beings, it is perhaps not surprising that human territoriality has remained for so long 'a neglected sociological dimension' (Lyman and Scott, 1967).

It was, in fact, mainly left to the writer Robert Ardrey, in his popular book *The Territorial Imperative* (1966), to bring into general focus the idea that much of human behaviour could be better understood if it were seen in relation to a territorial need or instinct, and, further, that man's territorial need was indeed genetically rooted with very apparent evolutionary precedents. Ardrey was very critical of the Watsonian influence in psychology and he argued forcibly for a reinstatement of instincts in the analysis of human behaviour. In arguing this way, Ardrey is asserting that man has a need for territory, its acquisition, maintenance and defence, in just the same way that he has a biological need for food and water (although one may wonder whether the territorial need has such intensity or whether it is more like sex which, though not strictly necessary for an individual's survival, is nevertheless essential to species survival). The concept of instinct, however, has fared badly in modern psychology because of its genetic connotation, and Ardrey has served the useful function of raising it again and with it the exceedingly important 'nature-nurture' debate. Over and above this, however, he has *orientated* behaviour theorists towards an inclusion of territory, *alerted* us to territorial behaviour when it occurs, *warned* us that there are likely to be repercussions when interventions in established territorial systems are made and, because we ourselves as investigators are so bound up in our own territorial systems, *suggested* that the study of lower animals' territoriality may shed light on our own. But what functions does Ardrey see territoriality performing?

Firstly, a territory provides an animal with security and safety. Secondly, it provides a source of excitement, because when the animal ventures to the periphery of its own territory the likelihood of challenge by other animals is increased. And thirdly, it provides an animal with a physical expression of its own identity and importance to other members of its species.*

When territoriality is defined in terms of the functions it

---

*This is only one definitional framework. Altman (1968) compiled nine (including Ardrey's): Nice (1941), Burt (1943), Hediger (1950, 1955, 1961), Carpenter (1958), McBride (1964), Stea (1965), Sommer (1966), Pastalan (1968) and Ardrey (1966). Altman notes that all refer to a 'place', and that they are all associated with important needs and behaviours (e.g. child rearing, feeding, etc.) and they are marked out in some way and, when threatened, are defended.

performs, it matters little for human behaviour whether or not it has a genetic or biological basis. One can, in the human situation, start looking for phenomena which may be subsumed under such functions. It can serve as a reified umbrella under whose aegis data can be gathered to await the theoretician. We can ask now whether human beings do seem, in the normal course of events, to have territories. If their living spaces or working areas turn out to be describable in this way, we can ask how people signify to others that they are territories. We can also inquire into the developmental processes involved – whether and how children become territorial; or just how effective environmental variables are in the development of territorial behaviour; and whether such variables play a part in individual differences in territorial behaviour that are almost certain to exist. We can ask how modifiable adult territorial behaviour is – is it really necessary for people to feel they have 'a place of their own' and so on. Bearing in mind Altman's (1968) warning that in humans territoriality is far more likely to be expressed symbolically than in lower animals, let us now turn to some studies that have been carried out in the human arena.

Esser *et al.* (1965) looked at the territorial behaviour in a psychiatric ward of schizophrenic patients. He pointed out that throughout the animal kingdom high status or dominance in a social group is found in conjunction with the possession of more territory. Did a similar relationship exist on the psychiatric ward? To answer this the investigators marked out the ward into squares of 3 square feet. Thus they were able to observe, from behind the one-way glass of their centrally located observation booth, both the spatial behaviour of the patients during the day and a. the number and durations of interactions with other patients and staff, b. the actual number of different patients interacted with and c. which patient took the initiative. From the pooling of this information a dominance hierarchy of the patients was drawn up. It was found that the top third of the patients on the dominance hierarchy were 'free to move wherever they want and do not seem to need to establish ownership of a spot'. In other words the ward as a whole was their territory. The patients in the middle third of the hierarchy had established territories but only in places where interaction was likely (e.g. on traffic lines) and the bottom third 'were moderately restricted in range and found themselves secluded spots in which to withdraw with a markedly lower chance of being contacted'. Thus the original relationship postulated – between territory and status – is borne out.

This raises many interesting questions. Firstly, knowing something about the territorial behaviour of these severely disturbed patients reveals a lot about the status relationships that exist. Could it be that there is a 'language of space' which functions as an unwritten system of rules which *govern* or at least play more than just a second-fiddle role to social interaction? Secondly, Esser *et al.* were observing the behaviour of people who had been, or chose to be, withdrawn from the world outside – the inference being that their behaviour outside was such that it no longer fell into some arbitrary 'normal' range. They were diagnosed as 'ill' and institutionalized. If one follows for a moment the argument that has been developed over the years by physician Thomas Szasz (e.g. Szasz, 1972), who regards mental illness as a myth ('illness can affect only the body; hence there can be no mental illness' p. 275), the territorial behaviour may take on a new significance. Szasz claims that what people describe as mental illness is 'not something a person has, but is something a person *does* or *is*' and that it may be best understood by looking at human behaviour not in terms of the motives that we construct to account for it but in terms of the rules (that need not be related to motives) that guide it. An appreciation of the rules of social and personal conduct will give us far more understanding of human behaviour (mainly in terms of predictability) than a motivational analysis (*à la* Freud).

These schizophrenic patients were quite clearly following rules concerned with occupancy of space. High-status individuals had more rights over territories, had more territorial freedom than low-status individuals. So even though the more readily observed human rules in the outside world, i.e. rules based on language, and verbal interactions between people, were inoperative – or had degenerated to a considerable degree – the spatial rules were still very much in evidence. Perhaps as Esser claims such spatial rules are *more* salient because of the institutional setting. Are we thus talking about a rule system of a primitive biological nature that is fallen back on when people become unable to cope with the more sophisticated human interactions which are more dependent on speech and person perception? If so it might have therapeutic implications. For, if Szasz is correct in his assertion that life is a game played to rules, then presumably to play the game well a person has to be well grounded in the rules. But these schizophrenic patients were – despite their condition – still following rules, if only spatial rules. Perhaps these spatial rules could be used as a foundation on which more sophisticated rules might be built, i.e. rule systems sophisticated enough to enable a return to a 'normal' community.

Another example of how territoriality has been studied in human situations can be seen in the work of Altman (e.g. Altman and Haythorn, 1967). This work bears a resemblance to Esser's, in that people are studied in 'captive' situations, in this case sailors who volunteered to spend ten days with one other individual, in a confined space (12 square feet) under conditions of comparative social isolation. Altman and Haythorn recorded amongst other things the territoriality displayed by their subjects, territoriality being defined by 'the degree of consistent and mutually exclusive use of particular chairs, beds, or sides of the table'. One of the conclusions from this study was that 'social isolation was associated with continuously high or growing territoriality for all areas and objects, while non-isolation (control groups following the same task schedule but not under conditions of social isolation) was accompanied by gradually declining territoriality in two cases' (which side of the table was used and which chair was used) 'and rising territoriality in the other' (beds). Accompanying this overall increase in territoriality for the isolated pairs was a gradual process of withdrawal from one another, or as Altman and Haythorn put it, 'there was a significant decline in together activities from early to later days and a significant elevation in time spent alone'. As in the Esser study there would appear to have been a fall back onto a spatial code of behaviour, with a concomitant lessening of normal social interaction. In the Altman and Haythorn study they deliberately engineered a social situation which one might intuitively suspect to be antithetical to normal human interaction, and, sure enough, the spatial codes became more apparent.

A final example concerning the specific issue of territoriality is given by Lipman's (1968) work in old people's homes. Before looking at the work itself, however, I would like to consider some of Lipman's (1968a) comments about the difficulties of carrying out such work. It seems that Lipman experienced a 'traumatic culture shock' in carrying out his semi-participant observational studies, because he was so unused to the kind of social system and the types of personal interaction found in the homes that he studied. For example, particularly upsetting to him were 'the way residents consigned certain of their fellows to social isolation, the personal vilification to which some were continuously subjected, and the acrimonious relationships which prevailed between the status groups found in the larger sitting rooms'. And also their 'sudden outbursts of temper, their apparently bitter arguments about issues which seemed trivial, or their cantankerous reaction to the comments of others, which they had misunderstood or misinterpreted'. And, most important for my argument, he goes on to note, 'Frequent exhibitions of customarily restrained emotions, such as open hostility . . . contrasted with the *mannered social constraints of everyday life outside the homes*' (my italics). So, just as was the case with Esser's and Altman's research, the veneer of culture surrounding more free-ranging human behaviour was not apparent. If so, we should be able to predict once again that there would be a fall-back onto the more primitive spatial codes or rules that were seen in the two former studies; that is, there should be marked territoriality in the behaviour of the residents. This expectation is borne out. 93 per cent of the 74 per cent of residents who responded to a questionnaire about a usual or preferred seat in the sitting rooms answered that they had such a preference and 84 per cent indicated the actual position of the preferred seat. From the observations Lipman made in the sitting rooms themselves these figures are, if anything, a conservative estimate. 'Those residents who regularly sat in the sitting rooms, over 92 per cent in the three homes, occupied the same chairs in the same positions each day.' Lipman takes this finding further by speculating about what functions such occupancy fulfils. Firstly, he says the claiming and defending of space – or chairs in this case – provides a physical manifestation of psychological identity. In an environment which – although not malicious in intent – removes many avenues through which individuality can be expressed and asserted, the chair becomes the vehicle through which the resident can hold on to some identity of his own. Thus, if others recognize *your* chair, they are symbolically recognizing you. Secondly, Lipman draws our attention to the typical chair layout of the sitting rooms. The chairs are arranged around the walls. This arrangement, he argues, serves to limit social participation and social interaction to a level that is within the old people's perceptions of their own capabilities (which might, of course, be conservative).

To summarize the argument from these examples, it seems that territorial behaviour is displayed in a fairly obvious way, and in captive settings may be a social-rule substitute for more sophisticated culture-dependent rule systems. Because territoriality seems to be displayed in conditions where the 'mannered social constraints' no longer apply, it is, perhaps, a more primitive system. It therefore follows that situations without an accepted social-rule system, or without precedent in an individual's experience, would result in the individual's greater dependence on territoriality or place-possession or association with place. This is a theme I shall take up again in the chapter on overcrowding. For the moment, however, I want to continue considering territoriality as a rule system, a primitive rule system, generally understood and used by people to communicate intention and meaning in their inter-actions with each other. The owned sitting-room chair attests a person's identity; the free-ranging behaviour of the ward patient attests his high status and so on. Spatial be-haviour such as this can be thought of as analogous to a 'language' of human communication – at least according to anthropologist Edward T. Hall. He has made a special study of the communication function of spatial behaviour (Hall, 1959; 1966; 1968) and identifies the study as *proxemics*, which he has defined as 'the interrelated observations and theories of man's use of space'. Although in a short space it is im-possible to do Hall's work justice, there is a central theme or argument which can be extracted.

Firstly, all our mental processes and behaviour take place within a cultural context which is itself a determinant of these processes. Thus, Hall would claim, no thought or behaviour can be 'culture-free'.

Secondly, this cultural cage is transmitted from one person to another through at least two channels – an obvious one, language, and one not as obvious, spatial behaviour. The way we use space, claims Hall, is deeply rooted in our culture and is a manifestation of that culture. Hall acknowledges his debt for this idea to linguist Benjamin Lee Whorf, who suggested that thought is relative to the language in which it is conducted, that language 'is itself the shaper of ideas, the program and the guide for the individual's mental activity, for his analysis of impressions, for his synthesis of his mental stock in trade'. Hall applies the same argument to the 'language' of space. Just as we learn our native tongue and therefore learn to think 'culturally', so too do we learn our spatial code and learn to behave 'culturally' with respect to space.

Thirdly, these spatial codes, like languages, will vary from culture to culture. As our 'sense of space' anyway is a com-pendium of many different sources of sensory information, e.g. sight, sound, touch, etc. (we have no sense organ of space) it would be expected, if cultures really are different in their spatial codes, that people of different cultures would place different emphasis on the cues that go to form the total space picture. An extreme example of this, though it has nothing to do with culture, is the blind man who is far more attuned to, and far more able to utilize, auditory information from the environment than is the sighted man even though his hearing may be just as good. Our perception of space, we know, is not something that is 'given in the understanding' but requires the activation through experience of inbuilt, highly ordered neural structures (Held and Hein, 1963; Hubel and Weisal, 1963). However, as there is far more sensory information coming into our brains than they can possibly cope with or utilize, some selection becomes inevitable. Apart from the mainly anecdotal evidence that Hall cites, there is some hard data to support this.

From his cross-cultural investigations Wober (1966) has gathered evidence to suggest that 'men in South Nigerian cultures . . . may represent . . . a "sensotype" different from "sensotypes" in western cultures . . . Western cultures typically put great stress on the visual world, to the detriment of the auditory and tactile and proprioceptive modes'. Hall (1966) himself cites olfaction (smell) and particularly body odours as having a far greater significance and therefore communicatory value for the 'Arab' than for the 'American' for whom body odours are something to be gotten rid of. By a sensotype 'is meant the pattern of relative importance of the different senses, by which a child learns to perceive the world and in which pattern he develops his abilities. These patterns may be predominantly visual in one culture, while in another culture auditory or proprioceptive senses may have a much higher relative importance.'

But, if it is true at a certain level of a culture, it could also follow that individuals within a culture may display similar individual differences. This too would appear to be the case. In the well-known work of Witkin and his colleagues (1954, 1962) it was found that individuals vary greatly in their ability to utilize proprioceptive information, that is information to do with balance, and the location of one's limbs in space.

Fourthly, Hall says that, in modifying space – in the building and rebuilding of our cities, creating and changing space – we are inevitably intervening in the processes of culture. To intervene knowledgeably means that we must understand the spatial language of that particular culture, which means we must get to know the sensory world in which its members live. We must learn, says Hall 'to read the silent communications (proxemics) as easily as the printed and spoken ones. Only by doing so can we also reach other people, both inside and outside our national boundaries, as we are increasingly required to do.'

As well as the question of the sensory composition of our space picture Hall also outlines some features of space usage in terms of the distances we put between ourselves and others in our interactions with them. It is quite possible, knowing the spatial relationship between people, to predict what sort of interaction they are engaging in. These 'rules' will of course vary from culture to culture and Hall developed the following from interviews with and observations of middle-class, adult Americans, native to the northeastern seaboard of the U.S.A. They probably have, however, a wider applicability than that. These zones of interaction are given below.

Intimate distance

a. *Close phase* – Actual physical contact as in lovemaking, wrestling, etc.
b. *Far phase* – (six to eighteen inches) Intimate exchanges between 'intimates'. 'The use of intimate distance in public is not considered proper by adult, middle class Americans.' In certain situations this intimate space is invaded unavoidably by non-intimates, e.g. in subways, crowds, etc. In those circumstances certain adaptations come into play – immobility, muscular tenseness, avoidance of eye contact, etc.

Personal distance

a. *Near phase* – (18 inches to 2½ feet) This distance between two individuals is expressive of a certain degree of intimacy: 'a wife can stay inside the circle of her husband's close personal zone with impunity. For another woman to do so is an entirely different story.'

b. *Far phase* – (2½ to 4 feet) Corresponds to 'keeping people at arm's length'. The sort of distance which non-intimates would maintain to exercise a certain degree of formality.

Social distance

a. *Near phase* – (4 to 7 feet) 'Impersonal business occurs at

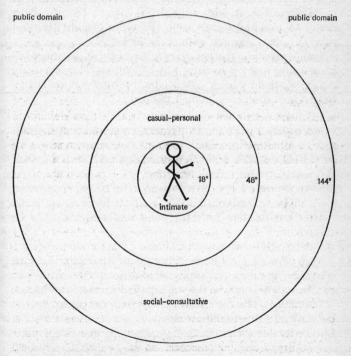

Fig. 13. Interaction zones.

this distance ... people who work together tend to use this distance. It is also a very common distance for people attending a casual social gathering.'

b. *Far phase* – (7 to 12 feet) A greater formality can be maintained at this distance for the same kind of activity that takes place at the near phase.

Public distance

a. *Near phase* – (12 to 25 feet) 'Well outside the circle of involvement.'

b. *Far phase* – (30 feet and over) 'the distance ... automatically set around important public figures.'

The elucidation of these distances was 'not only influenced by Hediger's work with animals (1955) ... but also by a desire to provide a clue as to the types of activities and relationships associated with each distance'.

Hall does stress the non-generality of these distances because space usage is so culturally dependent. He cites many examples (mainly based on anecdote) of intercultural space-behaviour differences. Some examples:

a. Americans unlike the English believe that residential propinquity automatically gives acquaintanceship rights.

b. To look into someone's room to a German counts as an intrusion. The equivalent for an American is physical entry into the room.

c. An acoustic screen to a Japanese can be paper thin and still be 'effective'. To the German, however, acoustic screens need to be thick, solid and soundproof to be effective.

d. An Englishman can shut himself off in public by putting up psychological barriers but for an American to do the same he needs actual physical barriers.

e. In Japanese houses the walls may move to accommodate function. The American pattern is for people to move to different functional areas.

f. To an American the space you occupy in a public place is yours during occupancy. To the Arab public space is genuinely public and is always open to challenge.

g. Arabs have a greater sensitivity to architectural crowding than Americans.

h. Americans are culturally under-developed in olfaction whereas the Arab uses smell unashamedly in communication.

i. The Japanese and Arabs have a higher tolerance of crowding in public spaces than have Americans.

j. Americans adopt a gridiron city plan whereas the French utilize the radiating-star framework.

k. The Japanese name the intersection of city streets, and houses are numbered in the order of construction. Americans name the streets themselves and the houses are numbered sequentially.

Differences h. and i. are particularly interesting in that they reveal a contradiction in Hall's work. He speculates (Hall, 1965) that the lack of development of the sense of smell in man allows him to withstand his present crowded condition, yet he tells us (above) that Arabs (with their well-developed olfactory abilities) have a *higher* tolerance of crowding.

Clearly these mainly anecdotally based assertions or hypotheses need putting to the test. Such an attempt has been made, notably by Watson and Graves (1966). One of their hypotheses (they had three in fact) was that 'Arabs will exhibit significant differences in proxemic behaviour from Americans, with Arabs being closer and more direct in their proxemic behaviour than Americans'.

Watson and Graves scored five of the eight categories of proxemic behaviour that Hall has outlined:

1. Sociopetal-sociofugal axis – score obtained by the relation of the axis of one person's shoulders to that of the other.

2. Kinesthetic factors – this score reflects the closeness of one person to another, and the potential each has for holding, grasping, or touching the other.

3. Touch code – scores the amount of contact during each interaction.

4. Visual code – scores the amount of visual contact present.

5. Voice-loudness – provides a measure for the level of a person's voice during interaction.

Using sixteen American and sixteen Arab college students as subjects, Watson found on all five proxemic categories that the hypothesis was confirmed 'with the Arab students confronting each other more directly . . . moving closer together, more apt to touch each other while talking, looking each other more squarely in the eye, and conversing in louder tones'.

Clearly Hall's ideas *are* a fruitful ground on which to base research. As international and intercultural social exchanges are becoming more frequent there is a greater likelihood of misunderstandings between people who are not aware of the differing proxemics of different peoples. However, just as we learn our culture, and our proxemics are a part of that culture, it follows that we learn our proxemic behaviour. If such behaviour is learned, just as surely it can be unlearned and a new one learned. Or an individual could learn a whole range of proxemic behaviours to be utilized when the individual found himself in the appropriate culture. Such exercises have in fact been carried out. Collett (1971) trained Englishmen in the non-verbal behaviour (mainly proxemic) of Arabs and found that the Arabs sampled preferred Englishmen who behaved *like themselves* rather than Englishmen who behaved like Englishmen. The trained Englishmen were trained on such things as, how close to sit, in what position, eye contact, when to touch and so on. As Collett points out, such a programme can aid intercultural understanding.

One thing that needs doing, and needs doing soon, however, (as Lynch, 1968, points out) is to move away from undifferentiated general categories – 'Americans', 'Arabs', 'Japanese', etc. – in order to be able to focus more precisely on status, and regional and individual characteristics. An example of how status distinctions can be communicated spatially is seen in the work of Duncan Joiner (1970). In studying a 'very ordinary life situation' (in the U.K.) – namely small office spaces – Joiner showed how the furniture arrangements could reveal information about the occupant, and about the behaviour the occupant expects from his visitors. '. . . academics generally sat sideways to their doors and adopted more open and less defined zone patterns than did the commercial and government occupants who predominantly sat facing their doors.' Thus academics could interact more freely with their usual visitor or visitors (students), while the commercial or government occupant could maintain the appropriate formality – yet another example of spatial arrangements being used as a means of communicating information.

To be meaningful, of course, what the spatial arrangements mean have to be held in common by all the people concerned. In Lipman's old people's homes it was accepted (though not necessarily spoken about as such) that a chair represented somebody even though the person was not present. What happens where we have a non-captive population – as we might have in a library where a person leaves a 'marker' to safeguard his territory while he is absent for a time? This is a question posed by, amongst others, Sommer (1969) who studied various kinds of marker: two notebooks and a textbook, four library journals piled in a neat stack, four scattered journals, a sportsjacket draped over a chair, etc., i.e. some non-personal, some personal. Personal markers kept intruders away more effectively than impersonal ones, but all markers were effective to some degree. When markers were ignored it was mainly by males. It is interesting to remark, however, in the light of the superiority of the personal marker noted above, that in a study by Hoppe (1970) in pubs in Victoria, British Columbia, a half glass of beer reserves a place better than a jacket. These examples do nevertheless show the existence of a spatial language or a way of interacting with the physical environment which is not idiosyncratic to the individual but is common to many individuals.

We have now looked at man as a territorial animal and at the language of spatial behaviour that stems from such territoriality. But a great many interactions between people occur on neutral ground where territorial rights in terms of either actual (or legal) ownership or even temporary physical possession are not clear, or are unspecified or ambiguous.

To understand these kinds of situation Sommer (1969)

has popularized the term 'personal space'. This refers to 'an area [should really be volume] with invisible boundaries surrounding a person's body into which intruders may not come'. That is the 'territory' that man carries around with him and regards as his. It is an emotionally charged space which will evoke reactions if penetrated. Sommer suggests that one of the best ways of studying this personal space bubble is to observe people's behaviour when the bubble is violated, to move closer and closer towards them and note their reaction. Thus investigators have sat too close to people as they are studying in a library (Felipe and Sommer, 1966); sat very close to psychiatric patients on benches (Sommer, 1969); had people walk over to hatracks and people to see how close they went (Horowitz *et al.* 1964; Dosey and Maisels, 1969); had people manipulate models of various persons in various situations (Little, 1965); had people reconstruct relationships using felt model figures (Kuethe, 1964, 1962a, 1962b), to mention only a few. Variables that have been shown to affect the size of the 'bubble' are *situational* – the physical context *where* the interaction is occurring; for example, open-air settings promote closer distances than contained settings (Little, 1965); *personalistic* – extroverts apparently tolerate physical closeness better than introverts (Williams; 1963), *acquaintanceship* – friends stand closer to one another than strangers (Little, 1965); and *sex* – when intrusion of another's bubble is unavoidable, females will intrude on another female's rather than on another male's (Leibman, 1970).

The personal space bubble can be conceived as an extension of 'self' that contracts and expands both according to circumstances and according to the person's own perception (conscious or unconscious) of how much protection the self requires. The amount of protection will depend in turn on the degree of threat provided by other people or by the physical environment. Certain people, of course, find the environment and/or persons more threatening than others do. Schizophrenics would appear to try and retain a larger 'extension of self' – personal space – than non-schizophrenics.

This was found to be so in an investigation of Horowitz, Duff and Stratton (1964). In this study people walked towards an inanimate object (a hatrack) and towards a person of the same sex and towards persons of the opposite sex, in an attempt to elicit the size of their personal space (or, as Horowitz *et al.* called it – their 'body buffer zone'). They also asked subjects to draw lines around figures – 'silhouettes of a nondescript male figure, seen from above, frontally and in profile', showing the distance they liked to maintain between 'themselves and others in ordinary conversations or approaches'. Using this method, it was found that, in general, schizophrenics preferred bigger body buffer zones than non-schizophrenics.

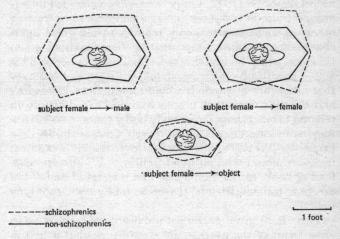

subject female ⟶ male   subject female ⟶ female

· subject female ⟶ object

－－－－schizophrenics
————non-schizophrenics

1 foot

Fig. 14. Body buffer zones (after Horowitz *et al.*, 1964).

A similar finding was reported by Kinzel (1971) who found that the body buffer zones of violent prisoners were almost all larger when compared to a group of non-violent prisoners. The figures are given as 29·3 square feet for the violent inmates as against only 7 square feet for the non-violent. In general, also, rear zones were larger than front zones in the violent group, which to Kinzel suggested 'A high level of homosexual anxiety'! Perhaps a less loaded explanation would be that they feared people approaching whom they couldn't see.

One could hypothesize in the light of this that the personal space or body buffer zone is performing a function very similar to that of the chairs in Lipman's old peoples homes – i.e. as a spatial extension of self. This is given credence by the fact that, when such space *is* violated without the accompanying desire for intimate exchange, people are either being *treated* as non-persons (as in the head-to-feet, horizontal storage of slaves in the slave ships plying between Africa and America in the eighteenth century; see Biderman *et al.*, 1963) or feel themselves to be non-persons – as on crowded underground trains at rush hour. Being a non-person, or treating others as such, means simply refusing to recognize interchanges (e.g. tactile contact) that in other situations would be emotionally highly charged. The body buffer zone is acting as a flexible filter regulating the degree of intimacy that others are allowed. It would appear from Horowitz's and Kinzel's work that people who do have difficulty in relating to others have larger body buffer zones. Also interesting in this connection is that introverts' zones are larger than extraverts (Williams, 1963) and introversion in this context means a person who is 'quiet, retiring . . . introspective, fond of books rather than people: he is reserved and *distant* except to intimate friends' (Eysenck and Eysenck, 1963; my italics).

There is, at this time, no natural history of *homo sapiens* in gross terms of the average amount of time that a person spends alone against the amount of time spent in the presence of other people. We have such natural histories for certain types of behaviour: sleep, for example, where we can say with a fair degree of certainty that when a man reaches sixty he will have spent about twenty years asleep, fifteen years of which will have been spent in subjective emptiness and five years of which will have been spent dreaming; or for sexual behaviour, where it would be possible to estimate the number of orgasms that an average male or female has over a lifetime, etc. (Kinsey *et al.* 1948, 1953). Such natural histories form a basic data bank out of which important questions about human nature can arise. Theorizing about sex, for example, was held up for decades because sexologists simply did not know how normal people behaved sexually. The arena of social behaviour, particularly, lacks such data. One aspect of social behaviour that is very obvious, however, is that in general most people do not either spend all their life in contact with others or all their life in solitude. People move from one domain to another in the natural course of events, or, as Barry Schwartz (1968) more forcefully puts it, 'patterns of social interaction . . . are accompanied by counter patterns of withdrawal'. Schwartz maintains that prolonged or sustained social contact becomes irritating and that in order for people to go on interacting with one another they have to periodically take their leave. This implies that selfhood – or some kind of central core of being – is not completely dependent on a social milieu for its existence but exists in its own right and is *presented* in social interactions.*

The idea represents of course a particular way of looking at man. Behind the idea lies the assertion that society serves individuals rather than the individual serving a superordinate society. In our western society individuality and the concept of individual worth are all-important ideals. In Lifton's study (1961) of Chinese thought reform the techniques are directed exactly against such an idea. Prisoners were 'forced to participate', they were 'drawn into the forces around them until they themselves began to feel the need to confess and to reform. This penetration by the psychological forces of the environment into the inner emotions of the individual person is perhaps the outstanding psychiatric fact of thought reform.' No chance for withdrawal, no chance to re-affirm the *particular* identity of self, only ever a chance of a personal existence in social interaction within a society or

---

* The wording here sounds very Goffmanesque (1959), but Goffman is much more preoccupied with the performance of the self in public rather than with the self as such.

social group. To maintain such a situation, privacy would have to be explicitly dénied.

But surely, one might argue, physical privacy is not essential, as the whole of one's experience is a private affair – and remains so unless communicated. Why should it be necessary to remove ourselves *physically* from others in order to retain the uniqueness of our experience and thus our self-hood? Could it be that we have not as yet learned to shut out the constant and insistent sensory data that others provide, and that this results in an incapacity to ponder on our experience? Pondering on our own experience, while at the same time receiving – however unwillingly – constant flows of information from others, may represent a condition of sensory overload, and its accompanying cognitive impairment (see chapter 3). This would indeed conform to the arousal theory presented in chapter 3, as from that theory one would expect introverts to be overloaded at a lower level of sense input than extraverts. Thus one would also expect to see behavioural adaptations. Such an adaptation could well be to preserve a larger body buffer zone, thereby enabling cerebral arousal to be kept within manageable limits. We could now hypothesize that Kinzel's violent prisoners and Horowitz's schizophrenics are over-aroused. Or put another way – would administration of an arousal-lowering drug also reduce the body buffer zone? Such ideas remain to be explored.

If, however, instead of looking at privacy as an attempt to reduce overload, we actually see what behaviour is most associated with privacy, a somewhat different analysis emerges. As Kira (1966) points out, privacy is sought a great deal for the conduct of the 'entire sex/elimination amalgam' and also for the maintenance of personal hygiene. Our cultural norms strongly encourage an association of embarrassment and shame with such functions and privacy for them becomes essential. It is fairly common, I think, for people in a public lavatory to retain their faeces within their rectum if other people come within earshot – even though visual privacy is assured – so that the splash as the stool hits the water will not be heard by others, and will not thereby cause embarrassment. Others adopt the tactic of placing lavatory paper on the surface of the water to lessen the impact, while in one extraordinary case reported to me a person actually defecated (in situations in which she could be overheard) into hand-held paper and then *placed* the stool in the water!* While it is irrelevant to defend or attack such practices, it is surely quite clear that there are very many aspects of our behaviour over which, although we know perfectly well they are performed by everybody, a discrete veil is drawn. Exactly to what such modesty attaches itself is variable in a given culture at a given moment in history, as only a glance at Havelock Ellis's *Studies in the Psychology of Sex* (1896–1928) shows. Perhaps it serves the function of preserving a private self as against a public one – giving a *raison d'être* for 'the counter pattern of withdrawal'. It is in discussing such questions that simple descriptive data for widely different social systems is essential if we are going to be able to comment intelligently about the necessity for maintaining such a schism. What is especially interesting in this context is the treatment meted out to those who have difficulty in coping with such a system.

In Goffman's now classic work, *Asylums* (1961), he gives account after account of the mechanisms that make the 'counter pattern of withdrawal' impossible. The removal of possessions, the wearing of apparel that is not the inmate's own, the necessity of doing things in public that would normally be performed in private, etc. All – though perhaps without deliberate attempt – specific mechanisms for making withdrawal for the purpose of self-confirmation impossible, if indeed withdrawal does serve that purpose. In a culture which values individuality, it seems that those who don't make it have the opportunity removed.

But what about those who have made it but perhaps made it too well? If our culture puts a premium on individuality which, as we have seen, is based on being able to withdraw, then some individuals will perhaps learn the lesson too well

* See Baxter (1973) for further examples.

and become unable to balance their withdrawal with periods of interaction. Or, to put it in spatial terms, such people might find body-buffer-zone penetration, both their own and others', very hard to bear. Intimacy here (meaning physical intimacy in a wide sense) is avoided for fear of reducing the saliency of self. This is no doubt a tremendous over-simplification, but it does 'fit' certain therapeutic procedures that are popular at this time. One of the aims of 'encounter groups' (see Bayne, 1972) is the discovery of self; and notably a method of achieving this is by the unembarrassed penetration of the personal spaces by others; thus breaking down spatial rules of conduct that specifically encourage 'performance' and role playing. The techniques developed by Masters and Johnson (1970) for reversing sexual dysfunction rely to a large extent on a similar paradigm. Instead of the more usual psychotherapeutic methods of treatment, i.e. of talking about the problem, their method is based on the dysfunctional couple (one partner is not conceived of as being 'responsible', since the dysfunction exists in the relationship, so it is the relationship that is treated) unembarrassedly learning about each other's bodies by exploring them. They discover and explore each other's preferences and dislikes of physical contact. They establish an intimate *physical* relationship with the psychological intimacy following rather than leading. To put it in a way that I'm sure Masters and Johnson never would, the couple are learning new proxemics with respect to each other – the intellectual adjustments trailing. The Masters and Johnson sex-therapy programme is the most successful ever for a wide variety of sexual dysfunctions, so the therapeutic concepts must have a great deal of empirical veracity.

The implication for environmental psychology is plain. Once we understand something of the individual and internal mechanisms of spatial behaviour, we can start looking at such behaviour in its own right and not as something which merely forms a backdrop to other behaviours or experiences. The potential for the manipulation of people's behaviour and experience is enormous; so is the problem of deciding exactly what it is we wish to manipulate. Easy enough to say we'd like to remove all sexual dysfunction from society, or all schizophrenic illness, but should we also train people to adapt to the increasing closeness and quantity of other people in the world? If we did that, would we ever stop over-producing?

In summary, we have seen that it is useful to view man as a territorial animal, that identity and social communication are both inextricably involved with the physical environment. We have seen that people's treatment of space is a language in its own right and although displaying enormous cultural variations is perhaps a very primitive communication channel, a system which is heavily utilized when the veneer of sophisticated social interchange loses its lustre. We have seen how the transportable territory – the personal space – is very much a reality and could itself serve not only as an indicator of personality type but also of the background culture and possibly, through its direct manipulation, could serve as a method for effecting behavioural change. This increased understanding further highlights the moral problem of deciding how and to what end such information is to be used.

7
Space and the Larger Scale

Some children who want to put their name and address on all their books and belongings write addresses that are often longer than is strictly necessary. The number of the house, the road, the postal area, the town and the county would be adequate, but they go on to name the country, the continent, perhaps the hemisphere, 'The Earth', 'The Solar System', 'The Galaxy' and 'The Universe'. It is as if they have realized the enormity of the spaces 'out there' and the relationship of their own directly experienced space to the larger space of which it is a part. Sommer (1969) formally distinguishes these two types of physical environment calling them the *proximate environment*, which includes 'everything that is physically present to an individual at a given moment', and the *macro environment*, which describes the out-of-sight but in-mind large-scale environment. Other investigators have used different names, for example Stea (1967) coined the phrase 'invisible landspace' to describe the macro environment, invisible because 'it is generally unavailable to, or unused by, the dwellers within [a given] habitat'. While Brian Goodey (1968) suggests that the 'invisible landscape' be further extended to take in 'those areas of the world which man perceives but of which he has no direct experience', and calls the study of such perceptions 'extra-environmental'.

These three concepts, the macro environment, the invisible landscape and the extra environment are similar, and the unifying idea behind them is that man is alert and responsive not only to the here-and-now physical environment, but also to environments that at any one time are not directly experienced. The suggestion is that we carry around in our heads some kind of 'mental map' or 'schemata' which provides a mental analogue to an outward physical reality inferred from primary and secondary sense sources. Such mental maps might relate to something as large as the world or a continent, or as small as the route we follow to work, or the neighbourhood in which we reside and so on. Indeed in the view of Professor T. R. Lee psychology can contribute a great deal to those professions concerned with shaping space by trying to understand how we build up such maps. Specifically with respect to architecture he says, 'The whole relevance of psychology to architecture lies in the fact that the subjective world does not directly correspond to the physical environment of agreed measurement,' (Lee, 1967) and again, 'The spatial schemata or inner representations of space are perhaps the most fruitful phenomena for architectural psychologists to study' (Lee, 1969). It is to these spatial schemata or inner representations of space that we now turn, specifically to that space called a 'neighbourhood'.

If one were to ask people what features of their neighbourhood they liked or disliked they would probably after a little thought be able to tell you. What they probably would not do would be to question whether or not they lived in a neighbourhood – they would take that as self-evident. People have neighbours, are neighbours and live in neighbourhoods. Indeed sociologists have long used the concept of neighbourhood in trying to understand urban behaviour. Very often it has been used synonymously with the word community, and that perhaps highlights a problem. What exactly do such terms mean? Is a neighbourhood or a community a group of relatively homogeneous people? Does it describe a physical area? Does it describe *both* a physical area *and* a type of people? Which is more important – the area or the people? Mann (1965) tells us, for example, that 'attempts to define the boundaries of the physical neighbourhoods may be sterile in that they bear so little relation to social relationships. It is more useful to consider social relationships themselves rather than to worry about where neighbourhoods begin and end.' But, as well as having different meanings depending on who is using the terms, 'neighbourhood or community' can, as Dennis (1958) points out, carry an implicit ideology. Dennis asserts that it is the ideological component that makes the concept so popular, and he goes on to describe the beliefs that make up the ideology. Firstly, there is the belief that, if people live in cohesive locality-based communities, there will be fewer social problems – people feel they belong to and can find support from their neighbours and neighbourhood. One might describe this belief as a desire to return to things as-we-think-they-used-to-be, i.e. the friendly village-y atmosphere of a time past, where everybody knew everybody else and where, therefore, controls over people's behaviour were far easier to effect, and where a group of houses would probably be a significant social group, as it was the only group around.

Related to this belief, the neighbourhood could be seen as a vehicle for dispersing the great masses of the working classes that were built up in confined enclosures in cities during the industrial revolution and who would as time went on constitute a greater and greater threat to the way society was organized, as their numbers increased and their spaces got smaller. If they could be spread out into designed neighbourhoods around the city and its perimeter, such a threat would be reduced and personal and social problems minimized.

Finally, there are the political aspects of the neighbourhood ideology. It is worth quoting Dennis at length:

The political doctrines which are associated with the neighbourhood ideology are those which talk particularly of the inherent wisdom, harmony and integrity of the community. In the science of human behaviour, the neighbourhood ideology is fed by those schools which equate 'maturity', etc. with competence in interpersonal relationships. All these views tend to be highly acceptable, because the reality component in each is reinforced by the fact that they can easily be used to justify the existing order of things, and to minimize the value of non-conformity; that is, they are amenable to the view that difference, conflict, and the desire for change, are essentially unrealistic and pathological phenomena.

Stacey (1969) is no more charitable to the concept of community, doubting whether it refers to *anything* useful. She takes one of Konig's (1968) definitions of community: 'an original social phenomenon, namely the local unity of a group of human beings who live their social, economic and cultural lives together, and jointly recognize and accept certain obligations and hold certain standards of value in common,' and one through which 'the human being is first introduced to social relationships extending beyond the confines of the family,' and she claims that it is 'so vague as to be nonsense'.

Hillery (1955) managed to find ninety-four definitions of community and he commented: 'all the definitions deal with people. Beyond this common basis, there is no agreement,' although a majority of the definitions include the following as elements (in order of increasing importance) *area*, *common ties* and *social interaction*.

This to-ing and fro-ing as to exactly what a neighbourhood or a community is might appear to be just another semantic/academic problem of interest only to certain specialists. This would be the case were it not for the fact that planners and architects do use these terms as if they had a very real meaning, and they serve as a background against which or around which 'massive environmental transformations' are made. For example, the concept of 'the neighbourhood unit' has been extremely influential in town planning ever since Clarence Perry introduced it in America in 1929.

I want first to explain this concept, then, in the light of what little we know psychologically about neighbourhood and mental maps, examine its assumptions. One of the unstated assumptions of the neighbourhood unit philosophy, unstated because so 'self-evident', was that it is of course possible to create 'communities' through physical design, i.e. through the design determinism discussed in chapter 4.

Perry defined what he meant by neighbourhood as 'that area which embraces all the public facilities and conditions required by the average family for its comfort and proper development within the vicinity of its dwellings'. These facilities Perry delineates as an elementary school, retail stores and public-recreation facilities. The conditions 'which the family most consciously seeks' are good residential tone and street safety. In order to create a neighbourhood, Perry does not propose any specifically detailed plan, 'since there are many local conditions which a specific plan would not meet', but states principles and standards in terms of definite objectives. Perry in fact outlines six such principles:

a. The neighbourhood unit should be of such a size that one elementary school is required. Perry claimed that, on average, in American cities about one sixth of the population would be of elementary school age and, as 'authorities in school administration' give a figure between 1,000 and 1,600 children to be accommodated in a typical public (i.e. state) school, this gives a neighbourhood population of between 6,000 and 9,600. Perry in fact suggests a range of 3,000 to 10,000 in order to give latitude to the educational service. The density of population would also need to be taken into account, because Perry does not want his children walking much more than a quarter of a mile to school. This is in fact below the educators' recommendations of a half to three quarters of a mile.

b. The neighbourhood should have distinct boundaries – namely arterial streets – to serve the dual function of enabling traffic to by-pass the centre of the neighbourhood and to serve the psychological function of allowing residents and strangers alike to 'visualize it as a distinct entity'.

c. There should be a system of small parks and recreation spaces. Perry suggests around 10 per cent of the neighbourhood space should be used for this purpose. The major social objective of this is to provide play space for the 'children and youths' of the apartment-house districts.

d. Like the school, other buildings providing a service to the neighbourhood should be grouped at the centre. If there is to be a community hall, for example, it should be centrally located although Perry sees no reason why such a place should not be combined with the school. There is no reason why the school, the hall, the library and the church should not be grouped together in the centre – around a square, in fact, which could also be the site of the flagpole and serve as the focal point for local celebrations.

e. The shopping districts (one or more) should be laid out on the periphery of the unit. One of Perry's reasons for this was that such areas would be aligned with the 'portals' of the neighbourhood. The shops would receive their supplies from vehicles using the arterial road system and the shops themselves would not defile the high residential quality of the neighbourhood.

f. The streets of the neighbourhood should be proportionate to their traffic load. They should discourage through traffic but facilitate internal circulation. Perry tells us that 'the street pattern produced by this method may seem like a maze to stranger-visitors and department-store delivery trucks but this difficulty can be met by posting maps of the neighbourhood, under weatherproof frames, in police booths and at the portals of the district'.

The fulfilment of these principles would achieve certain objectives: the neighbourhood unit would stand out geographically as a distinct entity, and the residents would have an affection for it. To quote Perry 'when it has complete equipment for the vicinity needs of its families; when the public services are nicely adapted to population requirements and all its component parts are integrated by a comprehensive plan – then you have a neighbourhood community that is bound to be marked because of the esteem in which it is held by its residents'.

Perry's proposals are clear, simple and straightforward and it is these very qualities of his proposals which have made the concept of the neighbourhood unit such an influential one. In this country it has until recently (Llewelwyn-Davies, 1972) been at the root of British town-planning policy, enshrined as it was in the Dudley Report (H.M.S.O., 1944) entitled *The Design of Dwellings*. This report maintained that 'a feeling of neighbourhood, of community' was 'one of the fundamentals of social well-being' and set out how this could be engendered through the design of the physical environment. Although the Perry-type clarity, simplicity and straightforwardness were still very much apparent, the Dudley Report did make certain modifications to the proposals. These have been documented by Goss (1961) as threefold:

1. The shops were to be situated at the neighbourhood centre rather than its periphery.
2. Open space was shifted from being within neighbourhood boundaries to the periphery where it could act as a buffer between neighbourhoods.
3. The size of the neighbourhood was not related to the size of the elementary (primary) school, but the figure, 10,000, was much in line with Perry's figure.

Thus in both types of neighbourhood unit there are still boundaries to give a geographical discreteness; the size is about the same; open space is also considered essential and the social objective of the unit is still paramount. The question of course is whether, in the case of the new towns, the neighbourhood unit formula has lived up to expectations.

Sadly such evaluations have rarely been made, and when they have little information is provided. For example, Goss (1961) from his 10 per cent sample of British New Town neighbourhoods found them to be very successful from a purely environmental or physical aspect, remarking: 'There is little doubt that most of the new neighbourhood units of British New Towns represent a qualitative advance over most pre-war housing estates', but, as for the social validity of the units, he is unsure, because of the 'general lack of information about how communities work'. But of course to Perry, and for that matter the New Towns Committee (H.M.S.O., 1946), the social values were paramount – the feeling of belonging and the sense of responsibility to a geographical community, serving as a much needed counter-balance to the 'most serious of modern urban ills', namely the weak sense of community membership. Lewis Mumford (1954), a staunch supporter of the neighbourhood-unit formula, puts this more graphically; 'In the neighbourhood, if anywhere, it is necessary to recover the sense of intimacy and innerness that has been disrupted by the increased scale of the city and the speed of transportation'; and in so doing can be rightly criticized for making assertions about the social consequences of physical planning that have no sub-stantive basis (Pahl, 1970). Jean Perraton (1967) would seem to have a more objective stance as regards the neighbourhood unit formula when, in a careful review of the evidence in favour and against the Perry-type ideology, she concludes: 'the research available tends to confirm doubts about the effectiveness of certain planning policies aimed at promoting local attachment, neighbourliness and community activity,' and goes on to point out that close neighbourly contacts and wider community activity may actually be antithetical. The general lack of evidence, however, has in no way prevented wholehearted commitment or condemnation, whether it be of the original Perry unit or variations of it – British, Swedish, Russian and German. Let us look at some of the criticisms.

A very voluble critic of the neighbourhood unit formula was Isaacs (1948), who maintained that as a concept it is totally inadequate to serve as a basis for town planning, because it only too readily serves as an 'instrument for implementing segregation of racial and cultural groups'. This is a view shared by Catherine Bauer (1945), who sees the planners' preoccupation with the physical detail (super-blocks or not, terraced v. detached, school-to-home distance, etc.) as a side-stepping of the more important issues of neigh-bourhood which centre around *class* and *race relations* in a democracy, *leisure, participation, population policy* and the like. Isaacs (op. cit.) went on to say that the proponents of the neighbourhood unit, in an effort to counteract what they see as the 'loneliness of the city', see it as a panacea in which, they believe, 'people can find friendliness, relaxation, convenience and safety, as well as opportunities for self-expression and citizenship on a manageable scale' – a sort of return to village life which ignores the incentives – 'new contacts, economic opportunity, anonymity and personal freedom' that go along with the 'flight from the farm'. There does seem to be quite a strong tradition of thought which says that city life and urbanism is, of itself, liable to produce bad rather than good effects – that man *basically* finds the city life, as opposed to rural life, an uncomfortable matrix. The eminent pioneer urban sociologist Louis Wirth seemed to hold such a view. In his now classic paper *Urbanism as a way of Life* (1938), in which he sought the beginnings of a theory of urbanism, he said, 'The close living together and working together of individuals who have no sentimental and emotional ties foster a spirit of competition, aggrandizement and mutual exploitation. Formal controls are instituted to counteract irresponsibility and potential disorder. Without rigid adherence to predictable routines a large compact society would scarcely be able to maintain itself.' He also writes of the loneliness of city life and the 'acceptance of instability and insecurity ... as a norm' and of the 'superficiality, the anonymity and the transitory character of urban social relations'. In doing so, Wirth must be comparing city life with something, as all his terms are comparative. Of course, his reference point is the rural way of life and the characteristics of such a life.

But why not turn the comparison around? Why not say rural life is changeless and restrained, repressive and controlled, and that a person's social relations are incarcerated or entombed within the prison-like enclosure of a limited number of people. Overstating the case, perhaps, but an argument nevertheless worth stating. Urbanity, being historically later, is bound to come off worse when compared to a *status quo*. And if such a comparison is believed, 'forward' progress becomes directed towards a re-instatement of the *status quo* – towards the disassembly of our cities to combat social malaise.

There *are* people who positively enjoy living in a city and who are not all the time pining for a life which the vast majority of people nowadays have not known anyway. It appears to me that what Wirth's pronouncements lacked was some evidence from people themselves. Just as Lansing and Marans (1969) found that a considerable discrepancy between planners' ratings of neighbourhood quality and the ratings of people who live in those neighbourhoods so Wirth might have found that urbanites themselves did not share his views. We need to do more than just stand outside and look in, we must enter into the world of the individual and try to understand that world from his point of view. Before doing this, however, let us look at one of the most trenchant and penetrating criticisms of the neighbourhood unit formula, which came from Herbert (1963–4).

Herbert maintains that Perry's doctrine is inherently inflexible and rigid, that the 'neighbourhood unit stands for commitment – commitment to a fixed schools policy, a fixed shopping system, an unchanging pattern of use. As such it shows itself not geared to change, inflexible, static.' And further: 'Not only has Perry, and those who followed him, failed to give consideration to the problem of growth, but the nature of the neighbourhood unit inhibits an organic growth pattern.' Herbert goes on to lay bare the assumptions on which the neighbourhood unit is based, namely:

1. That there is an optimum size for a community.
2. That such a community should be territory based and physically delineated.
3. That a city is an agglomoration of units plus specialized industrial units and a town centre.

The first assumption implies that for the development of an adequate personality a large primary group is essential and, says Herbert, there is no evidence that this is so. Nor is there any evidence that neighbourhoods themselves create 'community' or 'neighbourliness' or that they have any *social* significance. Perry's population claim is thus 'unsupported and arbitrary and rests on a misconception of [a] primary group' (Herbert, op. cit.).

In questioning the second assumption, the necessity of a specific territory, Herbert maintains that, if the neighbourhood is too large to serve as a primary group, it would follow that in the unit there would be a lot of overlapping groups performing primary group functions such that 'a social group is unlikely to be based on a specific geographic area' – mothers with young children and old people, who in their enforced immobility are likely to form a geographically based community, may be exceptions. If the first two assumptions *are* false, the third becomes an abstraction based on no social reality at all. In conclusion Herbert says, ' the neighbourhood unit concept is at best neutral and at worst antipathetic to the development of an integrated community life . . . basically because people are not contained or constrained in their behaviour by the planner's imposition of a territory based community, and because a delineation in territorial terms is neither desired nor perceived.' It seems as if on the planning side we have a *desire* to create communities through physical means while on the sociological side there is a desire – equally strong – to assert that physical planned environment is not a causative agent in the fostering of community and that the social structure and relationships are paramount. Clearly both these views reflect the interest of the proponents. What more natural than for the sociologist to be concerned about social relationships and for planners to be concerned with the physical, built environment? The discussion of neighbourhood certainly seems to be not short of dogmatic and doctrinaire views on both sides. Is there a solution?

I believe there is. What both the planner and the sociologist (whether Louis Wirth or Clarence Perry) leave out of their discussions is the individual person who actually lives in a neighbourhood or community. Earlier I mentioned how most people would acknowledge the validity of the concept of neighbourhood, but the questions that are only too rarely asked are twofold: do people see it in the same way as planners/sociologists? and do all people see the same thing?

These questions return us to the beginning of the chapter – to mental maps and people's conceptions of their 'invisible environment'. The question of how the individual sees 'neighbourhood' is a *psychological* question because it addresses the individual's perception of neighbourhood rather than the more traditional type of sociological question which has to do with social activities of a *group* of people, in an area *designated* a neighbourhood. To ask this psychological question may resolve the stalemate that has accrued around the concept of neighbourhood and it also has the potential of providing some usable information for the planners.

The first major contribution is that of T. R. Lee – now Professor of Psychology at Surrey University – who, despite an academically discouraging environment, made it the subject of his doctoral dissertation at Cambridge (Lee, 1954). The work was later published under the title *Urban neighbourhood as a socio-spatial schema* in 1968. I want to examine this work in some detail, not because it totally resolves the problems that surround neighbourhood (it raises as many as it solves), but because it is a pioneering piece of work which is now enabling students of the man–environment relationship to penetrate further in their understanding.

Firstly, Lee pointed out that the concept of neighbourhood has always been unsatisfactory, because no one has evolved a way of combining the geographical or physical aspect with the social characteristics. Thus we have the planners' insistence on the physical substance which they can manipulate and the sociologists concern with social relationships because they have tools to understand or manipulate these processes. Despite the lack of success in providing an adequate conceptualization of neighbourhood, however, it is recognized as a concept by most 'ordinary'(i.e. non-specialist) people. Fried and Gleicher (1961), for example, give credence to this. In a study of the residents of Boston's West End, they talk of the local area being a focus for 'strongly positive sentiments' and of the residents having 'sense of local spatial identity including both local social relationships and local places'. They also note that the 'belonging-to-an-area' phenomenon has been a consistent finding from research both in Britain and the United States. A solution to the difficulty of combining the social and physical aspects may lie in recognizing that each individual has his own *personal* conception of his neighbourhood, which may or may not coincide with the area which is designated a neighbourhood. It is of course likely to differ from individual to individual because it is, as Lee found, related to the number of friends in the locality. The obvious way to get at it, then, is to adopt a phenomenological approach; that is, directly to tap the experience of the individual.

To do this Lee interviewed 219 housewives in Cambridge, England. His wife Daphne went with him to allay suspicion and record the interview. Housewives were selected by taking every fortieth household from the electoral register. The main section of the interview was concerned with social behaviour and in particular 'with number and whereabouts of friends and acquaintances'. Background demographic information was also collected. During the course of the interview Lee produced a map (covering about $2\frac{1}{2}$ square miles) on which the interviewee's house was at the approximate centre and marked with a large cross. He then asked them: 'Please draw a line round the part which you consider acts as your neighbourhood or district.' 165 of the 219 interviewees (75 per cent) were able to draw the map; of the rest twenty-four (11 per cent) said the request was too vague, fourteen (6 per cent) lacked the necessary ability and sixteen (7 per cent) 'gave the impression that their willingness to cooperate was approaching its limit'. With this information Lee was able to compare the 'presented' environment with the 'accepted' neighbourhood. He drew a circle on the map of radius $\frac{1}{2}$ mile around the individual's house – this he calls the *locality*, or presented environment – and compares what is contained therein, in terms of houses, shops and amenity buildings, with what is contained in the area the housewives designated as their neighbourhood or district, for which he uses the word *schema*.

The word schema is an old one in psychology. It was first used by the neurologist Henry Head (Head, 1920) to describe the 'model' of our body that we carry around in our heads, against which changes in posture and movement are regi-

stered. It was extended in its use by Bartlett and formed a
central concept in his theory of remembering (Bartlett, 1932).
Bartlett defined it as 'an active organization of past reactions,
or past experiences, which must always be supposed to be
operating in any well-adapted organic responses'. In other
words the schema is used as a kind of continuously modifiable model of past realities, constructed out of past realities,
but used as a basis for comparing and accommodating
present realities. It is in this way that Lee is using the term
when he characterizes the urban neighbourhood as a 'socio-
spatial schema', in that people have built up a model of the
'environment–person' setting in which their own behaviour
and experience occurs. What is interesting is that this 'model'
or schema displays certain characteristics that are familiar to
psychologists from work in other areas. For example, the
Gestalt psychologists (one of the early 'schools' of psychology,
e.g. see Koffka, 1935), claimed, from their work on the
process of perception, that our perceptions of the world (they
were, however, mainly concerned with visual perception)
were 'organized' in certain ways; objects are seen as distinct
from their background, they have shape or contour, they
display continuity and closure (see Fig. 15), as indeed did the
schema produced by Lee's housewives. They differentiated
their neighbourhood from the surrounding environs, so that
it stood out as a figure against a background. They gave it
contour by drawing a particular line on a particular map,
giving it shape. They gave it closure, there being an outside
and an inside, and they also gave it continuity, in that the
space enclosed was continuous, i.e. an entity as opposed to
being made up of discrete elements. Thus the features that
are descriptive of relatively simple visual perceptions are
present in the perception of this complex 'invisible landscape' – the neighbourhood.

From the 165 schemata produced, Lee tentatively suggests
a typology of neighbourhoods as perceived by his subjects,
namely:

1. The social acquaintance neighbourhood which is a small

physical area, in which the people very much 'keep themselves to themselves' and where the main support in times of trouble is from kin rather than neighbours. This kind of neighbourhood is much more a function of people rather than locality – that is, it could be found in a variety of localities but only amongst a certain kind of person.

figure and ground reversed

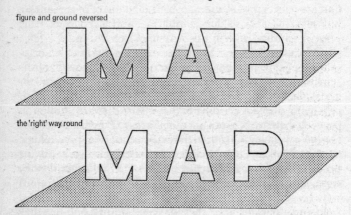

the 'right' way round

note too that 'closed' 'contours' produce 'continuous' surfaces

Fig. 15. Figure/ground; contour, continuity, closure.

2. The homogeneous neighbourhood. Here the perception of the schema includes greater awareness of physical aspects as well as people. An underlying principle is not only that the neighbourhood is comprised of 'people like us' but also of 'people who live in houses like ours'.

3. The unit neighbourhood. This, Lee tells us, most closely approximates the planners' conception of neighbourhood. Schemata here are large, contain a balanced range of amenities and have a heterogeneity of population and house types.

Now, if the neighbourhood maps do actually represent some amalgam of physical and social factors, then clearly specifiable connections between these factors should emerge if sought after. They do. For example, the number of local friends housewives said they had was positively related to the area of the schema – the more friends, the bigger the map ($p < 0.001$); also the more friends, the more houses there were in the schema ($p < 0.02$). It was the same with amenity buildings ($p < 0.05$) and shops ($p < 0.05$). Social behaviour and the physical characteristics *are* related. Having validated the concept in this way, Lee went on to develop a measure whereby people's schemas can be compared one with another. The reason for developing such a measure is of course that each person's schema is drawn out of a different environment, making direct meaningful comparisons impossible. Lee's measure is obtained by expressing the schema as a *ratio* of the locality – the number of houses, shops, etc. in the *schema* compared to the number in the *locality*. Utilizing these components (area, houses, shops, amenity buildings), Lee arrives at what he calls 'the neighbourhood quotient' or NhQ. The NhQ is comparable to an intelligence quotient, in the sense that, just as we can talk about a child's intelligence irrespective of his age, we can now talk about a person's neighbourhood irrespective of where he lives.

Having obtained the neighbourhood quotient, Lee found that it was related to social class – for example, class IV's (in Lee's terminology unskilled manual) average NhQ is significantly ($p < 0.05$) lower than class I's (professional managerial). He also found that NhQ was related to length of residence – increasing steadily after five years. Further, NhQ was related to the location of the husband's work – being higher if the husband worked in the locality. Non-native status was also shown to be related to high NhQ, and finally the NhQ of housewives living in both detached houses and terraced houses was higher than the NhQ of housewives living in semi-detached houses.

As well as being able to look at the way NhQ was related to information provided by the housewives, one can also use the NhQ to provide information about the collective aspects of neighbourhood. If, for example, one takes a discriminable group of people (say on the basis of social class, or geographical location), then the mean or average of the NhQs would

dwelling units

shops

amenity buildings

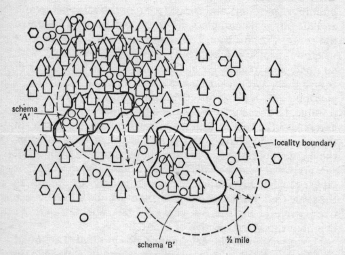

schema 'A'

locality boundary

schema 'B'

½ mile

Fig. 16. Schemata and localities (after Lee, 1968). An average NhQ subject from a high-density locality (A) and a high NhQ subject from a low-density locality (B).

reflect the level of the socio-physical involvement of that group while the spread or range of the values of the NhQs (more accurately the variance) would serve as a measure of that group's agreement or, as Lee calls it, 'consentaneity'. Doing this, Lee has found evidence to support the Perry assertion that a neighbourhood with well-defined boundaries will have an associated high level of social participation. In Lee's terms this is equivalent (though not *only* equivalent) to saying that high consentaneity (low spread of quotient values) should be found in conjunction with high NhQ means. And there does seem to be at least an indication that this is so. Lee found that median NhQ is significantly correlated to variance or spread of social classes ($p < 0.05$). This means that participation increases with heterogeneity of population in terms of social class, and it throws some empirical light on the usually emotive 'one-class-or mixed' arguments often surrounding public housing developments.

From the foregoing Lee felt able to make constructive suggestions to the planner – suggestions based on measurement which itself depends on certain theoretical assumptions. His recommendations include:

1. That planning should be directed towards heterogeneous physical and social layouts, deliberately emphasizing the local (and therefore most effortless) satisfaction of needs.

2. That because schemata tend to show concordance around prominent boundaries, and because schemata are territory and not density based, and taking into account that the typical schemata area for Lee's sample was 75 acres, then at current density developments the population would range from 5,000 to 7,500 'and this would be sufficient to support a good range of shops and amenity buildings'.

In this work Lee has made a significant contribution. He has not only found a way of measuring something never before measured with any degree of sophistication but he has also offered his findings for practical application, with the knowledge that his recommendations are empirically derived rather than based on intuition or on 'common' sense (cf. Lewis Mumford's size recommendation).

Let us now compare the injunctions offered by Perry for a neighbourhood unit with those recommendations made by Lee.

1. *Size.* Perry advocated a neighbourhood population of between 6,000 and 9,600 and based this figure on the approximate population size to support an elementary school – which in turn he derived from the 'educational authorities'. Lee advocates between 5,000 and 7,500 – thus there is a broad bond of agreement between the two recommendations. Lee, however, bases his figure on territory (75 acres) – the typical or modal size of the schemata – and derives the population size from the currently fashionable

density figures (up to 100 persons per acre – but see chapter 8). Both finish up with more or less the same answer, but in each case it is based upon some unverified assertion. For example, compare the following two statements concerning density figures: 'no one contends that families living at densities over 100 persons per acre is ideal' (M.H.L.G., 1970); 'Given favourable circumstances, and some self-selection of tenants, much higher densities [than 136 p.p.a.] are possible and may sometime be highly desirable in an urban renewal programme' (Smith, 1961). Just as educational authorities are liable to opine differently about optimum numbers for a school, so are planners about optimum numbers for a neighbourhood. Perhaps the value of Lee's work here is to demonstrate the unimportance of numbers when considering the neighbourhood unit, in that people's conceptions of their neighbourhood are not linked to density but rather to territory. Lee, in fact, directs our attention to the important role played by neighbourhood amenities. If local satisfaction of needs is important, then it should be possible to arrive at a minimum population size necessary to support a given range of amenities, which is an economic rather than psychological question.

2. *Distinct boundaries.* Lee and Perry would seem also to concur on this point. Distinct geographical features do seem to act as psychological boundaries. Lee found that consentaneity and participation were related, and, if this were causal, another injunction would follow; namely that, as distinct boundaries promote similar schemata and similar schemata tend to go with high participation, distinct boundaries should be planned to encourage neighbourhoodness.

3. *Parks and recreation spaces.* Again Perry and Lee agree. Perry implied that provision should be within the neighbourhood unit. Lee actually demonstrates that the use of local amenities is directly related to the number of amenities provided in the locality. Although Lee doesn't specifically mention parks, his 'amenities' include 'recreation rooms'. 'There is an increase in the ratio of "joiners" to "non-

joiners" that is directly proportional to the absolute number of amenity buildings in the locality and which shows no evidence of saturation over a range of provision extending as high as sixty-five amenity buildings per locality' (Lee, 1968).

4. *Central siting of community provisions*. Here Perry and Lee disagree. Perry is all for central siting, Lee for siting that provides minimum energy expenditure in terms of travelling distance, as he has shown (see above) that siting of social clubs should be many and spread out rather than few and concentrated (Lee, 1963).

5. *Shopping areas*. Lee does not here commit himself as Perry does to having shopping centres at the periphery of the neighbourhood, but points to the interesting phenomenon that housewives prefer to go to shops which are in the direction of the town centre rather than away from it even though the actual distance may be greater (see also Lee, 1962 and 1970).

6. *Internal Street System*. Again a similarity between the views of Lee and Perry, Lee additionally favouring path-access housing and the use of traffic ways as boundaries.

One aspect that Lee emphasizes that Perry does not is the need for heterogeneity of population – Lee being very strongly in favour. Also the Lee neighbourhood unit, in contrast to the Perry unit, is far more jumbled and less orderly, for example in the siting of amenities and shops. Thus the criticisms of the Perry unit – that it is static and supportive of the *status quo* – are not appropriate to the Lee unit. The ideology of the twenties and thirties re-emerges, but in a far more respectable form and with a far firmer empirical foundation.

In my opinion Lee's work is a landmark. He has not only with his phenomenological approach solved the problem of combining the physical and social factors, but he has also developed a measure that makes possible comparison between persons and/or groups of people. He is thus able to comment on planning practices from a platform of knowledge. Lee has expanded the horizons of traditional psychology, he has attacked an urgent social problem and has suggested some practical procedures. Perhaps above all he has shown that the possibility of a profitable exchange across disciplinary boundaries is very real indeed.

But, impressive as Lee's work is, it does contain serious flaws. When I first came across his work in early 1969 (a previous account had in fact been given in Lee, 1964), I immediately started asking people to draw lines on maps around their district or neighbourhood and was a little disturbed – particularly considering the small size of my sample – at the attitude of my respondents. They would ask me; 'Well, what do you mean by neighbourhood?' or 'Do you mean where I feel at home/at ease or not like a stranger?' or 'The parts that I know well or am familiar with or go to often?,' or 'Do you mean that part that feels like home when approaching it when returning from a holiday?' and so on. Later that year one of my students worked as a research assistant to Alan Lipman, Reader in the Welsh School of Architecture, in his research into territoriality with reference to housing (Watkins, 1970) and she experienced exactly the same problem. She thought she would circumvent it somewhat, however, by substituting the phrase 'home area' for neighbourhood (a change which might be thought to add to rather than reduce confusion), but she still found people giving it different meanings. Such meanings included just the respondent's house or one or two surrounding houses, or the local shops, or the whole estate, and Watkins was not at all happy about the validity of the maps that had been generated. Indeed she suggested that the home-area maps might be of at least three varieties (and this could just as easily apply to the neighbourhood maps):

1. An area to which a person feels she (housewives again!) belongs.
2. An area which is known and used frequently, for which she suggested the term facility map.
3. An area which is known but not necessarily used.

This delineation is not totally dissimilar to Lee's typology of neighbourhoods, given on page 161, but the important point is that one single question or request for a map could be understood in at least three ways, and simply because a person elects one way does not mean that she could not have produced either or both of the other two, had the original question been more specific. Could it be that the *word* neighbourhood has very many different meanings to people and the maps they draw are a function of the particular meaning they attach to it, so that the data they generate are incomparable? If you asked people, 'what is the population of the U.K.?' for example, you would get a range of answers, and one would be able to determine how correct these were and thus learn something about people's perception of population size in the U.K. However, if you asked them how many people could ride on a bus, the answers given would not be comparable unless you first knew how the people giving the answer had perceived the question: a single-decker bus or a double-decker? going on a holiday or coming home from work? packed or comfortably seated? and so on. Before learning something about their perceptions of buses *vis-à-vis* people, you would *have* to learn something about their perceptions of what the question actually *meant*. It is my contention that Lee's question is one involving this double perception – firstly, how do people perceive the *word* neighbourhood, and secondly, given their particular perception of the word, how do they perceive their actual neighbourhood of which they themselves are a part? The work of D. Spencer (1972, 1973) will perhaps allow me to make this point more clearly.

Spencer was particularly interested in the problems encountered not only when using different methods of eliciting the 'invisible landscape' (verbal, pictorial, cartographical) but also when eliciting such images (or schemata) from working-class people. Spencer found that it was very important to them 'whether or not they were convinced there was a right or wrong answer' and, significantly, that the difficulties seemed less when the neighbourhoods were *verbally* described or delineated than when they used a map. Some respondents refused to draw the map and Spencer says of these that 'lack of self confidence, inability to map read, and concern for giving the ''correct answer'' were important factors'. It would seem that the map drawing request could very easily be seen as a 'school-type' exercise. A very frequent response was: 'What do you want me to say?' That kind of situation lends itself very sweetly to prompting by the interviewer and thus introduces experimenter bias. Take Lee's question itself – 'Please draw a line *round the part* . . .' – this very phrase surely gives the respondent clues about how she should respond? It is being assumed that the respondent's neighbourhood or district can be contained within a single boundary. Why then be surprised at the features of the schemata that Lee documents – that it has figure and ground (it must have – the respondents are being asked to produce a figure on ground); contour (they are being asked to draw a *line*); and continuity ('draw a line *round* the part . . .') and so on. In other words what I am suggesting (and Spencer is producing the evidence) is that there are certain expectations *built in* to the Lee methodology that may lead one to look at the results in a somewhat different light. As Spencer goes on to say, 'Lee's method assumes that all features within the ''schemata'' are perceived by the respondents as integral parts of their neighbourhoods' and that his 'analysis is based on this assumption'. Perhaps if a different methodology were adopted, different results would accrue.

In 'imaging' the large-scale environment, Kevin Lynch (1960) takes a different starting point from Lee. Lynch was concerned with almost the complete opposite to Lee, in that Lee's respondents were to pick out an area from a larger area to which a special designation (neighbourhood) could be given. In arriving at the NhQ, Lee gave each house in the schema an equal value; the same with shops, amenities, etc. Lynch, on the other hand, wanted to find out from a given area what were the features of *special* importance which gave that area (and he is basically concerned with the cityscape) its 'imageability'. For imageability Lynch also used the terms 'visibility', 'legibility' and 'apparency'. He defined legibility as an aspect of visual quality which described 'the

ease with which [the] parts [of the cityscape] can be recognized and can be organized into a coherent pattern'.

Lynch described the image of the city as having five
elements: paths – channels along which the observer moves;
edges – boundaries and barriers of various kinds; districts;
nodes – focal points of various kinds; and landmarks. One
could, of course, conceive of using a Lynch-type analysis on
a Lee-type question, i.e. ask people to characterize or describe their neighbourhood not by drawing round it on a map
but by eliciting the elements of the neighbourhood image.
One of the procedures used by Lynch was to ask his respondents to draw sketch maps of the area in which he was interested (his investigations were conducted in Boston, New
Jersey and Los Angeles) and to describe the physical features
seen on the ordinary trip taken to work (the respondents were
all natives of their cities). He found little correspondence
between the two attempts (verbal and cartographic),
perhaps indicating again that methodology determines
results. Lynch's techniques have, however, been used in
other places, e.g. by de Jonge (1962) in the Netherlands and
Gulick (1963) in Tripoli.

Still other methods are being developed to elicit the
perceptions of large-scale environments. Lowenthal (1970)
for example had 300 people going individually on ten-mile
walks in Cambridge, Boston, New York and Columbus, Ohio.
Subjects then filled out a twenty-five-item five-point bi-polar
scale (e.g. natural-artificial, rich-poor, beautiful-ugly). He
found that different cities were typified by different cluster-
ings of adjectives: 'For example, observers in Columbus are
unique in connecting *smooth*, *uniform* and *horizontal*, observers
in Cambridge alone strongly link *contrast* with what is seen
as *rich*, *fresh* and *pleasant* ... New Yorkers associate *vertical*
environments with *people* and find such milieus *beautiful*;
Bostonians associate *verticality* with *things* and find it *ugly*,
drab and *artificial*.' This kind of approach could be used for
getting at people's perceptions not merely for urban environments but for natural environments also, and environments within buildings.

On a still larger scale Gould and White (1968, 1974) have mapped the 'residential desirability' of Britain as seen by school leavers. They were asked, with a map of Britain in front of them, to 'order their own, quite individual notions of residential desirability on the assumption that they would have an absolutely free choice to live where they wished "other things being equal"'. The map showed county boundaries and important towns. From the data produced Gould and White were able to produce a 'desirability map' exactly analogous to a contour map. The contour lines, instead of representing height, represent the strength of perceived residential desirability. Describing the mental map obtained, Gould and White pointed to some typical features of the maps produced by school leavers from a variety of locations 'starting from a ridge of high desirability along the entire South Coast, the surface falls steeply to a sinkhole centred over the metropolitan area. However, two prongs of residential desirability extend through East Anglia and the counties bordering Wales, to produce a "mental cirque" in the Midlands. Generally the entire surface declines with a considerable degree of regularity northwards to Scotland, with a major anomaly of a mental dome centred over the Lake District.' This particular technique of mental mapping of Gould and White could have important uses. It could help throw light on migratory movements, or help in anticipating problems arising from the location of new industrial developments. The general task Gould and White set themselves was the same as Lee's, Lynch's and Lowenthal's – to understand the relationship between the physical geography and the perceptual schema; their techniques, however, differ, and different data thus accrue.

It looks very much, then, that, if we are going to look at the broad question of how we conceive of our large-scale environment – whether it be our neighbourhood, city or country – we ought to invest some considerable effort into the methodologies that are even at this time available. This surely represents a worthwhile challenge to perceptual psychologists. A challenge that at least some psychologists have already risen to, for as Stea (1969) points out:

> Soviet psychologists have been directing attention for some time to the mental representation of large environments, and to problems of location, orientation and movement within these environments, [but] American psychologists – strongly rooted in the behaviouristic tradition – have shied away from the same problems.

Besides the problem of delineating the properties and meanings for behaviour of such maps (as Stea begins to do), it is also very important to understand the processes through which they are learned.

A very interesting investigation by Blaut and Stea (1970) attacks just this question. By defining map reading in a preliterate child as the ability to deal with scale, the ability to project and abstract when presented with an aerial photograph, Blaut and Stea suggest 'that mapping behaviour is a normal and important process in human development, and that map learning begins long before the child encounters formal geography and cartology'. In a recent review of the development of spatial cognition Hart and Moore (1973) have shown that psychological theories are available – namely those of the Swiss psychologist Jean Piaget (see Piaget and Inhelder, 1956) and Werner (1948), which can promote our understanding of this development. As our physical environment becomes increasingly man-made and as our cities continue to grow and become increasingly difficult to navigate, the understanding of such mental activity becomes paramount. If urban man is ever going to understand his own urban behaviour, he must know how he cognizes his self-created urban scene.

8
Overcrowding and All That

In Roman times London's population was around 15,000 (Collingwood and Myres, 1936). By today's standards that is not even a good-sized football crowd.

Only 123 years ago there were four cities in the world whose population topped a million. In 1961 that figure was 141 (Toffler, 1970).

There are two processes at work here, one is urbanization and the other is population growth. The population of the world is increasing at an exponential rate, and an increasing proportion of those people are leaving the rural areas in favour of the urban, bringing about the enormous urban agglomerations that are so much a feature of modern life.

These urban agglomerations, containing vast numbers of people, seem to raise two types of fear in the minds of concerned people. Firstly, the fear that, because such agglomerations are intensive energy and resource users, the limits of spaceship earth will soon be reached and social breakdown will result (see Ehrlich and Ehrlich, 1970; Ehrlich, 1971; Rattrey Taylor, 1972; Commoner, 1971; etc). The 'energy crisis' of early 1974 dramatically gave this fear reality. The second fear is that the sheer pressure of people within the relatively confined areas of cities is going to lead *itself* to a breakdown of the social processes that keep our societies intact, and society will simply fall apart. This second fear is the subject of chapter 8. What is overcrowding? How much people pressure can man adapt to? Are the effects good or bad? – these are the sort of questions I want to examine, and they have arisen only relatively recently, as man's image of himself in interaction with his physical and man-made environment has undergone change. Change from extolling man's propensities for the taming and exploitation of nature, to doubting that this propensity is in his own long-term interest. If the propensity is to be de-emphasized, then the environmental pressures which call it forth will have to be lessened. One such pressure is the overgrowth of world population.

The Ehrlichs (Ehrlich and Ehrlich, 1970) point out that the doubling time of the world population around 8,000 B.C. was about 1,500 years; and now – the population having itself increased 600 times – the doubling time is a mere thirty-seven years. Thus we have not only 800 times as many people but a doubling time forty times greater. The question is not whether this exponential growth should be allowed to continue, but rather *when* it will be generally recognized that it *cannot* continue if man is going to have a future at least as long as his history? In the modern world no nation is, or can afford to be, independent of other nations. Practically no nation is self-sufficient or unaffected by the activities of another nation, and thus no nation can remain uninvolved in the struggle to reduce population growth. Indeed the English, who inhabit the third most densely populated country in the world, should be particularly aware of this, but it would appear that the concern about the population size and growth centres on individual and social issues rather than on resources or pollutional aspects. Indeed the Royal Commission on Environmental Pollution (1971) saw 'no cause for alarm or for "crash" programmes of research'. The Abortion Act of 1967 allows termination to safeguard the *mental health* of the pregnant woman 'or any existing children of her family'. The prime intention of the Family Planning Association is to introduce choice in terms of number and spacing of children, rather than to effect a broad societal programme of population regulation.

There are signs, however, that some sort of awareness of the population problem is dawning on those who walk the English corridors of power. For instance, the conclusion from the first report of the Select Committee on Science and Technology (H.M.S.O., 1971) was that 'The Government must act to prevent the consequences of population growth becoming intolerable for the everyday conditions of life'. The regret of course is that the prevention of population growth was not focused on, but rather attention was directed to the consequences. However, the Select Committee did go on to recommend the setting up of a special office directly responsible to the prime Minister, with a duty to 'publicize the effects of population levels and their consequences'. This recommendation appears very laudable, but one cannot help wondering what information *could* be legitimately distributed concerning the psychological or social effects of population level, because there is very little such information available.

Zlutnick and Altman (1972), in a review of crowding and human behaviour, divide what evidence there is available into three sections:

1. Laboratory-oriented research involving some type of controls.
2. Correlational studies in natural settings involving use of records, such as crime rates, census data, etc.
3. Popularized speculations and guesses.

They comment that 'the last category is the most voluminous, the first least evident in the scientific literature'. There was certainly a noticeable lack of empirical work in the evidence presented and discussed by the Select Committee. The nearest the Committee gets to any experimental evidence concerning the behavioural consequences (pollution and resources problems are treated) of overcrowding occurs in the examination of the witness Sir George Godber by Mr Parkyn:

MR PARKYN: ... it has been argued that increasing population densities, particularly when associated with crowding in large cities, is now leading to stress, mental ill health, development of aggression and even crime. Have you any views on this?

SIR GEORGE: I have no views based on facts and I don't think anybody has.

MR PARKYN: There have been some studies which showed that if you put a lot of rats together in a small cage, they get aggressive.

Has that kind of experiment any serious validity, would you say?

SIR GEORGE: I suppose it might have a serious application if we ever got anywhere near the density of those rats in those cages, but we are a long way from that.

MR PARKYN: Can you lead from experience with animals to people in these matters?

SIR GEORGE: . . . I do not think that this kind of experiment has yet gone anywhere near indicating that such and such will happen with the kind of population movement that we have now.

Notwithstanding the above, there still comes across in the report the undercurrent of feeling that herding a lot of people together will have evil consequences. Comments of witnesses before the Select Committee like: 'a village man myself' (p. 139); 'I find it a fantastic thing that everybody wishes to get together into more and more dense areas as opposed to going off into the open spaces' (p. 53); 'I regard it as being a higher standard of living to live with the car and the television and my garden away from the big metropolis and high density than to live in the high-density area within a half hour's bus ride of the opera house' (p. 238); 'the problems of crime, hooliganism and mass disturbance . . . are essentially manifestations of high-density living' (p. 230), all convey the impression of 'high density = high pathology', that there is something intrinsically bad about high concentrations of people. Zlutnick and Altman (1972) actually compiled a list of some of the popular conceptions of the effects of crowding, citing no less than seventeen categories – from physiological breakdowns, unemployment, crime, riots, mental illness and loss of freedom to family disorganization. These 'stereotypes' (stereotypes because the evidence for them is either ambiguous, contradictory or absent) are fed by the so-called 'animal studies' to which a reference was made in the extract above. For example, G. M. Carstairs, addressing a Planned Parenthood Federation conference (1967) asked: 'What will be the consequences for mental health of a massive increase in population?' And he replied: 'as yet the science of human behaviour is not sufficiently developed to answer this question with precision or even confidence. Nevertheless it is possible to learn from studies of animals, both in their natural environment and under experimental conditions, and to note certain *apparently invariable* consequences of severe overcrowding: with due caution one can infer similar repercussions of overcrowding in man' (my italics).

Mayer Spivak (1970) in a similar vein has asserted that 'it is almost certainly true that the dynamics of behaviour under overcrowded conditions – so far only studied in dense animal populations – are to some extent operating in our own human social systems'.

Fawcett (1970), is, however, as regards the Human Condition, rather more accurate:

The deleterious effects on mental health of unwanted pregnancies, oversized families and urban crowding have been commented upon by a number of writers. Typically, reports dealing with the effects of population variables on mental health are based upon *clinical impressions* or *unsystematic observations*.

Some studies relate population density and urbanization to statistical data on the incidence of crime, delinquency and mental illness, but causal effects are not established and intervening psychological processes not specified (my italics).

and Freedman *et al.* (1971) are frankly sceptical: 'it is an entirely open question whether high concentrations of humans are inherently harmful. The fact is we do not know what effect population density *per se* has on human beings.' But which are the animal studies that tend to feed the stereotype of 'high density = high pathology' – the 'apparently invariable consequences'?

By far and away the best-known work on overcrowding in animal populations is that conducted by John B. Calhoun (1962, 1962a). It is to some parts of this programme of research that we now turn.

Starting with a population of wild Norway rats in a $\frac{1}{4}$-acre enclosure and allowing unlimited breeding to occur, Calhoun calculated a projected population of 5,000 after twenty-seven months. The actual population stabilized at 150. The reason was the very high infant mortality rate that developed. To delineate more exactly the factors involved, Calhoun started a series of laboratory experiments using specially constructed enclosures. One such enclosure – a room of 10 feet × 14 feet × 9 feet was divided into four equal areas by partitions. These areas were connected by ramps to give topographical linearity (i.e. pens 1 and 4 were not joined).

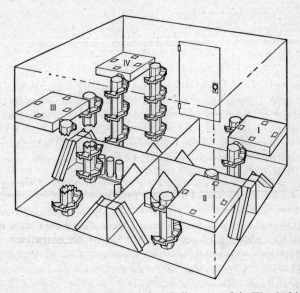

Fig. 17. Calhoun's enclosure (after Calhoun, 1961). The habitat. Dimensions 10 × 14 × 9 feet. Partitions 24 inches high formed four pens, PI, PII, PIII and PIV. The elevated square platforms connected to the floor by spiral staircases represent artificial 'burrows'. The four square openings on the surface of each provided access to a system of tunnels and nesting boxes. V-shaped ramps provided communication between PI and PII, PII and PII, PII and PIV. At all times a superabundance of food in each pen was available from the conical-topped hoppers. Similarly in each pen a superabundance of water was always available from a series of 2-quart bottles. A 3- by 5-feet glass window on the roof of the room enabled observations of rats recognizable as individuals through coded spots of dye on the fur.

The population in the enclosure was then allowed to increase to twice its 'normal' number (Calhoun was working this time with domesticated rats) whilst being closely observed for sixteen months. The behavioural changes resulting from increased density in this environment were:

a. Disruption of female nest-building. Mother rats would no longer organize the paper strips which were available for nest building into a nest and, as time went on, they would not even bother to collect the paper strips from outside their burrows.

b. Inadequate transport of the pups. In moving her pups from place to place (when pups had been disturbed, for example), the mother rat would frequently drop pups and fail to retrieve them. Such pups would eventually die and be eaten by other rats.

c. Inappropriate sexual behaviour. Males would mount unreceptive females, other males, and immature rats. Courtships ritual also disappeared.

These disruptions of behaviour were not, however, equally spread throughout the four pens. As can be seen from Fig. 17, pens 2 and 3 have two points of access, whereas pens 1 and 4 have only one. Furthermore, the height of the burrows above floor level varies. In pens 3 and 4 the burrows are 6 feet off the ground, in pens 2 and 1 only 3 feet. As Calhoun says: 'This introduced an "income" factor in the environment since rats living in pens 1 and 2 had to expend only half the effort in going to the floor to secure food and water as did rats in pens 3 and 4.' Considering these two physical features of the total environment together would lead us to expect the highest residential probability in pen 2 which has both a 'low' burrow and two access points. This was what Calhoun found. In addition, something funny started happening to the eating habits of the rats. Although food and water hoppers were provided in each pen, so that rats did not have to go elsewhere to eat, they favoured food hoppers around which they had a greater chance of social contact. Calhoun writes: 'Once the number of rats in a room increased above a certain level, this frequency of contact while eating increased sufficiently that the rats *developed a new definition of the feeding situation to include the presence of another rat*. Gradually eating in the other pens declined until 60–80 per cent of all food consumption was in this one of the four pens' (my italics). In other words, there developed an abnormal pattern of behaviour – an atypical aggregation of individuals in a space only a fraction of the area totally available.

Thus a combination of factors in the physical environment has brought about changes in behaviour at the social level. This atypical aggregation of individuals Calhoun describes as a 'behavioural sink'. It is within the behavioural sink that the main pathologies of behaviour occur. Some of the males in the sink Calhoun categorizes as 'probers' – hyperactive, hypersexual, homosexual and cannibalistic; others displayed complete passivity – 'they moved through the community like somnambulists' – ignoring all other rats. But when the behavioural sink became established, the rats in the two end pens (1 and 4) seemed the least disturbed. In these pens the lowest infant-mortality rate was observed and the females generally made good mothers. Changes from the norm were apparent, but not such as to threaten survival in the dramatic way that it was threatened in the behavioural sink. In the two end pens the tendency was for a dominant male to take over exclusive territorial rights. This male established a 'harem' of female rats, and prevented other males from entering. The behavioural sink, however, was not the inevitable concomitant of sheer numbers for, when Calhoun tried a different type of feeding (powdered food in an open hopper instead of pellet food in a wire mesh hopper that required several minutes of effort to gain satisfaction), the redefinition of the eating to encompass social contact did not occur. Although severe social pathologies did evolve, these were not as serious as those formed in the behavioural sink. Thus the particularities of the situation would seem to have great importance in mediating the final behaviour resulting from high population density.

It is this 'behavioural sink' phenomenon that has been

selected as an analogue for the densely populated, human, urban scene found in our larger cities.

Carstairs (1967), for example, comments on what a far cry such studies are from the human condition, indicating that an important difference is the *compulsory* confinement. But he then goes on to say – 'In human populations, however, boundaries can be set by social institutions and by communicated attitudes and values, and these boundaries can under certain circumstances create a sense of confinement no less demoralizing than the bars of a cage.' René Spitz (1964) notes, 'however farfetched the analogy, the activities of the juvenile gangs (of our major urban centres) are strangely reminiscent of Calhoun's "probers". And in reading Calhoun's description of the "withdrawn rats", one gets the uneasy feeling that we have heard of something not too dissimilar in our own culture (and in older ones too). One is reminded of the cultists, of the beatniks, of the strange little communities found on the so-called lunatic fringe.'

Although at a superficial level such views seem reasonable, when scrutinized they appear less so. Carstairs implied a direct analogy between a physical and a psychological barrier but this must surely be regarded as an empirically unverified speculation. And, as for Spitz's 'uneasy feelings' about what could be regarded as deviant groups in society, why single out beatniks instead of psychoanalysts? Are juvenile gangs (or groups of young people) really all the same in their behaviour propensities? Archer (1970), in a very comprehensive review of the effects of population density on behaviour in rodents, castigates those who would seek to relate directly these animal studies to human behaviour (e.g. Querido, 1966; Spitz, 1964; Russell, 1966), claiming that 'their writings demonstrate only a superficial understanding of the animal literature', and he declines to take their ideas seriously.

Archer's concluding paragraph is perhaps revealing, where he says, 'the *usual* response to increased population density in natural populations is emigration'. Only when emigration is prevented for one reason or another is there an increase in aggressive behaviour, and changes in social structure. The question which seems to arise *vis-à-vis* the human population is: what exactly are the mechanisms through which man comes to know and act upon undue concentrations of population? If the sub-human animal kingdom's 'natural' response to overcrowding is emigration, there is the implication that density (or the other side of the coin – pressure on resources) is in some way perceivable and likely to stimulate avoiding or adaptive behaviour. As Chitty warned (Chitty, 1971), the sorts of density that Calhoun achieved with his rats and mice simply would not occur under natural conditions. Overcrowding must surely, then, have *at least* two meanings – firstly, higher than normal densities which occur in natural settings (with emigration resulting) and, secondly, the very high densities achievable under specific confinement regimes, to which the response is bizarre behaviour. If we look at man and assume that bizarre behaviour is being produced (which as I hope to show below is not the case), then the question becomes – what is it that is preventing him from emigrating to less dense regions? In answering that question we must inevitably consider Carstairs's 'social institutions, attitudes and values' as presenting effective *physical* barriers to mass movements. However, before accepting this speculation, let us consider another piece of animal research – the work done by Dr A. Kessler (1966, 1967).

A notable finding of Kessler's research into 'the interplay between social ecology and physiology, genetics and population dynamics of mice' was the enormous population sizes that resulted from allowing the mice to reproduce freely in the specially constructed enclosures. Kessler studied three mouse populations (A, B and C) all based on genetically similar founder mice. Populations A and B were the experimental groups in the specially designed enclosures, while population C served as a control group for behavioural, physiological and genetic comparison, and was kept in pairs in separate cages. As Kessler says: 'Both populations [A and B] grew to sizes that are several times larger than those of any

closures, Kessler specifically aimed at reducing the effects engendered by the particularities of the layout of the enclosures. Calhoun's 'behavioural sink', for example, was related to features of the physical enclosure (burrow height and pen accessibility) and as a phenomenon was not apparent in other situations. Figs. 18 and 19 show Kessler's layout which 'aims to avoid behavioural and physiological differentiation based upon distance from food source'.

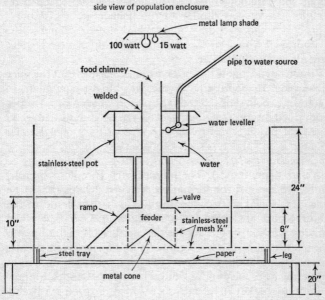

Fig. 19. Kessler's enclosure, side view (after Kessler, 1966).

The free growth of populations A and B to these final high densities (eighty-five and sixty mice per square foot) was accompanied by changes in behaviour which Kessler summarizes as follows:

1. Disappearance of circadian activity peaks.
2. Decline in frequency of fighting per male but an increase in unusual aggressiveness.

3. Aberrations of sexual behaviour.
4. Deterioration of maternal care.
5. Cannibalism.
6. Striking decrease in social responsiveness.

There are similarities between the behaviour of these mice and the behaviour of the rats observed by Calhoun. The 'queueing' type of sexual activity – that is, packs of six to ten male mice making repeated brief mounts (up to fifty) on single females – is similar to the behaviour of Calhoun's 'probers'; the dropping and abandonment of pups, the withdrawal from activity of some mice, the aggressiveness, are all strikingly similar.

But what accounts for the enormous densities that the mice achieved? In population A this was almost equivalent to 'standing room only'. Surely the picture of over a 1,000 mice contained in 13·33 square feet of space and still in good 'general physical health' is an extraordinary one. Kessler relates it to 'the types of animals used, to the *number of individuals in the founder nuclei* and to the *physical structure of the enclosures*' (my italics). The physical structure, for example, militated against the formation of status groups (based on age, sex, social status), as all animals had to come to the central part enclosure for food and water, so that social mixing was inevitable. About the number of original population members (thirty-seven males and thirty-seven females in each population) Calhoun (1970) hypothesized that, right from the very beginning, individuals have far less opportunity to make any 'enclosure indentification with any portions of the physical environment' (because of the large numbers) and as time goes on 'very little crowding exists because personal space has become reduced to the boundaries of the individual's skin'. Both these factors may have implications for a definition of human overcrowding, because quite clearly more is involved than just a consideration of numbers or for that matter resources.

However, before going into this problem, another aspect of Kessler's work deserves attention. At the end of the fifty weeks of observation of population B, and when the mice in population A enclosure had been removed, Kessler joined up the two enclosures, so that he could make an emigration study.

Population B – although identical in all aspects to population A – had not achieved the same density. A peak population of 800 mice was achieved during the first six months, but for six months after that not a single new mouse had been born. Ten days after the joining of the two enclosures the numbers of mice in each one was roughly equal and also stable. However, there were obvious behavioural differences between the sub-populations. Three times as much fighting occurred amongst the emigrants, and this fighting was both more

emigration study

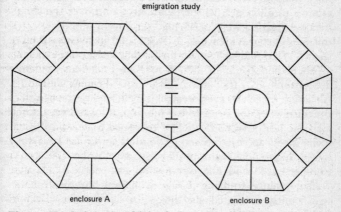

enclosure A   enclosure B

Fig. 20. Kessler's enclosed joined, floor plan (after Kessler, 1966).

intense and more prolonged. There were, however, only one third as many attacks on the females in the emigrant population. There was an increase in mating frequency, especially of normal matings and, about five weeks after the enclosures were joined, there was an 'outburst' of births: scattering and cannibalism of pups was uncommon amongst the emigrants, but persisted in the stay-puts. Live births were six times as common amongst the emigrants although the mortality rate was greater. After two months had elapsed – two months which saw population increases for the first time in thirty-five weeks – Kessler closed off the enclosures from each other, having returned all the emigrant population and its additions to the original enclosure. The date was 12 March 1965. The mice entered a period of hyperactivity which went on for at least twenty hours. On 15 March Kessler reported 'a chattering-like sound was audible on entering the room housing the population enclosure. In marked contrast to the previous hyperactivity, most of the mice were standing still, head down, bodies drawn together. Many of the mice had ruffled coats. There were more than forty dead mice. Of 500 mice 292 showed one or more gross signs of disease . . . Twenty-two mice had purulent conjunctivitis, eighteen had visible subcutaneous abscesses (in the pelvic area and over the shoulders). Autopsies were performed on fifty randomly selected mice and gross evidence of disease found in twenty-seven of them.' What had happened during that fateful three days?

There had been, in fact, a massive infectious epidemic attributable to the micro organism Proteus mirabilis. Although there was every reason to believe that the health of the mice was good prior to the reunion, it looked very much as if the adaptive capacities of the mice to this additional social stress were stretched beyond their limit. It is very interesting to note at this point the work of Rahe *et al.* (1964) who presented evidence to show that – in people – 'a cluster of social events requiring change in ongoing life adjustment is significantly associated with the time of illness onset' (Holmes and Rahe, 1967). It seems not to matter whether the changes required are associated with positive or negative effect – the 'life change' itself is the critical factor. The implication of this for the study of crowding is clear. Whether or not a particular crowded situation is a stressful one will be at least partly determined by how far that situation deviates from the one in which the individual was previously engaged. In other words – how much adjustment is required? Again, this emigration study of Kessler's is leading us to look at what may be the superordinate factors operating in the crowded situation as opposed to the species' specific outcomes and to produce hypotheses suitable for testing or speculating about in human populations. Kessler's conviction (based on his own highly convincing evidence and other field studies) that social behaviour and social ecology govern population dynamics (p. 177), and that population growth *can* follow on social disorganization, are examples of such hypotheses.

This now pinpoints the question of exactly what the parameters of the 'crowded situation' are. It is a question taken up by Calhoun (1970), who sees it as a question of real importance, because, as he says, 'The implications of Kessler's study suggest that for all practical purposes, to where food and shelter are limiting variables, man can go to standing room only'.

Calhoun maintains that there are *at least* four factors which contribute to crowdedness. Firstly, the actual density measured in number of organisms per unit space. This is obviously dependent on the space which a particular individual of the population occupies. In human populations one could ask whether children feel as crowded as adults at similar objective densities. This would perhaps be related to the size of their 'personal spaces' about which there is little information. A second factor is the homogeneity or the degree of harmony of the value systems of the population. Calhoun (1967) cites an interesting example of disharmony amongst a rat population. This study involved the use of an instrument Calhoun called S.T.A.W. – Socialization Training Apparatus Water. This device had two levers which when pressed delivered water to the rats which were pressing them. Pairs of rats were separated from each other by a perspex screen. The apparatus was built so that it could work in three ways: (i) each lever press produces water independently of whether the other lever is pressed; (ii) the levers are both locked unless both levers are being pressed (i.e. two rats have to cooperate to get water – hence Calhoun called this the COOP condition); (iii) either lever only works if the other is *not* being operated (the DISOP – disoperation – condition). Both the COOP groups and DISOP groups of rats very quickly got the hang of their S.T.A.W. *modus operandi*. One day, however, a DISOP rat learned how to get from its pen with its fifteen peers into a neighbouring pen which happened to be a pen of sixteen COOP rats. Of course every time the DISOP intruder found the S.T.A.W. free he would go in for a drink; and every time a COOP rat saw him do this it would join him in the other half – a behaviour which according to the DISOP rat's values or expectations was completely wrong. He would come out of his half of the apparatus and pull the COOP rat out of the other half by the tail. Although Calhoun kept putting this adventurous DISOP rat back in his home cage, it insisted on returning, and within a period of weeks had 'macerated the tails and hind feet of all the COOP rats. Most lost all their toes. Seven died from these wounds. And yet the invading male was never attacked. To the COOP rats this invading DISOP male was always behaving correctly when it entered the S.T.A.W. and their ethical standards dictated that they come to his rescue.' A case surely for asserting that while sixteen were company seventeen was definitely a crowd!

A third aspect of crowding, and probably the limiting one for the human global population, is the amount of competition for resources. Travelling on a London tube at rush hour is one thing, but being contained at the same density in the hold of a ship as a Japanese P.O.W. (see Stewart, 1961) with insufficient air is quite another. People's attitudes towards their density make a difference. For example, Biderman *et al.* (1963), in their review of historical incidents of extreme overcrowding, make the point that modern-day citizens seeking shelter refuge following nuclear attack would probably *not* be able to survive at the sorts of density sustained by African slaves on the slave ships of the eighteenth and nineteenth centuries. The physical state of modern man would be likely to be one of hyperactivity as opposed to the dulled apathy and probably lowered metabolic rates of the brow-beaten slaves.

The fourth and final factor listed by Calhoun has to do with the rate of social contact between individuals. In a given space with a given number of individuals there will be a certain chance of any two individuals coming into contact with each other. Social contact alternates with patterns of withdrawal (see Schwartz, 1968, chapter 6). The social contact itself can be seen as tripartite, consisting of initiation, interaction and termination. If one then assumes, for either an individual or a species, that the withdrawal/contact cycle has a 'natural' period of oscillation and that the contact must occupy a minimum time to be intense enough to be satisfying, then it follows that there will be an optimum number of individuals that can be contained in a given spatial enclosure of fixed area. As with Kessler's mice, for example, when densities rose there was a cutting down on the initiation part of the interaction, with mice going straight into the interaction (fighting or copulating, etc.). As densities rose still higher, 'social' withdrawal occurred despite the extremely close configurations of animals (see also Marsden, 1972). Calhoun maintains that a particularly common optimum size for many mammalian species is one consisting of a core of twelve mature individuals. Where this is overly exceeded emigration will be the result, or, if this is impossible, alterations of behaviour will occur.

The implication in this chapter has been that abnormal behaviours are in some way undesirable, but Calhoun provides an anecdotal example to question this implication. In his observations of one of his studies of wild rats he noticed that the 'withdrawn' rats (the density was such that this behaviour was now being manifest) made a discovery that on a human level 'would be comparable to developing the wheel'. In fact what they did was to invent a more efficient way of removing excavated material in the making of burrows. Instead of, as is more usual, pushing and kicking the loosened dirt back towards the entrance, they packed together forty or fifty wads of dirt into a round ball just smaller than the tunnel diameter and rolled it out! Well-adjusted rats living in normal, non-crowded settings were never observed to make this creative leap. The question being raised is: Can or does social pathology provide a framework or seedbed for creativity?

Returning to the Select Committee's report from considering these animal studies we can now comment further on the stereotype that seemed to be popular: 'high density equals high pathology'. The most notable finding that has emerged from the animal work is that there is far more to overcrowding than can possibly be incorporated in density figures. This is a general and not a species-specific conclusion.

It is interesting to note that this finding is essentially the same as the one arrived at by Biderman *et al.* (1963). In this review they considered human situations as varied as concentration camps, slums, mental hospitals, slave ships and suchlike in an attempt 'to gain knowledge of possible hazards to life and health under conditions of overcrowding that might occur in civil defence shelters'. They indicate that:

> Physical crowding, *per se*, is not regarded as a fruitful unitary concept for examining the differences between high- and low-casualty events. For most of the range of densities, physical crowding has significance only in interdependent relationship with many other variable features of the entire situation, including environmental, structural, temporal, psychological and social features. The acts of oppressive captors and epidemic disease were the most frequent causes of high fatality in the incidents reviewed. Similarly, refinement of definition is required for considering the sociological aspects of overcrowding.

This conclusion might seem banal were it not for the fact that the space/person or person/space type of index is the most usual one when the topic of overcrowding is being considered. Take some examples:

1. *The U.K. Royal Commission on Population* (1949). The Commission was set up originally in 1944 because of rising concern about declining population growth of the U.K. (Holmans, 1964). In their section on housing *vis-à-vis* deterrents to parenthood, it was suggested that one room (size unspecified) per person was an ideal standard: 'They [five-roomed houses, three bedrooms] appear to us to be adequate on modern standards for the needs of a family containing a husband, wife, and three young children' (p. 202); 'one room per person [gives] the size of house appropriate to each

size of family' (p. 202); 'The five-room house does not meet the needs of the family with more than three children' (p. 203). In the Commission's view overcrowding existed where these conditions were unfulfilled.

2. *The measure used in the 1951 and 1961 censuses.* Here again actual size is unspecified – the unit being a room. It is calculated by dividing the number of persons in the household by the number of rooms in the house. A kitchen is counted if it is used for eating or sleeping in. If the ratio of people to room is greater than 1·5 the household is considered overcrowded.

The 1966 sample census, however, included all kitchens, whatever ancilliary purpose they served, thus bringing about a dramatic apparent reduction in the number of overcrowded households (Petzing and Wedge, 1970). Then there are the sorts of figures utilized by planners:

3. *Residential densities.*
a. Overall residential density. This is applied to a town, and is the number of people divided by the acreage occupied, excluding undeveloped or agricultural land.
b. Gross residential density. This is applied to a neighbourhood and is the number of people divided by the acreage occupied, including facilities, but excluding industrial land, secondary schools and town centres.
c. Net residential density. This definition, used as a normal basis for development control, is people divided by acreage, including gardens, incidental open space, half the width of surrounding roads, but not shops, primary schools and most open space. Instead of using people, 'habitable rooms' (not kitchen or bathroom) or 'dwellings' are used.

These density measures are taken from a ministry report published in 1962. This same report, although acknowledging that density control need not necessarily be related to overcrowding, implies that there is an upper limit – for example (p. 6), 'no one contends that families living at densities over 100 persons per acre is ideal', and 'Development or redevelopment at net densities much above 140 persons per acre . . . should seldom be necessary'.

Indices 1 and 2 are clearly referring to something different from 3. The former are concerned with the internal aspect of the dwelling (the internal living environment, I.L.E.), while 3 is referring to the intensity of dwellings in the open environment (the external living environment, E.L.E.). There is no work I know of that combines the two aspects in a consideration of crowding. One could ask for example whether a large I.L.E. would 'make up for' a highly dense E.L.E., i.e. ask what the rate of exchange between E.L.E. and I.L.E. is (if there is one at all). Inevitably involved in such an investigation would be the way people actually utilized the environments, and this would introduce behavioural aspects into such an index.

Many countries now, of course, have – if not statutory, then obligatory – standards for both I.L.E.s and E.L.E.s (see National Swedish Institute for Building Research, 1967). The U.K.'s I.L.E.s are based on the Parker-Morris report, *Homes for Today and Tomorrow* (H.M.S.O., 1961). This report eschews the idea of specifying sizes of rooms (just as the 1944 Dudley report had done), but gives standards in terms of net floor area. As net floor area includes features such as staircases and chimney breasts, it will vary per person depending on both the number of people in occupancy and the type of dwelling, but a family of four living in a semi-detached house would have about 190 square feet/person. If such space standards are going to be made to serve as indices of crowding, I would suggest that they should at least be investigated in conjunction with an E.L.E. index. The E.L.E., however, would present problems and would probably have to be established on a comparative phenomenological basis (like Lee's method in chapter 7), because, quite clearly, one would not expect a town planner's boundaries in which an E.L.E. is calculated to coincide necessarily with a resident's. Thus, just because the planner talks about a particular development having a certain net residential density, we still have no guarantee that the resident will feel himself to be living within the same boundaries. This again raises the question (dis-

cussed in chapter 7) of how people perceive the invisible
landscape.

All this leads us inexorably away from (as we would now
expect) any simple person/space crowding index. It also
might be pointed out at this stage that the relationship between space and space/person (considering just the E.L.E.)
is itself not a linear one (see James, 1967) – the land acreage
saved by higher and higher densities becomes progressively
less (see Fig. 21).

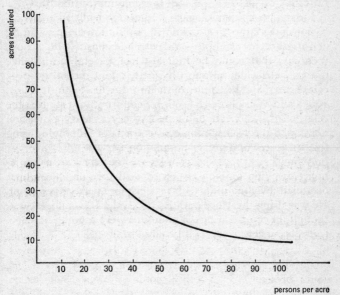

Fig. 21. Graph shows relationship between acreage required at
different levels of P.P.A. for 1,000 people.

Lee's (1968) finding that the neighbourhood schema relate
to territory rather than to density, is pertinent here, for it may
be that the cognitive mechanisms for perceiving the densities
of E.L.E.s are non-existent. It is clearly a question needing
investigation. In short, the effects of 'overcrowding' are not

going to be understood until the concept of overcrowding is accurately delineated.

Lack of definitional depth and conceptual clarity have not, however, stopped some of the more intrepid behavioural scientists and others from looking at the human scene. There aren't very many studies (and I make no claim that my list is exhaustive) but those there are substantiate not only that crowding is an extremely complex phenomenon but also that some of the variables the animal work has shown to be important may be just as important in the human situation.

Firstly, the epidemiological studies. Typically such investigations take large areas of known population density – using census tracts for example – and correlate density with various measures that could be indicative of societal health, like disease rates (mental and physical), infant mortality rates, crime rates, etc. Examples of such studies are Schmitt (1957, 1963) and Winsborough (1965). Schmitt (1957) studied the relationship between delinquency, crime and population density in the twenty-nine census tracts of Honolulu, using five measures of density: population per net acre; average household size; married couples without their own household; dwelling units in structures with five or more units; occupied dwelling units with 1·51 or more persons per room. He was using therefore both E.L.E. and I.L.E. indices (not, though, in combination). The results were as follows: (number of census tracts is given in brackets)

a. *Persons per net acre (E.L.E.).*

	less than 20 (9)	20–59·9 (12)	60 and over (8)
delinquency rate per 1,000	15·8	18·2	20·0
crime rate per 1,000	0·66	0·68	1·72

b. *Household size (I.L.E.)*.

	less than 3·75 (7)	3·75–4·99 (15)	4·50 and over (7)
delinquency	12·7	18·6	23·5
crime	1·18	0·63	1·09

c. *Married couples without own household.*

	less than 12% (9)	12–15·9% (11)	16% and over (9)
delinquency	15·7	20·5	19·6
crime	0·62	0·81	1·31

d. *Dwellings in structures of five or more.*

	less than 5 (14)	5–19·9 (8)	20 and over (7)
delinquency	19·5	17·9	15·9
crime	0·77	0·59	1·40

e. *Dwellings with 1·51 or more persons per room (I.L.E.).*

	less than 10% (9)	10–19·9% (14)	over 20% (6)
delinquency	12·5	20·2	26·1
crime	0·56	0·78	1·92

Schmitt remarks that 'it is apparent that the various measures of density were not uniformly associated with delinquency or crime. Only two – population per net acre and per cent of units with 1·51 or more persons per room – showed a consistent and strongly positive correlation with juvenile and adult offender rates.'

Perhaps this is not surprising if – as the figures themselves strongly suggest – the same census tracts, give or take a couple, are appearing in the same relative categories. This suggestion is of course *strictly* unwarrantable but it does again raise the question of the distinction between the E.L.E. and I.L.E. For example, using the density indicator of 'dwellings in structures of five or more', there is a disparity between adult and juvenile figures, delinquency displaying an overall decrease, with crime almost doubling; the actual physical structure of the housing seeming to exert a differential effect. Schmitt goes on to suggest that other factors like economic status, parent–child relationships (see chapter 5) 'are undeniably operative', but continues: 'It is nevertheless likely, from other evidence, that high densities predispose a resident population, either juvenile or adult, to illegal acts.' He does not, however, cite this 'other evidence'.

Winsborough's (1965) study attempts to control a factor which Schmitt thinks important – socio-economic status of individuals. Winsborough worked with the seventy-five community areas of Chicago – areas which 'demonstrate a considerable variability in population density', but he was not as sophisticated in his measure of density as Schmitt. Winsborough utilized only gross population density. He did mention room occupancy as a component of total density in a footnote, to say that the patterns of correlation with this measure were similar to those found for overall density – implying that E.L.E.s and I.L.E.s are synonymous. The five variables he chose to associate with density were: infant death rate, public assistance rate (adjusted for age), rate of public assistance to under eighteen year olds, T.B. rate and overall death rate. The first three correlated significantly with density ($p < 0.01$) – the higher the density the higher the rates. The T.B. rate was also positively correlated though at a lower level of significance ($p < 0.05$), while overall death rate showed no significant relationship. However, as Winsborough suggested, these relationships were confounded with socio-economic status. Using a statistical technique which controls for this effect (partialling out) and the effect of quality of housing and migration, a very different picture emerged. Deaths, T.B. and public assistance rate all now become significantly *negatively* associated with density ($p < 0.01$), i.e. the higher the density the fewer the deaths. Infant deaths, however, remained the same, while the relationship of density to public assistance to under eighteen year olds lost significance. The problem, however, with partialling out as many variables as Winsborough did is that one cannot then be absolutely sure of what is left, as the effect of say socio-economic class might effectively have been removed more than once if it was related to migration or housing quality. It seems implausible that T.B. rate should be *negatively* associated with density, as T.B. is highly contagious. An interpretation that Winsborough himself puts on the changed pattern of correlations is 'that the effects of density on the young seem to be different from the effects on the adult population'. This seems a cautious but reasonable conclusion.

Schmitt's (1963) second study adds to the complications. In this study he looks at density in Hong Kong which is one of the most densely populated territories in the world. Some individual neighbourhoods had over 2,800 persons per acre with average floor space per person in the region of 32 square feet (figures collected in 1962). Schmitt points out that American density figures – both overall and city – are, with one or two minor exceptions, well below comparable Hong Kong figures which would lead 'orthodox planners' to expect 'death, disease and social disorganization rates on a scale unparalleled in low-density American cities'. The figures that Schmitt quotes demonstrate anything but such expectations, although it is certainly not clear why Schmitt chose to compare H.K. rates with the overall U.S. rates when a more detailed breakdown would provide more information. His figures were as follows:

	H.K.	*U.S.*
deaths/1,000	5·9	9·3
infant mortality/1,000 live births	37·7	25·2
maternal deaths/1,000	0·45	0·32
psychiatric hospitalizations/1,000	0·3	over 3

	H.K.	U.S.
T.B./1,000	4·0	less than 0·4
murder/manslaughter/100,000	0·8	approx. 4·8
all serious crimes/100,000	4·78	approx. 1,000

Even though H.K. rates for maternal deaths and infant deaths exceed U.S. rates, the overall picture – particularly in terms of mental illness and crime – is very far removed from the picture of social pathology and disorganization anticipated. Schmitt attempts to explain the figures by citing four factors: a. Chinese traditions and family cohesiveness, with the associated strict social controls; b. low space expectations of the populace – having never had much space, they didn't know what they were missing (recall that Calhoun's explanation of the Kessler standing-room-only mice population was largely in these terms); c. luck, medical science and efficient administration; d. low car-to-person ratio. We could, perhaps, speculate from this that the social structure is a crucial factor mediating people's behaviour under high-density conditions.

Perhaps the most sophisticated attempt on epidemiological lines is Russell Murray's (1971, 1971a, 1973). Looking at schoolboys' behaviour, Murray found two factors that were associated with withdrawn behaviour. One was whether or not the boy lived in a high-rise flat, and the second 'was concerned with overcrowding as a result of family size independent of the spatial aspects of the home'. Thus, not only is an I.L.E. involved but also the actual structure of the physical environment. Murray has in his study collected data on forty-two different factors: fourteen to do with the child's neighbourhood, nine concerned with household features (floor space, number of rooms, family size, etc.) and nineteen psychological variables (teachers' ratings, friendships, scores on various psychological tests, etc.). Murray reduced this array of variables to a set of ten by a factor analytic technique. Two of the factors related to the housing features. These two are particularly interesting in that one is 'loaded highly on the indices of crowding – space per person and person per

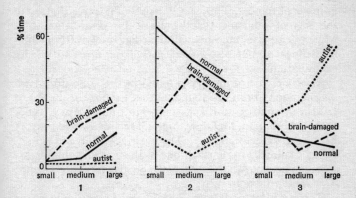

Fig. 22. Differential effects of density (after Hutt 1971).

1: Shows the amounts of time spent in aggressive and/or destructive behaviour by the different types of children in the small, medium and large groups. The autists show virtually no aggression; the brain-damaged subjects, on the other hand, show increasing aggressive and destructive behaviour as group density increases; in the largest group the brain-damaged subjects tended to be successful in nearly all their fights over possessions. The normals only showed an appreciable amount of aggressive behaviour when the group was largest.

2: Shows the relative amounts of time spent in other social encounters by the different children. The most remarkable finding was that the normal children reduced their interactions as the number in the room increased. The social encounters of the autists in the large group consisted largely of approaches to the adults – they appeared to be seeking refuge from the scramble going on around them.

3: Shows the amounts of time spent within one metre of the periphery of the room under the different group-size conditions. Here the most notable finding is that the autists withdrew themselves more and more from the centre of activity as group density increased.

room – and on the spatial aspects of the home – floor space and number of rooms' and the other is 'loaded highly on indices of crowding and family size, but not on floor space or number of rooms'. This, surely, is proof positive that, with the sort of refinement and statistical sophistication that Murray employs, not only will the concept of overcrowding be delineated but also its effects will be open to precise examination.

A second line of inquiry is found in the laboratory-type investigations, or in investigations that confine themselves to I.L.E.s as opposed to E.L.E.s, viz. Hutt and Vaizey, 1966, 1966a; Hutt and McGrew, 1967; Freedman *et al.*, 1971; Ehrlich and Freedman, 1971; Desor, 1972; Griffitt and Veitch, 1971; Skolnick, 1971. Each one of these studies highlights some particular variable or factors, or spawns new concepts. To consider them in turn:

Corrine Hutt and Jane Vaizey used fifteen children as their subjects, five diagnosed as autistic, five with gross brain damage and five normal, all aged between three and eight. Using only two or three of the subjects at any one session (the rest of the group was made up of other children), they observed the behaviour displayed in a free-play situation in a room of 27 feet × 17·5 feet at three levels of density – under six children (small), between seven and eleven (medium) and twelve and over (large). They recorded the incidence of aggressive/destructive behaviour, social interactions and time spent on the boundary of the room. Fig. 22 shows the results.

The outstanding conclusion to emerge is that the density has differential effects on the different types of children. Hutt and Vaizey explain their findings in terms of the arousal theory presented in chapter 3. Thus autistic children – already highly aroused – attempt to reduce the extra arousing conditions of high density by retreat to the boundary. The response of normal and brain-damaged children to increased density is an increase in aggressive/destructive behaviour. This increase cannot be explained by greater competition between children for the same number of toys, as Freedman *et al.*, (1971) suggest, as the number of toys was increased proportionately with the number of children (Hutt, 1972).

The study also suggests that, at least on the small scale, there are perceptual mechanisms sensitive to density, because both the normal and autistic children 'resorted to methods for regulating the frequency of social encounters, under high-density conditions' (Hutt and Vaizey, 1966a). The question of exactly what the specific sensory inputs are that mediate the perception of density remains to be explored – is it noise, body heat, smell, sight or a combination, or what?

The next study – that by Hutt and McGrew (1967) – makes two very important points. Firstly, that density can be construed in two ways. An experimenter can examine *social* density 'by observing groups of different numbers within the same spatial area. Or he may examine *spatial* density by observing the same-sized groups in different spatial areas.' This distinction takes on a special significance when Russell Murray's two household factors (see above) coincide almost exactly with such a delineation. The second point concerns the *form* of the enclosures studies. (They were again studying children's free play.)

The 27 feet × 17·5 feet rectangular playroom was supplemented with a clover-shaped room with a central area of 6 feet × 6 feet with three 'leaves' 10 feet square, and Hutt and McGrew comment: 'The move from the previous rectangular playroom to the clover shaped one ... had a marked effect upon the social behaviour of the children. This effect was most dramatically manifested in the children's territorial behaviour.' Such behaviour – guarding a physical space against intruders – was rarely seen in the rectangular room. Territorial behaviour, they continue, 'was more dependent on the characteristics of the environment than on the number in the room'. Clearly, density effects *per se* could – for the unwary – easily be confused with the effect of environmental form.

The next piece of research, that of Freedman *et al.* (1971), represents an attempt to illuminate the effects of density *per se*. Their paper in fact reveals a somewhat naive approach to the question. While they review much of the work quoted above, they seem to imagine that high density has some kind of unitary meaning. They review Schmitt (1957, 1966) and Winsborough (1965) and find them wanting, and wrongly explain away the results of Hutt and Vaizey (1966). They make a great play on the fact that their experiments have relevance to the population explosion and imply that by learning about 'density *per se*' useful information will accrue. While I would in no way wish to prevent them studying 'density *per se*', I would question the relevance of the results, as not only the animal investigations but also the work on the human scene suggest that 'density *per se*' is a rather meaningless abstraction. Notwithstanding this criticism their results are interesting. The questions they ask are straightforward viz.:

1. What effect does density have on performance of simple and complex tasks?
2. What role do temporal factors play?

In the light of my conviction that high population density and crowding are very far from being the same thing, their results assume an especial significance. They make it very clear that it is the effects of density they are trying to get at, and *not* any of the things with which it tends to be associated like 'lack of air, physical discomfort, restriction on movement, high temperature, odours', rather, they continue, 'we were interested in the individual's reactions to the high density itself, *to their feelings of being crowded* when these other variables were eliminated or controlled' (my italics). One could argue that a person's feelings of being crowded are related exactly to those variables they have sought to remove or eliminate, so while they are certainly studying the effects of population density I do not think that the experiment is necessarily related to people's 'feelings of being crowded'.

Freedman *et al.* carried out three experiments. In the first, groups of five and nine subjects (Californian High School children – 126 in all) performed both simple and complex tasks in three conditions of density – in a room of 160 square feet (uncrowded condition), in one of 80 square feet and in one of 35 square feet, which was the crowded condition. The children were seated in wooden chairs with a desk-type arm on which they could write. They were physically comfortable, the rooms being air conditioned, fairly quiet and with a water cooler from which drinks could be obtained. Their performances were recorded on seven tasks ranging from a twenty-minute group discussion to having to count clicks sounded without fixed rhythm at the rate of three per second. Of the results Freedman *et al.* say: 'there were no effects of any kind attributable to the level of density in the rooms.' This is perhaps surprising because, despite the fact that many of the sensory stimuli that might be thought to contribute to a feeling of crowdedness had been eliminated, nine people were, for four hours, performing where 'it would have been difficult to imagine anyone else in the room with them'. Because of the lack of a density effect in the first experiment, they decided in the second experiment to make the tasks more boring. The rationale behind this change was that the subjects in the first experiment were so involved and interested in their tasks they had little time to 'take in' the density factor. But even in this second experiment 'density did not affect performance'. For the third experiment they again tried a different tack. High-school students, they reasoned, might be an unrepresentative sample of people. As the experiments were carried out during the summer vacation, many of the subjects were looking for something to do, wanted the money ($1·75 per hour), found taking part in a psychology experiment interesting in itself and were in addition both young and probably highly adaptable. So, to find out whether students were unusual in their response to density, Freedmen *et al.* turned to an employment agency and hired 180 woman between the ages of twenty-five and sixty, untrained in any skills and with little motivation, since payment was made without regard to how hard they worked. The agency was not given a report of their performance, so this could not produce motivational effects. The results? '. . . once again there were no effects of any kind of density on performance.' In discussing these results, the investigators are led to the inevitable speculation that only when density is found with other *situational* variables does its effect begin to show up. The fact that the dense situations were in these studies highly structured and formal, that people were static, had no opportunity to get in each other's way, that it was short term, that the subjects had no anticipation of long-term relationships with each other, might account for the lack of results. Thus, the negative attributes often thought to be associated with overcrowding reveal themselves only when density *and* other factors combine. Again a crowding index *cannot* be based on density without regard to other situational variables.

In later studies (Ehrlich and Freedman, 1971) social interactions liable to generate emotional feelings in the participants were used. The hypothesis here was that density combined with high *affect* might produce results. The high-school subjects who were the subjects of the experiments had to discuss various topics, play a game requiring a high level of coordination between partners and then a game requiring that the subjects be cooperative or competitive, with money being used as an incentive. If the subjects were competitive, they could make more money, although the risk also increased. If they were all cooperative, they made less money, but the risk of losing it was also less. Here, for the first time, a density effect did emerge but, strangely, so did a clear sex difference. Boys responded more competitively in the smaller room and for the girls this effect was in reverse. More experiments were run with another less 'atypical' sample, composed of men and women aged over eighteen, from a variety of ethnic origins and educational and income levels. These groups of subjects listened to tapes of courtroom cases and then served as a jury. A similar sex difference emerged from these experiments. Crowded men tended to give severer sentences than the non-crowded men, liked their fellows less and found the experience more unpleasant. The women on the other hand were more lenient when crowded, and found the other members more likeable and friendlier. Ehrlich and Freedman suggest a cultural hypothesis – that women are taught, indirectly, that physical closeness is O.K. and have fewer hang-ups about touching each other than men have. (Kuethe, 1964, provides some substantiating evidence for this.) Thus women will see being crowded as a less threatening situation than will men. If this cultural hypothesis can be shown to be correct, then it repeats a point which was raised in chapter 6: if people *learn* their spatial code (just as they learn the highway code), they can unlearn it, learn a new one or learn a wide variety of different codes. If one could specify the processes involved, people (particularly men) could be taught to cope with crowded conditions. As man does seem hell bent on producing an S.R.O. world (standing room only), maybe psychologists could help him develop the skills to handle it in a non-self-injurious fashion!!

Freedman *et al.* have again shown that density *per se* and *over*crowding are not synonymous. Overcrowding is density plus: plus the social situation, plus the environmental form and plus, perhaps, a sex component. Studies by Desor (1972) and Griffit and Veitch (1971) lend support to this. Desor, for example, in putting forward a psychological theory of crowding, suggests that 'being crowded is reception of excessive social stimulation and *not merely a lack of space*'. Using scale models, she showed that, if a room (35 feet × 15 feet × 8 feet) was divided by partitions, more 'people' (3·75-inches-high round-ended clothes pegs) could be placed in it to make it 'crowded' than if it did not have partitions. Further, rectangular rooms could 'take' more people than square rooms, rooms with two doors more than rooms with six doors, and of course crowdedness depended on the on-going activity of the 'clothes pegs' – whether they were just standing around or were at some social gathering like a cocktail party. The feeling of crowdedness can thus be influenced by architectural form. This study, taken in conjunction with that of Griffit and Veitch (1971), who manipulated population density and temperature and found that people under high-density/high-temperature conditions express significantly more negative social-affective behaviour towards presented written profiles of strangers, suggest that perceptual mechanisms mediating crowdedness include non-animate features. It follows that as non-animate environmental features can be manipulated so can people's feelings of crowdedness.

One final experiment to do with human overcrowding, and perhaps one of the most ambitious, remains to be discussed. This is the work by Paul Skolnick *et al.* (1971), who attempted to simulate the urban and non-urban condition in the laboratory. They reasoned that the urban condition is characterized chiefly by 'large numbers of people living at high density', whereas the non-urban condition is typified by 'small numbers of people living at low density'. In other words two factors, density *and* numbers, are being *deliberately* confounded; that is, their effects are being studied when they operate *with* each other rather than separately. This point is, of course, an arguable one, as the size/density feature of the urban scene does not provide a total description. The well-housed urban dweller (as opposed to sections of the urban population living in spatially sub-standard homes and/or overcrowded on a number-of-people-per-room index) is part of the size/density complex in certain situations only – on the streets, in public-transport systems, going shopping, at football matches or at the cinema, etc. These situations have certain characteristics: they are over in a relatively short period of time; they occur with minimal social interaction (people become physical objects to avoid skilfully); there is a rapid turnover in people 'met' where the population is mobile; either mobility is a feature (e.g. commuting), or strict territoriality is a rule (e.g. football match). Thus the overcrowded situation has *structure*, exists for some purpose or, if not, each individual is attempting to achieve some personal objective. Furthermore an individual is able to withdraw from it, perhaps to his own dwelling, which (if he is lucky) is not overcrowded on an I.L.E. index. Thus the urban scene could be more accurately described as a periodic immersion in an impersonal size/density complex, with a counterpattern of withdrawal to a comparatively small-size, low-density situation within limited territorial boundaries.

This takes on an added significance in the light of Vere Hole's (1965) finding that standards in minimum housing in this country in the last hundred years have increased 'at the rate of about 1 square foot every two years' (reiterated by Cherry, 1969).*

It is technologically possible (though of course astronomically costly) for this trend to continue, to go on increasing standards for the I.L.E. and reducing them for the E.L.E. To continue such a trend would force conceptual refinement of the term overcrowded. It would also make decisions about the allocation of space for new developments more difficult. Champion (1970) tells us that recent master plans for new towns are taking 10 acres more land per 1,000 people than previously, and that 'over half of this increase is being used to provide extra open space'.

But with this in mind let us return to Skolnick's experiment. The experimenters used groups of volunteer college students. One group of fifteen students was confined in a room 22 feet × 11·5 feet (i.e. at 16 square feet per person) for twelve hours (10 a.m. to 10 p.m.), while the other group of eighty-eight students were confined in a room approximately 28 feet × 26 feet, giving them 8 square feet each. This latter group was described as the 'urban' condition. One wall of each room was a one-way mirror through which observations could be made. Each individual had four bathroom passes, and two meals and two snacks were provided. Before confinement, subjects filled out personality tests which measured self-esteem, need for approval, authoritarianism, introversion and extraversion and a questionnaire covering their need for privacy and general demographic background. During the twelve-hour period of confinement Time Sample Observations (T.S.O.) of five minutes each were taken. These consisted of a video-tape sweep, a motion picture and several still pictures. In addition there were eight observers watching the crowded room and four observing the non-urban condition.

*But see Bauer, 1951, p. 16 – 'The average new house [U.S.A.] has been getting steadily smaller.'

The differences in the behaviour of the two groups were large. Skolnick *et al.* list them as follows:

a. *Cohesiveness*. The non-urban group remained a group for the twelve-hour duration of the experiment. The subjects engaged in 'group' activities and reacted to the experimenter-planned 'crises' as members of a group rather than as separate individuals. One such crisis occurred when the experimenters announced over the public-address system that the fire marshal had ruled that the rooms were too crowded and three people would have to leave the crowded room, and one would have to leave the uncrowded room. In the uncrowded room, after a discussion, the subjects announced that, if one of them went, they would all go. Skolnick *et al.* comment: 'Wishing to continue the study, the experimenters "yielded" to this group's decision.' In the crowded room on the other hand two subjects immediately volunteered, and after a delay so did a reluctant third.

b. *Aggression*. More aggressive behaviour was observed in the urban group and, significantly, some of it was directed at the experimenters, even though a subject's presence in that room was entirely voluntary. For example, subjects covered the clock (a crucial part of the video-tape data) and they turned out the lights when the food was late, making observation of their behaviour impossible. Towards the end of the twelve hours everyone began batting about an inflated beach ball in such a way that precluded interpersonal cooperation. The investigators interpreted this as 'an overt sign of aggression'. In the uncrowded room, apart from the hostility towards the experimenters over the fire marshal crisis, aggression was absent.

c. *Territoriality*. As might be expected from the discussion in chapter 6, in which territoriality was seen as a more 'primitive' rule system adopted in situations that lack the more 'mannered social constraints of everyday life', the subjects in this experiment displayed greater territoriality that was *well* beyond the normality of the everyday situation. Thus it was in the crowded room that people occupied particular places in the room, and kept to them. Subjects did not 'visit' other areas of their room. In the uncrowded room territorial behaviour was not apparent.

d. *Recreational activity*. The general finding here was that the activities in the uncrowded room were person-centred – people amusing themselves in 'chat', the chat being an end in itself. In the crowded room, however, activities centred on 'things rather than persons – card playing, paper folding, decorating the room, and the generation of a forty-page newspaper'. One wonders whether, as with Calhoun's withdrawn but 'creative' rats, the presence of so many others was so physically overloading that psychological safety was sought through involvement with things rather than with people.

e. *Noise*. The students' reactions differed also with respect to the 'city sounds' the experimenters played over the speakers. In the uncrowded room it was taken in good humour – the students talking and laughing about it. In the crowded room they covered the speaker with coats and thus effectively blocked themselves off from these city sounds. This could be interpreted as part of the aggressive milieu which developed in the large room, where much aggression was directed towards the experimenters.

It must be remembered that all the subjects in this experiment were volunteers and the psychological characteristics of volunteers are in themselves important factors in many types of psychological situation. For example, a person having volunteered for an experiment (particularly if that subject is being paid) will – in most cases – be trying his best to 'obey' the instructions, to play the role of 'being a subject in a psychological experiment'. (This effect is reviewed at length by Rosnow and Rosenthal, 1970.) It will, of course, be easier to fulfil the 'demand characteristics' if the demands do not involve anything which threatens a person's self-identity. Where such threats do exist, as with Stanley Milgram's pioneering studies on obedience in which people were asked to give others electric shocks that might have resulted in death (Milgram, 1963), one might expect one of two effects: *either* subjects will react by calling the experimenters' bluff – by discontinuing to play the role of subjects *or* play out the whole scene losing sight of the game aspect of the situation, ceasing to play the role but *becoming* the person they were formerly playing the role of. I would suggest that in the uncrowded room all the subjects were role playing: still behaving as 'good' experimental subjects, being good-humoured and generally cooperative. After all, the situation they were in was not without intrinsic interest.

In the crowded room, on the other hand, the situation was, surely, more stressful and ego-threatening, but, because of its even greater deviation from everyday life, it was even more intrinsically interesting than the uncrowded room. In the crowded room subjects stopped playing the role of good experimental subjects. The diminishing individual responsibility that appears to be a concomitant of large crowds could have made this easier (Latané and Darley, 1970). Subjects had re-defined the experiment in their own terms. They didn't want to stop the experiment, perhaps because it was particularly interesting (remember they had trouble in getting the third volunteer to leave), but nor would they, willy nilly, accept the experimenters' manipulations of them. At one point the experimenters lost control of the situation when the subjects turned the lights out, making observation impossible – a complete role-reversal between manipulator and manipulated!! It seems that something had happened which is perhaps unique in the history of experimental laboratory research. The crowded subjects hadn't simply acted out the role of subject, nor had they withdrawn from doing so, nor had they *become* their roles, but they *had* demonstrated their power over the experimenters without having to opt out of the situation. The uncrowded group, it may be argued, had done something similar, though not quite, in taking a united stand against the experimenters when a volunteer to leave was called for in the fire marshal crisis. The difference between that and the sort of behaviour the crowded group displayed (covering the clock, turning out the lights) was that the uncrowded group was potentially opting out, whereas the crowded group was not. The crowded situation seemed to have generated processes for its own continuance, with the experimenters being assigned the role of persecutors, or at the very least jailers, against whom the group had a united hostile attitude, and there were group processes operating to maintain solidarity or togetherness (cf. Calhoun's behavioural sink) even though relationships between individuals in the group were not necessarily harmonious (see below). It is possible that Skolnick *et al.* had found the conditions necessary to create a 'group mind'.* If so, then the crowded room as an urban simulator might have to be jettisoned because the urban dweller has no identifiable persecutor, unless, alternatively, we can look more carefully at the urban scene to see if there is anything there that serves a persecutory function. We should do this only if we think we can see behaviour emergent in the experimental situation which is analogous to behaviour in the urban one.

f. *Eating and environmental maintenance.* There were also differences in the 'eating behaviour' and the environmental maintenance behaviour between the two groups. When the food trolleys were wheeled in, the subjects in the uncrowded room were orderly and helpful to each other, while in the crowded room it was everyone for themselves, indeed some subjects took more than their fair share, so that others actually had to go without. The amount of activity put into keeping the rooms clean and tidy was also different in the two rooms. By the end of the experiment the crowded room was 'almost ankle deep' in 'trash' and this despite an attempt by 'an irate individual to organize a clean up'. In the uncrowded room clean ups *were* organized after each meal. Skolnick *et al.* remarked: 'Apparently when population density is high, individuals living under those conditions do not identify with or relate to the environment and, therefore, neglect it.'

Two findings that emerged after the experiment are par-

* For a modern analysis of this very old concept see Roger Brown (1965).

ticularly noteworthy. One was the subjects' general willingness to participate in experiments like this one again, whether they had been crowded or uncrowded. The other finding was the lack of relationship between the personality tests and demographic data and the behaviour of subjects (Skolnick, 1972).

Skolnick *et al.*'s final remark is: 'the data are consistent with the hypothesis that high-population density and crowding have detrimental effects on human behaviour including the environment in which it occurs'. I do not believe, however, that the conclusion is as depressing as it appears. If we do, for a moment, accept that the Skolnick situation is an urban simulator (but see pp. 208ff.), we might imagine that, when high-density urban dwellers are released into or visit low-density rural areas on their vacations, they become the extreme despoilers of the natural environment – carrying over their accepted and learned patterns of behaviour to the country scene. There is, however, a basis for optimism. Catton (1969) informs us that it is amongst the educationally sophisticated urban dwellers that a 'wildernist value orientation' is more likely to be found than amongst people socialized in rural environments. And, of course, institutes for advanced educational dissemination and enlightenment are only to be found where there are concentrations of population. It could be that Skolnick's environmental despoilers were reacting to the specific experimental set up, for as Catton says, the person who takes his vacations in a wilderness or natural environment does so 'partly because he has learned how to ask interesting questions of nature'. Thus the urban milieu *can* generate an increased environmental sensitivity. The problem is that, because of biases in the educational system and the differential reward structure of society, this environmental sensitivity is engendered in a comparative minority. Until man is educated to see himself in relation to his physical matrix, Skolnick may be right to associate the despoilation of the environment with high density, but the inevitability of such an association has to be proven. This again raises the question of how the environment is perceived.

The perceptual question this time is not how the 'here and now', invisible landscape is perceived (as it was in chapter 7) but how the behaviour *vis-à-vis* the presented environment will affect a *future* invisible landscape. For example, D. B. Luten (1963) worked out that the global population, growing at the present rates, will reach S.R.O. (standing room only – 5 square feet per person*) in 800 years – not a long time even compared to the history of man, but an infinitesimal fraction of time in the history of the planet. If this state were actually perceived as an outcome of present trends, then there would surely be no population problems, as most people would regard S.R.O. as intolerable and would thus not continue reproducing irresponsibly. It is obviously not that simple.

It should be fairly clear by now that overcrowding and space/person cannot be regarded as being identical. 'High density = high pathology', even if it does occur, is mediated by other variables, many of which can be easily manipulated. We are undoubtedly going to learn how to 'fit' more and more people into less space without societal collapse. Even the work discussed above provides several adaptive strategies – environmental structure can be manipulated, arousal-damping drugs, if this is what we decide to use, can be administered and proxemic re-education can be undertaken (Mercer, 1973). It seems that the potential for adaptation via knowledge based on scientific study is enormous. This unfortunately makes the problem more difficult. Even if we wholeheartedly did wish to achieve an S.R.O. state (what then – smaller people?) and our psychological knowledge could facilitate our adaptation to it without societal breakdown, it still would not come, for reasons that have nothing to do with psychology – namely the finite-resources problem. If we are to extend human life on this planet (and there's no real reason why this should be considered desirable in any absolute sense), we must reduce population-growth rates. If we were to rely simply on people's sense of being overcrowded to reduce the birth rate, we would be misguided. People will

---

*This seems a somewhat generous figure. My estimation is around 190 square inches.

adapt, or *be* adapted to, or the urban environment will be restructured to accommodate, higher and higher densities. It *could* be that we do have cognitive mechanisms for perceiving high densities (although Wynne-Edwards, 1965, thinks we've lost them), but all they will bring into operation when activated is, not lower reproduction, but adaptive and manipulatory accommodations.

Lest this seem an unduly pessimistic view (but it gives great credit to man's ingenuity), consider the findings of L. D. Barnett (1969). Barnett was looking at women's attitudes toward family life and U.S. population growth. He had found previously (Barnett, 1968) that the view existed, amongst 56 per cent of his 'probability sample survey of adult women living in a small city', that 'America is rapidly reaching a point where she'll have too many people'. This being the case, one might expect that such concern about population growth would have *some* influence on the reproductive behaviour of these women. Not so. From his sample of 462 women over eighteen years old living in Flagstaff, Arizona, Barnett's evidence supports the proposition that 'Americans view the continued expansion of their country's population as an abstract problem, having no bearing on their immediate life situation', and concludes that the links between family-planning behaviour and national population have yet to emerge if population growth is to be halted. Having myself made a overland trip round the U.S.A., I do not find this lack of relationship surprising. The country is so enormous. How can anyone possibly imagine that the country as a whole is overcrowded when you can travel for hundreds of miles without seeing another human being? Perhaps Kaplan (1972) is right (see chapter 3) when he says that for man to act intelligently with respect to the future he needs to have strong vivid imagery about such futures. To expect anyone to conjure up the image of an S.R.O. population level at a time when there is still so much space available for exploitation and when children are not yet an unacceptable economic burden would surely be stretching the power of most people's imagination just a little too far.

If we do accept the finite-resources argument that population growth should be halted, how then can such a programme be brought about if – as we now know – we cannot rely on people's direct perceptions of there being 'too many people' to curb their reproductive rates? And even if we could, we would need to assume that people have got free access to and knowledge of contraceptive techniques, which of course they have not. Even in this country the Family Planning Association has had an extremely hard time. In our so-called 'permissive times' Schofield (1968) tells us that eight out of ten episodes of sexual intercourse amongst the unmarried young occur without contraceptive precaution. Also the topic of sexual and contraceptive education for children is still likely to raise an enormous emotional holocaust. Indeed in an introductory course I gave to paramedical students at the University Hospital of Wales in 1971 (see Mercer, 1972) a lecture on the psychological principles and therapeutic concepts of the sex researchers, Masters and Johnson (1970), provoked a mass walk-out of the physiotherapy students at the instruction of their principal! I am not suggesting that the topic of sex and/or family planning should be a topic free of an emotional aura, but what I would strongly assert is that this emotional aura can be used to cloud what is now the real issue confronting man – that of global population regulation. For example, most family planning programmes stress the element of free choice – 'have *only* the number of children you want *when* you want' is the main principle. The basic tenet is that of free determination of your own reproductive destiny (see Wilbur Cohen, 1967). And that is exactly what it is – *own* destiny not society's destiny. Even if the absolutely desirable aim of free access and use of contraceptives were established, people would still have more children than necessary to achieve zero population growth (Barnett, 1970, Gustavus and Nam, 1970).

There are signs, however, that research effort into the psychology of population and birth planning is at last becoming respectable. 1969 marked the publication of Edward

Pohlman's excellent book *The Psychology of Birth Planning*, and 1970 James Fawcett's *Psychology and Population* and 1973 his *Psychological Perspectives on Population*. In 1969 the American Psychological Association – the largest single body of psychologists in the world – established a Task Force on Psychology, Family Planning and Population Policy, which has since resulted in the creation of a separate division within the association. Through this expansion of interest we learn more about people's motives for parenthood; how such motives can be regulated to suit the resource situation and so extend man's time on earth (see Berelson, 1964; Pohlman, 1971; Buckhout, 1971; Davis, 1967; Kangas, 1970; Spengler, 1969 and Lipe, 1971, as starters). Dewey Lipe's (1971) excellent paper on the use of incentives for effecting fertility control represented an interesting attempt to establish a 'conceptual framework regarding incentives that will insure that no major incentives are ignored in the research'. It was made even more interesting because of the reaction it evoked from Jennifer MacLeod (1972). It is worth quoting her in full:

It is incredible that a serious researcher could go on and on for eight pages on the subject of incentives to fertility control, and how to get women to limit their families, without a single mention of this obvious hypothesis: If you raise girls to be mothers, and if you deny them fair and equal access to every occupation except housewifery and motherhood, it should not surprise anyone that they insist on becoming mothers not just once or twice, but three or four or six times.*

Does it even occur to Dr Lipe that the best way to discourage excessive reproduction might be to permit women equal access to the satisfactions of life other than parenthood?

If we – as a species – do manage to solve the problem of population multiplication, we might even get a better society. It seems that the knowledge which is bound to accrue over the next few years will enable us to, on the one hand, facilitate progress to an S.R.O. world or, on the other hand, to promote

*Women tolerate crowding better anyway (Freedman *et al.*, 1972).

a population level congruent with resources. As this chapter demonstrates, the stereotype 'high density = high pathology' is a great oversimplification. Thus we cannot rely on a self-limitation of reproductive behaviour evoked directly by conditions of high-density living.

This is where we came in. In the first chapter I raised some questions about what man was doing to himself through his massive environmental transformations, and whether it was 'good' or 'bad' for him.

One of the themes running through this book is that scientific inquiry alone cannot offer directives to people about how they should behave or about what is good or bad. The scientific inquiry of environmental psychology cannot answer the questions of what is the best environment for man and the best man for the environment; all it can do is to make the inevitably value-loaded answers to these questions slightly less than complete shots in the dark. It can delineate more exactly the range of possibilities that lie open to us, so that we can make more rational choices about our future. It leaves man free to exercise the ultimate control over his own destiny, and I believe that to be the most worthwhile of all possible human endeavours.

References

Abortion Act, (1967) H.M.S.O.

ABRAMS, R. H., (1943) 'Residential propinquity as a factor in marriage selection', *American Sociological Review*, 8, 288–94.

ALTMAN, I., (1968) 'Territorial behaviour in humans: an analysis of the concept', paper presented at 'Explorations of spatial-behavioural relationships as related to older people' conference, Institute of Gerontology, University of Michigan.

ALTMAN, I., (1973) 'Some perspectives on the study of man-environment phenomena', *Representative Research in Social Psychology*, 4 (1).

ALTMAN, I., and HAYTHORN, W. W., (1967) 'The ecology of isolated groups', *Behavioural Science*, 12 (3), 169–82.

ARCHER, J., (1970) 'Effects of population density on rodents', *Social behaviour in birds and mammals*, J. H. Crook, (ed.), Academic Press.

ARDREY, R., (1966) *The Territorial Imperative*, Atheneum, New York.

ARGYLE, M., (1967) *The Psychology of Interpersonal Behaviour*, Penguin Books.

BARKER, R. G., (1941) 'Frustration and regression: an experiment with young children', *University of Iowa Studies in Child Welfare*, 18, No. 1.

BARKER, R. G., (1965) 'Explorations in ecological psychology', *American Psychologist*, 20 (1), 1–14.

BARKER, R. G., (1968) *Ecological Psychology*, Stanford University Press.

BARNETT, L. D., (1968) 'Education and religion as factors influencing attitudes toward population growth in the United States', unpublished manuscript, California State College at Los Angeles.

BARNETT, L. D., (1969) 'Women's attitudes toward family life and U.S. population growth', *Pacific Sociological Review*, 12, 95–100.

BARNETT, L. D., (1970) 'U.S. population growth as an abstractly perceived problem', *Demography*, 7, 53–60.

BARTLETT, F. C., (1932) *Remembering: A study in experimental and social psychology*, Cambridge University Press (paperback 1967).

BAUER, C., (1945) 'Good Neighbourhoods', *Annals of the American Academy*, 104–15.

BAUER, C., (1951) 'Social questions in housing and community planning', *Journal of Social Issues*, 7 (1), 1–34.

BAYNE, R., (1972) 'Psychology and encounter groups', *Bulletin of the British Psychological Society*, 25 (89), 285–9.

BERELSON, B., (1964) 'On family planning communication', *Demography*, 1, 94–105.

BIDERMAN, A. D., LOURIA, M., BACCHUS, J., (1963) *Historical Incidents of Extreme Overcrowding*, Bureau of Social Science Research, Washington.

BINDER, A., (1972) 'A new context for psychology: social ecology', *American Psychologist*, 27 (9), 903–8.

BITTERMAN, M. E., (1965) 'Phyletic differences in learning', *American Psychologist*, 20, 396–410.

BLAKE, R. R., RHEAD, C. C., WEDGE, B., MOUTON, J. S., (1956) 'Housing architecture and social interaction', *Sociometry*, 19, 133–9.

BLAUT, J. B., and STEA, D., (1970) 'Studies of geographic learning', paper for the annual meeting of the Association of American Geographers.

BRITISH BROADCASTING CORPORATION, (1968) 'High Living', a *Man Alive* programme, 9 April 1968.

BROADY, M., (1966) 'Social theory in architectural design', *Architectural Association Journal*, 81, 149–54.

BROWN, R., (1965) *Social Psychology*, Collier-MacMillan.

BRUNER, J. S., GOODNOW, J. S., AUSTIN, G. A., (1956) *A Study of Thinking*, John Wiley & Sons, New York.

BUCKHOUT, R., (1971) 'The war on people. A scenario for population control', *Environment and Behavior*, 3 (3), 322–44.

BUILDING PERFORMANCE RESEARCH UNIT, STRATHCLYDE, (1970) 'Building appraisal: St Michael's Academy, Kilwinning', *Architects' Journal*, Information Library, January 1970, 9–50.

BURBRIDGE, M., (1969) *High-density housing – a social perspective*, Ministry of Housing and Local Government, London.

BURT, W. H., (1943) 'Territoriality and home range concepts as applied to mammals', *Journal of Mammalogy*, 24, 346–52.

BYRNE, D., and BUEHLER, J. A., (1955) 'A note on the influence of propinquity upon acquaintanceships', *Journal of Abnormal and Clinical Psychology*, 51, 147–8.

CALHOUN, J. B., (1961) 'Determinants of social organisation exemplified in a single population of domesticated rats', *Transactions of the New York Academy of Sciences*, Ser. 11, Vol. 23, No. 5, 437–42.

CALHOUN, J. B., (1962) 'Population density and social pathology', *Scientific American*, 206 (2), 139–48.

CALHOUN, J. B., (1962a) 'A "behavioral sink"', *Roots of Behavior*, E. Bliss (ed.), Paul Hoeber, New York, chapter 22, 295–315.

CALHOUN, J. B., (1967) 'Ecological factors in the development of behavioral anomalies', *Comparative Psychopathology*, Grune and Stratton, New York.

CALHOUN, J. B., (1970) 'Population', *Population Control*, Anthony Allison (ed.), Penguin Books.

CANTER, D. V., (1970) *Architectural psychology: proceedings of the conference held at Dalandhui, 1969*, R.I.B.A. publications.

CAPLOW, T., and FORMAN, R., (1950) 'Neighbourhood interaction in a homogeneous community', *American Sociological Review*, 15, 357–66.

CAREY, L., and MAPES, R., (1971) *The Sociology of Planning*, Batsford.

CARPENTER, C. R., (1958) 'Territoriality: a review of concepts and problems', *Behavior and Evolution*, A. Roe and G. G. Simpson (eds.), Yale University Press, New Haven.

CARSTAIRS, G. M., (1967) *Impact of population growth on mental health*, from the proceedings of the 8th international conference of the International Planned Parenthood Federation, Santiago, Chile, 68–72.

CATTON, W. R., (1969) 'Motivations of wilderness users', *Pulp and Paper Magazine of Canada*, 19 December 1969, 3–8.

CHAMPION, A., (1970) 'Recent trends in new town densities', *Town and Country Planning*, 38 (5), 252–5.

CHERRY, G. E., (1969) 'Overcrowding in cities', *Official Architecture and Planning*, 32 (3), 287–90.

CHITTY, D., (1971) Personal communication.

COHEN, H., (1951) 'Social surveys as planning instruments for housing: Britain', *Journal of Social Issues*, 7 (1/2), 35–46.

COHEN, W., (1967) 'Freedom of choice', *Studies in Family Planning*, 23, 2–5.

COLLETT, P., (1971) 'Training Englishmen in the non-verbal behaviour of Arabs', *International Journal of Psychology*, 6, 209–15.

COMMONER, B., (1971) *Science and Survival*, Ballantine Books, New York.

COLLINGWOOD, R. G., and MYRES, J. N. L., (1936) *Roman Britain and the English Settlements*, Clarendon Press.

CRAIK, K. H., (1966) 'The prospects for an environmental psychology', *I.P.A.R. Research Bulletin*, University of California (mimeo).

CRAIK, K. H., (1968) 'The comprehension of the everyday physical environment', *Journal of the American Institute of Planners*, 34, 29–37.

CRAIK, K. H., (1970) 'Environmental psychology', *New Directions in Psychology*, Vol. 4, Holt, Rhinehart & Winston, New York, 1–121.

CRAIK, K. H., (1973) 'Environmental psychology', *Annual Review of Psychology*, 24, 403–22.

DARKE, J., and DARKE, R., (1969) *Physical and Social Factors in Neighbour Relations*, Centre for Environmental Studies, Working paper 41.

DARKE, J., and DARKE, R., (1969a) *Social Class and Social Status*, Centre for Environmental Studies, Working paper 42.

DARWIN, C., (1859) *On the Origin of Species*, Murray.

DARWIN, C., (1871) *The Descent of Man*, Murray (2nd edn 1885 cited in text).

DAVIS, K., (1967) 'Population policy: Will current programs succeed?', *Science*, 158, 730–39.

DAVISON, P. L. *et al.*, (1970) 'Research in action: an integrated design study applied to schools' development', *Journal of Architectural Research and Teaching*, 1, 4–19.

DEAN, J. P., (1949) 'The myths of housing reform', *American Sociological Review*, 14, 281–8.

DEESE, J., (1972) *Psychology as Science and Art*, Harcourt Brace Jovanovich, New York.

DE GROOT, I., (1967) 'Trends in public attitudes toward air pollution', *Journal of Air Pollution Control Association*, 17, 679–81.

DE JONGE, D., (1962) 'Images of urban areas', *Journal of the American Institute of Planners*, 28, 266–76.

DENNIS, N., (1958) 'The popularity of the neighbourhood community idea', *Sociological Review*, 6 (2), 191–206.

DESOR, J. A., (1972) 'Towards a psychological theory of crowding', *Journal of Personality and Social Psychology*, 21 (1), 79–83.

DEUTSCH, M., and COLLINS, M. E., (1952) *Interracial Housing: a psychological evaluation of a social experiment*, University of Minnesota Press, Minneapolis.

DOMINIAN, J., (1968) *Marital Breakdown*, Penguin Books.

DOSEY, M., and MAISELS, M., (1969) 'Personal space and self-protection', *Journal of Personality and Social Psychology*, 11 (2), 93–7.

DUDLEY REPORT, (1944) *The Design of Dwellings*, H.M.S.O.

EHRLICH, P., (1971) *The Population Bomb*, Ballantine.

EHRLICH, P., and EHRLICH, A., (1970) *Population, Resources, Environment*, Freeman & Company, San Francisco.

EHRLICH, P., and FREEDMAN, J., (1971) 'Population, crowding and human behaviour', *New Scientist and Science Journal*, 1 April, 1971, 10–14.

ELLIS, H., (1896–1928) *Studies in the Psychology of Sex*, Random House, New York, 2-Volume edn 1936.

ESSER, A. H., CHAMBERLAIN, A. S., CHAPPLE, E. D., KLINE, N. S., (1965) 'Territoriality of patients on a research ward', *Environmental Psychology* (1970), Proshansky, Ittleson and Rivlin (eds.), Holt, Rhinehart & Winston, New York.

EVANS, H. (ed.), (1972) *New Towns: The British Experience*, Charles Knight & Co.

EYSENCK, H. J., (1967) *Fact and Fiction in Psychology*, Penguin Books.

EYSENCK, S. B. G., and EYSENCK, H. J., (1963) 'The validity of questionnaire and rating assessments of E and N and their factorial stability', *British Journal of Psychology*, 54 (1), 51–62.

FANNING, D. M., (1967) 'Families in flats', *British Medical Journal*, 4, 382–6.

FARIS, R. E. L., and DUNHAM, H. W., (1939) *Mental Disorders in Urban*

Areas, University of Chicago Press (edn cited in text is the first Phoenix edn, 1965).

FAWCETT, J. T., (1970) *Psychology and Population*, The Population Council, New York.

FAWCETT, J. T., (1973) *Psychological Perspectives on Population*. Basic Books, New York.

FELIPE, N. J., and SOMMER, R., (1966) 'Invasion of personal space', *Social Problems*, 14 (2), 206–14.

FESTINGER, L., SCHACHTER, S., BACK, K., (1950) *Social Pressures in Informal Groups*, Harper & Brothers, New York (edn cited in text is Tavistock Publications, 1959).

FESTINGER, L., (1951) 'Architecture and group membership', *Journal of Social Issues*, 7 (1 and 2), 152–63.

First Report from the Select Committee on Science and Technology (1971), H.M.S.O.

FORM, W. H., (1951) 'Stratification in low- and middle-income housing areas', *Journal of Social Issues*, 7 (1 and 2), 109–31.

FREEDMAN, J., KLEVANSKY, S., and EHRLICH, P., (1971) 'The effect of crowding on human task performance', *Journal of Applied Social Psychology*, 1, 7–25.

FREEDMAN, J. L., LEVY, A. S., BUCHANAN, R. W., PRICE, J., (1972) 'Crowding and human aggressiveness', *Journal of Experimental Social Psychology*, 8, 528–48.

FREID, M., and GLEICHER, P., (1961) 'Some sources of residential satisfaction in an urban slum', *Journal of the American Institute of Planners*, 27, 305–15.

FREUD, S., (1915) 'Instincts and their vicissitudes', *Collected Papers of Sigmund Freud*, Vol. IV, Hogarth Press, 1949.

GALE, A., COLES, M., BLAYDON, J., (1969) 'Extraversion–introversion and the E.E.G.', *British Journal of Psychology*, 60 (2), 209–23.

GANS, H. J., (1961) 'The balanced community: homogeneity and heterogeneity in residential areas?', *Journal of the American Institute of Planners*, 27, 176–84.

GOFFMAN, E., (1959) *The Presentation of Self in Everyday Life* (edn cited in text Penguin Books, 1971).

GOFFMAN, E., (1961) *Asylums* (edn cited in text, Penguin, 1968).

GOODEY, B., (1968) 'Environmental, extra environmental and preferential perception in geography', *Proceedings of the North Dakota Academy of Science*, 22, 73–8.

GOODEY, B., (1971) 'Perception of the environment', *Occasional paper No. 17*, University of Birmingham Centre for Urban and Regional Studies.

GOODEY, B., (1974) 'Green fields and postures new: the image of British New Towns', paper at the annual conference of the Institute of British Geographers, Norwich.

GOSS, A., (1961) 'Neighbourhood units in British towns', *Town Planning Review*, 32, 66–82.

GOULD, P. R., and WHITE, R. R., (1968) 'The mental maps of British school leavers', *Regional Studies*, 2, 161–82.

GOULD, P. R., and WHITE, R. R., (1974) *Mental Maps*, Penguin Books.

GREENSPOON, J., (1955) 'The reinforcing effect of two spoken sounds on the frequency of two responses', *American Journal of Psychology*, 68, 409–16.

GRIFFITT, W., and VEITCH, R., (1971) 'Hot and crowded: influences of population density and temperature on interpersonal affective behaviour', *Journal of Personality and Social Psychology*, 17 (1), 92–8.

GULICK, J., (1963) 'Images of an Arab city', *Journal of the American Institute of Planners*, 29, 179–98.

GUSTAVUS, S. O., and NAM, C. B., (1970) 'The formation and stability of ideal family size among young people', *Demography*, 7 (1), 43–51.

GUTMAN, R., (1965–6) 'The questions architects ask', *Transactions of the Bartlett Society*, 4, 49–82.

HALL, E. T., (1959) *The Silent Language*, Doubleday, Garden City, N.Y.

HALL, E. T., (1968) 'Proxemics', *Current Anthropology*, 9 (2–3), 83–95.

HALL, E. T., (1969) *The Hidden Dimension*, Bodley Head (first published 1966).

HARRINGTON, M., (1964) 'Cooperation and collusion in a group of young housewives', *Sociological Review*, 12 (3), 255–82.

HART, R. A., and MOORE, G. T., (1973) 'The development of spatial cognition. A review', *Image and Environment: cognitive mapping and spatial behavior*, R. M. Downs, and D. Stea (eds.), Aldine, Chicago, 246–88.

HEAD, H., (1920) *Studies in Neurology*, Oxford University Press.

HEBB, D. O., (1955) 'Drives and the C.N.S.' (conceptual nervous system), *Psychological Review*, 62, 243–54.

HEDIGER, H., (1950) *Wild Animals in Captivity*, Butterworth's Scientific Publications.

HEDIGER, H., (1955) *Studies of the Psychology and Behavior of Captive Animals in Zoos and Circuses*, Criterion Books, New York.

HEDIGER, H., (1961) 'The evolution of territorial behavior', *Social Life in Early Man*, S. L. Washburn (ed.), Viking Fund Publications in Anthropology No. 31, New York.

HELD, R., and HEIN, A., (1963) 'Movement-produced stimulation in the development of visually guided behavior', *Journal of Comparative and Physiological Psychology*, 56, 607–13.

HELSON, H., (1964) *Adaptation–Level Theory*, Harper & Row, New York.

HERAUD, B. J., (1968) 'Social class and the new towns', *Urban Studies*, 5, 33–58.

HERBERT, G., (1963–4) 'The neighbourhood unit principle and organic theory', *Sociological Review*, 11–12, 165–213.

HERON, W., (1961) 'Cognitive and physiological effects of perceptual isolation', *Sensory Deprivation*, P. Solomon *et al.* (eds.), Harvard University Press, Cambridge, Mass., 6–33.

HILLERY, G. A., (1955) 'Definitions of community: areas of agreement', *Rural Sociology*, 20, 111–23.

H.M.S.O., (1946) *Final Report of the New Towns Committee*, Ministry of Town and Country Planning Dept of Health for Scotland.

H.M.S.O., (1961) *Homes for Today and Tomorrow*, Ministry of Housing and Local Government, London.

H.M.S.O., (1967) *The Needs of New Communities*, Ministry of Housing and Local Government, Welsh Office.

H.M.S.O., (1971) *The First Report from the Select Committee on Science and Technology*, London.

HOLE, W. V., (1965) 'Housing and standards and social trends', *Urban Studies*, 2 (2), 137–46.

HOLMANS, A., (1964) 'Current population trends in Britain', *Scottish Journal of Political Economy*, 11 (1), 31–56.

HOLMES, T. H., and RAHE, R. H., (1967) 'The social readjustment rating scale', *Journal of Psychosomatic Research*, 11, 213–18.

HOPPE, R. A., (1970) 'Territorial markers, requested protection and the good neighbour', paper presented at Western Psychological Convention, 15 April 1970.

HOROWITZ, M. J., DUFF, D. F., STRATTON, L. O., (1964) 'Body buffer zone', *Archives of General Psychiatry*, 11 (6), 651–6.

HOUSING REVIEW, (1966) 'Two new high density schemes for London boroughs', *Housing Review 15*, No. 2, 54–5.

HUBEL, D. H., and WIESEL, T. N., (1962) 'Receptive fields, binocular interaction and functional architecture in the cat's visual cortex', *Journal of Physiology*, 160 (1), 106–54.

HUDSON, L., (1966) *Contrary Imaginations*, Penguin Books.

HUDSON, L., (1970) 'The choice of Hercules', *Bulletin of the British Psychological Society*, 23 (81), 287–92.

HUTT, C., (1972) Personal communication.

HUTT, C., and MCGREW, W. C., (1967) 'Effects of group density upon social behaviour in humans', paper presented at Symposium on changes in behaviour with population density, at Association for the Study of Animal Behaviour meetings, Oxford, 17–20 July 1967.

HUTT, C., and VAIZEY, M. J., (1966) 'Differential effects of group density on social behaviour', *Nature*, 209, 1371–2.

HUTT, C., and VAIZEY, M. J., (1966) 'Group density and social behaviour', *Neue Ergebnisse der Primatologie*, 15, 225–7.

ISAACS, R. R., (1948) 'The neighbourhood theory: an analysis of its adequacy', *Journal of the American Institute of Planners*, 14, 15–23.

JAHODA, M., and WEST, P., (1951) 'Race relations in public housing', *Journal of Social Issues*, 7 (1 and 2), 132–9.

JAMES, T. R., (1967) 'Residential densities and housing layouts', *Town and Country Planning*, 35, 11, 552–61.

JAMESON, C., (1971) 'Social research for architecture'. *Architects' Journal* 154 (43), 917–54.

JAMESON, C., (1973) 'The impact of social research on planning procedures', paper at the Occupational Psychology Section conference: 'Man–Environment – a better fit', Oxford Polytechnic, 27 October 1973.

JAY, P., (1968) 'The interior environment: sense and nonsense', *Architectural Review*, February 1968.

JEPHCOTT, P., (1971) *Homes in High Flats*, Oliver & Boyd.

JOINER, D.. (1970) 'Social ritual and architectural space', proceedings of the architectural psychology conference at Kingston Polytechnic, 1–4 September 1970.

KANGAS, L. W., (1970) 'Integrated incentives for fertility control', *Science*, 169, 1278–83.

KAPLAN, S., (1972) 'The challenge of environmental psychology: A proposal for a new functionalism', *American Psychologist*, 27 (2), 140–43.

KATES, R. W., (1962) 'Hazard and choice perception in flood plain management', Department of Geography Research, paper No. 78, University of Chicago.

KENNEDY, R., (1943) 'Premarital residential propinquity', *American Journal of Sociology*, 48, 580–84.

KESSLER, A., (1966) 'Interplay between social ecology and physiology, genetics and population dynamics of mice', Ph.D. dissertation, Rockefeller University, University Microfilms, 67–9869.

KESSLER, A., (1967) 'Interplay between social ecology and physiology, genetics and population dynamics of mice', *Dissertation Abstracts*, 28 (3).

KEYFITZ, N., (1966) 'Population density and the style of social life', *Bio Science*, 16 (12), 868–73.

KINSEY, A. C., POMEROY, W. B., MARTIN, C. E., (1948) *Sexual Behavior in the Human Male*, W. B. Saunders Co., Philadelphia.

KINSEY, A. C., POMEROY, W. B., MARTIN, C. E., GEBHARD, P. H., (1953) *Sexual Behavior in the Human Female*. W. B. Saunders Co., Philadelphia.

KINGSTON POLYTECHNIC, (1969) *Architectural Psychology Newsletter*, Vol. 1, No. 1, published July 1969, ongoing.

KINZE, A. F., (1971) 'Body buffer zones in violent prisoners', *New Society*, 28 January 1971.

KIRA, A., (1970) 'Privacy and the bathroom', *Environmental Psychology*; H. M. Proshansky, W. H. Ittelson, L. G. Rivlin, (1970) (eds.), Holt, Rhinehart & Winston, New York.

KOFFA, K., (1935) *Principles of Gestalt Psychology*, Routledge & Kegan Paul.

KOHLER, W., (1925) *The Mentality of Apes*, Penguin Books, 1957.

KONIG, R., (1968) *The Community*, Routledge & Kegan Paul.

KRETCH, D., CRUTCHFIELD, R. S., BALLACHEY, E. L., (1962) *Individual in Society*, McGraw-Hill, New York.

KUETHE, J. L., (1962a) 'Social schemas'. *Journal of Abnormal and Social Psychology*, 64 (1), 31–8.

KUETHE, J. L., (1962b) 'Social schemas and the reconstruction of social object displays from memory', *Journal of Abnormal and Social Psychology*, 64 (1), 71–4.

KUETHE, J. L., (1964) 'Pervasive influence of social schemata', *Journal of Abnormal and Social Psychology*, 68 (3), 248–54.

LANSING, J. B., and MARANS, R. W., (1969) 'Evaluation of neighbourhood', *Journal of the American Institute of Planners*, 35, 195–9.

LATANÉ, B., and DARLEY, J. M., (1970) *The Unresponsive Bystander; Why Doesn't He Help?* Appleton-Century Crofts, New York.

LAZARSFELD, P., and MERTON, R., (1954) 'Friendship as a social process', *Freedom and Control in Modern Society*, M. Berger, T. Abel, C. Page (eds.), Van Nostrand, New York.

LEE, T. R., (1954) 'A study of urban neighbourhood', unpublished Ph.D. dissertation, University of Cambridge.

LEE, T. R., (1962) '"Brennan's Law" of shopping behaviour', *Psychological Reports*, 11, 662.

LEE, T. R., (1963) 'The optimum provision and siting of social clubs', *Durham Research Review*, No. 14 (September), 53–61.

LEE, T. R., (1967) 'The concept of space and the control of environment', *Architectural Association Journal*, 82, 172–5.

LEE, T. R., (1968) 'Urban neighbourhood as a socio-spatial schema', *Human Relations*, 21 (3), 241–67.

LEE, T. R., (1969) 'The psychology of spatial orientation', *Architectural Association Quarterly*, 1, 11–15.

LEE, T. R., (1970) 'Perceived distance as a function of direction in the city', *Environment and Behavior*, 2 (1), 40–51.

LEE, T. R., (1971) 'Psychology and architectural determinism', *Architects' Journal*, 154, Part One, 253–62, Part Two, 475–83, Part Three, 651–9.

LEIBMAN, M., (1970) 'The effects of sex and role norms on personal space', *Environment and Behavior*, 2, 208–46.

LIFTON, R. J., (1961) *Thought Reform and the Psychology of Totalism*, Penguin Books, 1967.

LILLY, J. C., (1956) 'Mental effects of reduction of ordinary levels of physical stimuli on intact, healthy persons', *Psychiatric Research Reports* 5, 1–9.

LIPE, D., (1971) 'Incentives, fertility control, and research', *American Psychologist*, 26 (7), 617–25.

LIPMAN, A., (1968) 'Territorial behaviour in the sitting rooms of four residential homes for old people', Welsh School of Architecture (mimeo).

LIPMAN, A., (1968a) 'Some problems of direct observation in architectural social research', *Architects' Journal*, 147 (24), 1349–56.

LIPMAN, A., (1970a) 'Strategies for architectural research – a comment', *Journal of Architectural Research and Teaching*, 1 (2), 56–7.

LIPMAN, A., (1971) 'Integrated design – its potential contribution to the development of a theory of man–environment behaviour', paper presented at the Conference on the Integrated Design of Building, University of Technology, Loughborough, 5–6 July 1971.

LITTLE, K. B., (1965) 'Personal space', *Journal of Experimental Social Psychology*, 1, 237–47.

LLEWELWYN-DAVIES, LORD, (1972) 'Changing goals in design: The Milton-Keynes example', *New Towns: The British Experience*, H. Evans (ed.), Charles Knight and Co. Ltd.

LOCKARD, R. B., (1971) 'Reflections on the fall of comparative psychology: is there a message for us all?', *American Psychologist*, 26 (2), 168–79.

LORENZ, K., (1966) *On Aggression*, Methuen.

LOWENTHAL, D., (1970) 'The nature of perceived and imagined environments', paper presented to the New England Psychological Association, November 1970.

LUTEN, R. B., (1963) 'How dense can people be?', *Sierra Club Reprint Series*, No. 7.

LYMAN, S. M., and SCOTT, B. B., (1967) 'Territoriality: a neglected social dimension', *Social Problems*, 15 (2), 236–49.

LYNCH, F., (1968) 'Comment on E. T. Hall's "Proxemics"', *Current Anthropology*, 9 (2–3), 102–3.

LYNCH, K., (1960) *The Image of the City*, M.I.T. Press, Mass.

MACLEOD, J., (1972) 'Lipe ignored obvious hypothesis' (comment) *American Psychologist*, 27 (3), 233.

MAISELS, J., (1961) *Two to Five in High Flats*, The Housing Centre, London.

MANN, P. H., (1965) *An Approach to Urban Sociology*, Routledge & Kegan Paul.

MARSDEN, H. M., (1972) 'Crowding and animal behaviour', *Environment and the Social Sciences: perspectives and applications*, J. F. Wohlwill, D. H. Carson (eds.), American Psychological Association.

MASTERS, W. H., and JOHNSON, V. E., (1970) *Human Sexual Inadequacy*, Churchill.

MCBRIDE, G., (1964) 'A general theory of social organisation of behaviour', University of Queensland papers, 1, 75–110, St Lucia.

MENDELSON, J. H., KUBZANSKY, P. E., LEIDERMAN, P. H., WEXLER, D., SOLOMON, P., (1961) 'Physiological and psychological aspects of sensory deprivation – a case analysis', *Sensory Deprivation*, P. Solomon *et al.* (eds.), Harvard University Press, Cambridge, Mass. 91–113.

MERCER, C., (1972) 'Towards an orientation course in psychology', *Occupational Therapy*, 35 (5), 309–14.

MERCER, C., (1974) 'A sense of place: who needs it?', paper at annual conference of British Geographers, Norwich.

MERCER, C., (1973) 'Towards standing room only', paper at the 3rd conference on Psychology and the Built Environment, University of Surrey, September 1973.

MERTON, R. K., (1948) 'The social psychology of housing', *Urban Housing*, W. L. C. Wheaton, C. Milgram, M. E. Meyerson (eds.), The Free Press, New York, 1966.

MILGRAM, S., (1963) 'Behavioural study of obedience', *Journal of Abnormal and Social Psychology*, 67 (4), 371–8.

MILGRAM, S., (1970) 'The experience of living in cities', *Science*, 167, 1461–8.

MINISTRY OF HOUSING AND LOCAL GOVERNMENT, (1962) *Residential areas. Higher densities*, H.M.S.O.

MINISTRY OF HOUSING AND LOCAL GOVERNMENT, (1970) *Families living at high density*, H.M.S.O.

MORRIS, D., (1969) *The Human Zoo*, Jonathan Cape.

MORUZZI, G., and MAGOUN, H. W., (1949) 'Brain stem reticular formation and activation of the E.E.G.', *E.E.G. Clinical Neurophysiology*, 1, 455–73.

MUMFORD, L., (1954) 'In defense of neighborhood', *Town Planning Review*, 24, 256–70.

MURPHY, D. B., and MYERS, T. I., (1962) 'Occurrence, measurement and experimental manipulation of visual hallucinations', *Perceptual and Motor Skills*, 15, 47–54.

MURRAY, R., (1971) 'Report on research', *Kingston Polytechnic Architectural Psychology Newsletter*, 2 (2) (unpaginated).

MURRAY, R., (1971a) Personal communication.

MURRAY, R., (1973) 'Influence of crowding on children's behaviour', paper at 3rd conference on Psychology and the Built Environment, University of Surrey, September 1973.

MYERS, T. I., MURPHY, D. B., SMITH, S., GOFFARD, S. J., (1966) 'Experimental studies of sensory deprivation and social isolation', Technical report, 66–8, Basic research, 6, Human Resources Research Office, The George Washington University.

NATIONAL COUNCIL FOR WOMEN OF GREAT BRITAIN, (1969) 'Guidelines for happier living in high blocks', October 1969 (mimeo).

NATIONAL PLAYING FIELDS ASSOCIATION, (1953) *Playgrounds for blocks of high flats*, London.

NATIONAL SWEDISH INSTITUTE FOR BUILDING RESEARCH, (1967) *Quality of Dwellings and Housing Areas*, Report 27, Stockholm.

NEWMAN, O., (1972) *Defensible Space*, MacMillan, New York.

NEWSON, J., and NEWSON, E., (1965) *Patterns of Infant Care in an Urban Community*, Penguin Books (first published Allen & Unwin, 1963).

NEWSON, J., and NEWSON, E., (1970) *Four Years Old in an Urban Community*, Penguin Books (first published Allen & Unwin, 1968).

NEWSON, J., and NEWSON, E., (1971) Personal communication.

NICE, M. M., (1941) 'The role of territory and bird life', *American Midland Naturalist*, 26, 441–87.

NOBLE, J., (1963) 'The how and why of behaviour. Social psychology for the architect', *Architects' Journal*, 6 March 1963, 531–46.

ORNE, M. T., and SCHEIBE, K. E., (1964) 'The contribution of non-deprivation factors in the production of sensory deprivation effects', *Journal of Abnormal and Social Psychology*, 68, 3–12.

PAGE, E. B., (1972) 'Behavior and Heredity', *American Psychologist*, 27, 7, 660–61.

PAHL, R. D., (1970) *Patterns of Urban Life*, Longmans, Green & Co.

PARR, A. E., (1964–5) 'Environmental design and psychology', *Landscape*, 14 (2), 15–18.

PARR, A. E., (1967) 'Urbanity and the urban scene', *Landscape*, 16 (3), 3–5.

PARR, A. E., (1970) 'The city as habitat', *Centennial Review*, 14 (2), 177–87.

PARR, A. E., (1970a) 'Heating, lighting, plumbing, and human relations', *Landscape*, 19 (1), 28–9.

PARR, R. E., and BURGESS, E. W., (1925) *The City*, University of Chicago Press.

PASTALAN, L., (1968) 'Spatial privacy and differential manifestations of the territorial imperative among the elderly in various congregate living arrangements', Institute of Gerontology, University of Michigan, Ann Arbor (mimeo).

PERRATON, J. K., (1967) 'Community planning – an analysis of certain social aims', *Journal of the Town Planning Institute*, 53 (3), 95–8.

PERRY, C., (1939) 'The Neighborhood Unit formula', *Urban Housing*, W. L. C. Wheaton, G. Milgram, M. E. Meyerson (eds.), The Free Press, New York, 1966.

PETZING, J., and WEDGE, P., (1970) 'Homes fit for children?', *New Society*, 10 September, No. 415, 448–50.

PIAGET, J., and INHELDER, B., (1956) *The Child's Conception of Space*, Routledge & Kegan Paul.

POHLMAN, E., (1969) *The Psychology of Birth Planning*, Schenkman, Cambridge, Mass.

POHLMAN, E., (1971) 'Population education – critical questions', *Environment and Behavior*, 3 (3), 307–21.

POLLARD, J. C., UHR, L., JACKSON, C. W. JR, (1963) 'Studies in sensory deprivation', *Archives of General Psychiatry*, 8, 435–54.

PROSHANSKY, H. M., ITTELSON, W. H., RIVLIN, L. G., (1970) *Environmental Psychology: Man and His Physical Setting*, Holt, Rhinehart & Winston, New York.

QUERIDO, A., (1966) 'Alone in a crowd', *World Health*, February–March 1966, 18–23.

RAHE, R. H., MEYER, M., SMITH, M., KJAER, G., HOLMES, T. H., (1964) 'Social stress and illness onset', *Journal of Psychosomatic Research*, 8, 35–44.

RAINWATER, L., (1966) 'Fear and the house as haven in the lower class', *Journal of the American Institute of Planners*, 32, 23–31.

RAND, G., (1969) 'What psychology asks of urban planning', *American Psychologist*, 24, 929–35.

RATTREY-TAYLOR, G., (1970) *The Doomsday Book*, Thames & Hudson.

REES, W., (1969) *Cardiff. A History of the City*, The Corporation of the city of Cardiff.

RESNICK, J. H., and SCHWARTZ, T., (1973) 'Ethical standards as an independent variable in psychological research', *American Psychologist*, 28 (2), 134–9.

ROHLES, F. H. JR, (1965) 'Consideration for environmental research in human factors', *Journal of Environmental Sciences*, June 1965 (reprint is without pagination).

ROHLES, F. H. JR, (1967) 'Environmental psychology: a bucket of worms', *Psychology Today*, 1, 55–63.

ROSENTHAL, R., (1966) *Experimenter Effects in Behavioral Research*, Appleton-Century Crofts, New York.

ROSNOW, R. L., and ROSENTHAL, R., (1970) 'Volunteer effects in behavioral research', *New Directions in Psychology*, Vol. 4, K. H. Craik, B. Kleinmuntz *et al.*, Holt Rinehart & Winston, New York.

ROYAL COMMISSION ON ENVIRONMENTAL POLLUTION, (1971) H.M.S.O.

ROYAL COMMISSION ON POPULATION, (1949) H.M.S.O.

RUSSELL, W. M. S., (1966) 'Aggression: new light from animals', *New Society*, 176, 12–14.

SCHMITT, R. C., (1956–7), 'Density, delinquency and crime in Honolulu', *Sociology and Social Research*, 41, 274–6.

SCHMITT, R. C., (1963) 'Implications of density in Hong Kong', *Journal of the American Institute of Planners*, 29, 210–17.

SCHOFIELD, M., (1968) *The Sexual Behaviour of Young People*, Penguin Books.

SCHWARTZ, B., (1968) 'The social psychology of privacy', *American Journal of Sociology*, 73 (6), 741–52.

SEARLES, H. F., (1960) *The Non-Human Environment*, International Universities Press, New York.

SKINNER, B. F., (1971) *Beyond Freedom and Dignity*, Alfred Knopf, New York.

SKOLNICK, P., MOSS, R., SALZGEBER, R., SHAW, J. I., (1971) 'The effect of crowded conditions on human behavior', paper presented at the Western Psychological Association, San Francisco, 21–4 April 1971.

SKOLNICK, P., (1972) Personal communication.

SMITH, M., (1961) 'Residential development densities', *Journal of the Town Planning Institute*, 47 (1), 9–10.

SOMMER, R., (1966) 'Man's proximate environment', *Journal of Social Issues*, 22 (4). 59–70.

SOMMER, R., (1969) *Personal Space*, Prentice Hall, Englewood Cliffs, New Jersey.

SONNENFELD, J., (1967) 'Environmental perception and adaptation level in the Arctic', in 'Environment, perception and behavior', D. Lowenthal, Dept of Geography Research paper 109, University of Chicago 1967.

SONNENFELD, J., (1969) 'Personality and behavior in environment', *Proceedings of the Association of American Geographers*, 1, 136–40.

SONNENFELD, J., (1969a) 'Equivalence and distortion of the perceptual environment', *Environment and Behavior*, 1 (1), 83–99.

SPENCER, D., (1972) Personal communication.

SPENCER, D., (1973) 'An evaluation of three techniques of image representation: A study of neighbourhood perception in Selly Oak, Birmingham', M. Soc. Sci. Thesis, Centre for Urban and Regional Studies, Birmingham.

SPENGLER, J., (1969) 'Population problem: In search of a solution', *Science*, 166, 1234–8.

SPITZ, R., (1964) 'The derailment of dialogue', *Journal of the American Psychoanalytic Association*, 12, 752–75.

SPIVAK, M., *et al.* (1970) 'Mental health implications of the organisation of the large-scale physical environment', From 'Hearings before the Select Committee on Nutrition and Human Needs of the United States Senate Ninety-First Congress, Part 6', Health and Housing, Washington D.C.

SPROTT, W. J. H., (1958) *Human Groups*, Penguin Books.

STACEY, B., (1969) 'Planning for people or people for planning', *Architectural Psychology Newsletter*, 1 (3) (unpaginated).

STACEY, M., (1969) 'The myth of community studies', *British Journal of Sociology*, 20, 134–47.

STEA, D., (1965) 'Space, territory, and human movements', *Landscape*, Autumn, 15, 13–16.

STEA, D., (1967) 'Reasons for our moving', *Landscape*, Autumn 17 (1), 27–8.

STEA, D., (1969) 'The measurement of mental maps: an experimental model for studying conceptual spaces', *Studies in Geography*, 17, Behavioural Problems in Geography: A symposium Northwestern University 1969.

STEINHART, J. S., and CHERNIACK, S., (1969) *The universities and environmental quality – commitment to problem-focussed education*, report to the President's environmental quality council, U.S. Government Printing Office, Washington D.C.

STEWART, S., (1961) *Give Us This Day*, Popular Library, New York.

STEWART, W. F. R., (1970) *Children in Flats: A family study*, National Society for the Prevention of Cruelty to Children, London.

SUEDFELD, P., (1969) 'Introduction and historical background', *Sensory Deprivation: 15 years of research*, J. P. Zubeck, Appleton-Century Crofts.

SZASZ, T. S., (1972) *The Myth of Mental Illness*, Paladin.

TAYLOR, C. W., BAILEY, R., BRANCH, C. H. H., (eds.), (1967) *Second National Conference on Architectural Psychology*, University of Utah, Salt Lake City.

THORNDIKE, E. L., (1882) *Animal Intelligence*, MacMillan, New York.

TINBERGEN, N., (1951) *A Study of Instinct*, Oxford University Press.

TOFFLER, A., (1970) *Future Shock*, The Bodley Head.

VERNON, J. A., (1966) *Inside the Black Room*, Penguin Books (first published 1963).

WATKINS, V., (1970) *Territoriality and Housing*, Welsh School of Architecture (mimeo).

WATSON, J. B., (1913) 'Psychology as the behaviourist views it', *Psychological Review*, 20, 158–77.

WATSON, J. B., (1925) *Behaviorism*, Norton, New York.

WATSON, O. M., and GRAVES, T. D., (1966) 'Quantitative research in proxemic behavior', *American Anthropologist*, 68, 971–85.

WELLS, B., (1965) 'Towards a definition of environmental studies: a psychologist's contribution', *Architects' Journal*, Information Library, 22 September, 677–83.

WELLS, B., (1969) 'Architectural Psychology: the evolution of a technology', *Architectural Association Quarterly*, 1 (3), 44–9.

WERNER, H., (1948) *Comparative Psychology of Mental Development* (rev. edn), International Universities Press, New York.

WHYTE, W. H., (1960) *The Organization Man*, Penguin Books (first published 1956).

WILCOCK, J., (1972) 'Comparative psychology lives on under an assumed name – psychogenetics', *American Psychologist*, 27 (6), 531–8.

WILLIAMS, J. L., (1963) 'Personal space and its relation to extraversion–introversion', Master's thesis, University of Alberta.

WILMOTT, P., and COONEY, E., (1963) 'Community planning and

sociological research: a problem of collaboration', *Journal of the American Institute of Planners*, 24 (2), 123–6.

WILNER, D., WALKLEY, R., PINKERTON, T., TAYBACH, M., (1962) *Housing Environment and Family Life*, The John Hopkins Press, Baltimore, Maryland.

WINSBOROUGH, H., (1965) 'The social consequences of high population density', *Law and Contemporary Problems*, 30 (1), 120–26.

WIRTH, L., (1938) 'Urbanism as a way of life', *American Journal of Sociology*, 44, 1–24.

WITKIN, H. A., DYK, R. B., FATERSON, H. F., GOODENOUGH, D. R., KARP, S. A., (1962) *Psychological Differentiation*, Wiley, New York.

WITKIN, H. A., LEWIS, H. B., HERTZMAN, M., MACHOVER, K., MEISSNER, P. B., WAPNER, S., (1954) *Personality through Perception*, Harper, New York.

WOBER, M., (1966) 'Sensotypes', *Journal of Social Psychology*, 70, 181–9.

WOHLWILL, J. F., (1970) 'The emerging discipline of environmental psychology', *American Psychologist*, 25, 303–12.

WYNNE-EDWARDS, V. C., (1965) 'Self-regulatory systems in populations of animals', *Science*, 147, 1542–8.

YANCEY, W. L., (1971) 'Architecture, interaction and social control', *Environment and Behavior*, 3 (1), 3–21.

ZLUTNICK, S., and ALTMAN, I., (1972) 'Crowding and human behavior', *Environment and the Social Sciences: perspectives and applications*, J. F. Wohlwill and D. H. Carson (eds.), American Psychological Association, Washington D.C.

Index

Acknowledgements

For permission to reprint the Figures and Tables specified we are indebted to:

The University of North Carolina for Fig. 1, from I. Altman in *Representative Research in Social Psychology*, Vol. 4, No. 1, 1973.

The *Journal of Environmental Sciences* for Fig. 2, from F. H. Rohles 'Considerations for environmental research in human factors', 1965.

Tavistock Publications Ltd; Stanford University Press for Figs. 8, 9 and 10, from L. Festinger *et al.*, *Social Pressures in Informal Groups*, 1959.

The American Medical Association for Fig. 14, from M. J. Horowitz in *Archives of General Psychiatry*, Vol. 11, December 1964.

Plenum Publishing Corporation for Fig. 16, from T. R. Lee in *Journal of Human Relations*, Vol. 21, No. 3, 1968.

The New York Academy of Sciences for Fig. 17, from J. B. Calhoun in *Transactions of the New York Academy of Sciences*, Series 2, Vol. 23, No. 5, 1961.

Charles C. Thomas for Fig. 22, from S. J. Hutt and C. Hutt, *Direct Observations and Measurement of Behaviour*, 1971.

R. E. L. Faris for Table 1, from R. E. L. Faris and H. W. Dunham, *Mental Disorder in Urban Areas*.

George Allen & Unwin Ltd; Aldine Publishing Co., for Tables 2, 3 and 4, from J. Newson and E. Newson, *Four Years Old in an Urban Community*, 1968.